STUDIES ON MODERN ASIA AND AFRICA

Volume 1

I0083835

CHANGING LAW IN DEVELOPING COUNTRIES

CHANGING LAW IN
DEVELOPING COUNTRIES

Edited by
J. N. D. ANDERSON

Routledge
Taylor & Francis Group

LONDON AND NEW YORK

First published in 1963 by George Allen & Unwin Ltd

This edition first published in 2022
by Routledge
2 Park Square, Milton Park, Abingdon, Oxon OX14 4RN

and by Routledge
605 Third Avenue, New York, NY 10158

Routledge is an imprint of the Taylor & Francis Group, an informa business

© 1963 George Allen & Unwin Ltd

All rights reserved. No part of this book may be reprinted or reproduced or utilised in any form or by any electronic, mechanical, or other means, now known or hereafter invented, including photocopying and recording, or in any information storage or retrieval system, without permission in writing from the publishers.

Trademark notice: Product or corporate names may be trademarks or registered trademarks, and are used only for identification and explanation without intent to infringe.

British Library Cataloguing in Publication Data
A catalogue record for this book is available from the British Library

ISBN: 978-1-03-215171-7 (Set)
ISBN: 978-1-00-324754-8 (Set) (ebk)
ISBN: 978-1-03-215778-8 (Volume 1) (hbk)
ISBN: 978-1-03-215790-0 (Volume 1) (pbk)
ISBN: 978-1-00-324567-4 (Volume 1) (ebk)

DOI: 10.4324/9781003245674

Publisher's Note
The publisher has gone to great lengths to ensure the quality of this reprint but points out that some imperfections in the original copies may be apparent.

Disclaimer
The publisher has made every effort to trace copyright holders and would welcome correspondence from those they have been unable to trace.

CHANGING LAW IN DEVELOPING COUNTRIES

EDITED BY

J. N. D. ANDERSON

Professor of Oriental Laws, Head of the
Department af Law at the School of
Oriental and African Studies and Director
of the Institute of Advanced Legal Studies
in the University of London

LONDON
GEORGE ALLEN & UNWIN LTD
RUSKIN HOUSE   MUSEUM STREET

FIRST PUBLISHED IN 1963

This book is copyright under the Berne Convention. Apart from any fair dealing for the purposes of private study, research, criticism or review, as permitted under the Copyright Act 1956, no portion may be reproduced by any process without written permission. Enquiry should be made to the publishers.

© *George Allen & Unwin Ltd,* 1963

PRINTED IN GREAT BRITAIN
in 11 *on* 12 *point Fournier type*
BY UNWIN BROTHERS LTD
WOKING AND LONDON

FOREWORD

The present volume finds its genesis in a series of lectures under the same general title given during the academic year 1961-62. This series, in its turn, was initially built up round the three University Lectures which Sir Kenneth Roberts-Wray was invited to give, under the auspices of the Board of Studies in Laws of the University of London, at the School of Oriental and African Studies; for it seemed appropriate to make these University Lectures the nucleus of a series of fortnightly lectures, extending throughout the session, in which members of the Department of Law at the School joined with distinguished guests in providing what might be regarded as somewhat analogous, within the field of their own particular interests, to the series on *Current Legal Problems* which University College has sponsored for so many years. This series seems to have met a distinct need, and to have aroused a sustained interest. Such, moreover, is the current importance of this subject that the decision has been taken to reproduce the papers in printed form—together with two further papers on the same subject—so that they may reach a wider audience.

In the present volume chapters one, three and four represent Sir Kenneth Roberts-Wray's three lectures, on 'The Authority of the United Kingdom in Dependent Territories', 'The Legal Machinery for the Transition from Dependence to Independence', and 'The Independence of the Judiciary in Commonwealth Countries', respectively. Sir Kenneth's experience as Legal Adviser to both the Colonial Office and the Commonwealth Relations Office during many years of unprecedented development gives him unique qualifications to provide an authoritative treatment of these subjects. It is particularly fitting, therefore, that his successor at the Colonial Office, Mr J. C. McPetrie, should contribute a 'Survey of Constitutions Drafted at the Colonial Office since 1944' as chapter two.

An outstanding characteristic of many of these constitutions is the inclusion, and often the entrenchment, of fundamental rights, so chapter five represents a study of this subject by Professor A. Gledhill, whose work in Constitutional Law has frequently centred round this topic, particularly in its context in the Indian Subcontinent. It was appropriate, therefore, to follow up this more general treatment of such rights by Sir Orby Mootham's University Lecture on 'Constitutional Writs in India'—a subject for which his previous appointment as Chief Justice of the Allahabad High Court gave him an abundance of personal experience. And the more general part of this volume is fittingly concluded by a historical examination of the phrase 'Justice, Equity and Good Conscience' provided by Dr J. D. M. Derrett, whose legal interests cover a very wide field.

Next the volume turns more particularly to Africa. Sir Sydney Littlewood, previously President of the Law Society, provides a chapter on 'The Legal Profession in African Territories'—a subject which he has very much at heart; for my own contribution I chose the subject 'Islamic Law in Africa: Problems of Today and Tomorrow'; Dr R. Y. Hedges, formerly Chief Justice of the Western Region of Nigeria, has provided a study of 'Liability under the Nigerian Criminal Code'; Dr A. N. Allott, a pioneer in many aspects of research in African law, has tackled the subject of 'Legal Development and Economic Growth in Africa'; and Mr J. S. Read, another specialist in African law, has contributed a paper on 'Women's Status and Law Reform'.

Finally, our attention is directed again to Asia. Mr N. J. Coulson, whose speciality is Islamic Law, discusses the recent legislation on Family Law in Pakistan, while Mr H. McAleavy, whose particular interest is Chinese Law, has contributed a paper on 'Chinese Law in Hong Kong: The Choice of Sources'.

No attempt has been made radically to change the style of these lectures as they were given, since it was felt that any resulting gain would be more than matched by a corresponding loss.

J. N. D. ANDERSON

CONTENTS

9

1

THE AUTHORITY OF THE UNITED KINGDOM IN DEPENDENT TERRITORIES[1]

*Formerly Legal Adviser to the Secretary
of State for the Colonies and the Secretary
of State for Commonwealth Relations*

The forms and processes of control and supervision exercised by the Government of the United Kingdom in dependent territories form a vast subject which could, without difficulty, be made to occupy weekly lectures throughout an academic term. On the other hand, it is possible to give (and, indeed, I have several times given) a fairly complete skeleton picture in less than an hour; but that would be of no use to one with experience of the subject, unless he were in need of sleep; and, as I know from experience, it would leave the less informed with nothing to take away with him except a state of bewilderment. For the empiricism and inhibitions of politicians and constitutional lawyers, reflected in scrappy and sometimes badly drafted Acts of Parliament (I am not thinking of present-day Parliamentary Counsel) have succeeded in producing a jigsaw puzzle which defies any attempt to combine brevity and comprehensiveness with clarity.

I therefore propose to compromise; to present a simplified overall sketch, but to discuss interesting points in detail. In particular I shall, at some length, presume to call in question a few generally accepted practices or propositions of law and I shall present one or two problems which do not appear previously to have been unearthed or fully discussed. I hope it is not necessary to make apologies for concentrating my attention on the specialist; for I feel that I should try to make a fresh contribution, however small, to a subject upon which a number of learned authors have written.

[1] The matters dealt with here and in chapters 3 and 4 are considered by the author at greater length in a book on Commonwealth and Colonial Law to be published shortly by Stevens & Sons Ltd.

II

EXECUTIVE AUTHORITY

First, a few words about executive authority.

Certain powers are reserved to the Queen or the Secretary of State by Order in Council or Letters Patent, by Royal Instructions, or sometimes by laws passed by Colonial Legislatures. These, however, are few. The Governor is the local head of the Executive and he is expected to act in accordance with any instructions which he may receive from the Secretary of State. But control of this kind is not available when action does not depend upon the Governor himself. He cannot insist upon the carrying out of United Kingdom policy where the local Executive are in a position under the constitution to assert their will and the Governor has no reserved power to override them; or where the matter at issue is not of sufficient importance to justify the use of the reserved power. Moreover, certain executive functions are conferred by statute, not upon the Governor or Governor in Council, but on statutory bodies or other authorities who are not obliged to carry out the Governor's orders.

PARLIAMENT

My main concern, however, is with legislative power, and it is to this subject that I want to devote the rest of this paper. First, there is the United Kingdom Parliament. The sovereignty of Parliament, as a principle of constitutional law, is so elementary that there is no need to discuss it. Not very long ago, a politician in the Caribbean area publicly claimed that the United Kingdom Parliament had no right to legislate for the Colony; but, as he was a member of the legal profession, one must assume that under cross-examination he would have said that he was talking of moral, not legal, right. During the trouble preceding the War of American Independence, a like claim in the American Colonies was responsible for the American Colonies Act, 1766,[1] in which Parliament solemnly declared that the Parliament of Great Britain had 'and of right ought to have, full power and authority to make laws ... to bind the colonies and people of America'. Did this piece of legislation serve any useful purpose? Where Parliament possesses legislative authority it requires no assertion; where Parliament has no power to make laws it cannot, by making one, give itself the power. It is true that United Kingdom Courts would presumably have given effect to the Act as such, but it is more to the

---

[1] 6 G. 3, c. 12.

point that the Courts in the American Colonies would probably not have done so. The Act could have made no difference to the law in force in the Colonies; it was either redundant or invalid. In point of fact, there can be little doubt that it was redundant.

A very similar question would arise if an Act of Parliament purported to extend to, say, a Protected State in which the Crown had not acquired jurisdiction in the subject matter of the Act. It is highly improbable that a United Kingdom Court would hold that an Act was invalid to the extent that it went beyond jurisdiction acquired. But what of local Courts? They would be quite justified in declining to give effect to an Act of Parliament which went beyond the Crown's jurisdiction. It is interesting to speculate how, if an appeal were brought to Her Majesty in Council, the situation would be dealt with by the Judicial Committee, bearing in mind that, when dealing with an appeal from a particular country, it sits as the highest appellate tribunal of that country. Unfortunately for students of Commonwealth jurisprudence, this absorbing problem is never likely to come before the Courts.

THE SOVEREIGN

The Sovereign possesses legislative and executive power derived, directly or indirectly, from the Prerogative, general Acts of Parliament and special Acts of Parliament. I shall deal with each in turn.

A large variety of types of instrument is available, though some of them are now rarely used. In the early days of the British Empire, Orders in Council, Charters, Letters Patent, Proclamations, Governors' Commissions, Instructions to Governors and Warrants seem to have been used more or less indiscriminately. Nowadays, each type of instrument is in practice reserved for particular purposes. An Order in Council is almost invariably employed to establish a constitution and for most other purposes; Letters Patent are principally used for the creation of offices, particularly those of Governor-General and Governor, for countries within Her Majesty's dominions and for delegating to the holders of such offices powers relating to such matters as the prerogative of mercy, the disposal of land and the appointment and dismissal of officers.

In the oldest Colonies, however, where the Crown does not possess general legislative power and elected legislative Houses are constituted under local laws, there are still Prerogative Letters Patent upon which the constitutions are to a significant extent dependent, and I shall have occasion to refer to these later. Thus, the Bermuda Letters Patent of 1888, as amended in 1953 and 1955, not only constitute the office of Governor and delegate powers to him; they also establish the Executive Council, set up the Legislative Council (the Upper House of the Legislature) confer the power to make laws and provide for disallowance. There are similar Letters Patent for the Bahamas and other Colonies in the Caribbean area.

Royal Instructions to the Governor are principally used to supplement Orders in Council and Letters Patent. It has from time to time been said that they are not law; but that is, to say the least, gross exaggeration. In general, Royal Instructions have the force of law. The only clear exceptions are statutory, notably section four of the Colonial Laws Validity Act, 1865,[1] which lays down that no Colonial Law shall be void or inoperative by reason only of any Royal Instructions 'with reference to such Law or the Subject thereof'. The section is very limited in its scope. As it applies only to instructions with reference to the law or its subject matter, it cannot extend to instructions regarding, for instance, the composition of the legislature. This section is of importance in relation to the giving of the Royal Assent and the reservation of Bills for Her Majesty's pleasure. As a rule, the Governor is given a general discretion to assent, refuse assent or reserve a Bill, but is required to reserve, or to assent only if certain conditions are satisfied, in the case of Bills falling within prescribed categories. If this requirement is in Royal Instructions it is caught by the section and if the Governor in fact assents when he should not have done so, his assent will, by virtue of the section, be valid. But that is not so if the requirement is in some other instrument, and Bills of first importance, such as those amending the constitution, have often been omitted from Royal Instructions and inserted in Orders in Council or Letters Patent as exceptions to the Governor's general discretion to assent, so as to ensure that no Bill within the prescribed class can become law until the United Kingdom Government has an opportunity to consider its terms.

Another distinction, not without importance, is that between Royal Instructions under the Royal Sign Manual and Signet, which are approved in draft by Order in Council and printed, and less formal instructions, conveyed as a rule by despatch or telegram through the Secretary of State to a Governor. The former are used only for giving instructions which have continuing operation, the latter rather for giving instructions of a more or less administrative nature. Sometimes

[1] 28 & 29 V., c. 63.

a provision in an Order in Council or Letters Patent requires a Governor to exercise powers or duties in accordance with instructions either under the Royal Sign Manual and Signet or through a Secretary of State. One result of this is that instructions under the Sign Manual and Signet can be, and occasionally have been, varied by instructions conveyed by despatch or telegram.

I now propose to consider the various Prerogative and statutory powers vested in the Sovereign in relation to different classes of territories. One major distinction which must be constantly borne in mind is that between the constituent power—the power to establish, amend or revoke constitutions for overseas countries—and the power to make law of other kinds, from the control of bicycles to the implementation of treaties.

THE PREROGATIVE

British Settlements. The extent of the Prerogative depends upon the territory concerned. At common law, British subjects who settle in a country without an organized government and legal system carry English law with them as their birthright; and though the Crown has a constituent power in such British settlements, it cannot make ordinary laws for them.

Some writers state that the Crown, in the exercise of the Prerogative, can grant only a constitution of the United Kingdom type, with an elected Lower House and a nominated Upper House or Council, but this alleged limitation does not appear to be supported by any judicial authority. Admittedly, it was usual for the Crown to set up legislatures analogous to that in Great Britain, but it was not obliged to do so. The practice was not uniform and it was more and more abandoned after the eighteenth century.

Nor is the Prerogative in settled Colonies limited to the power to establish a legislative body. The Letters Patent which I have mentioned, constituting the Office of Governor, delegating powers to him and providing for the Executive Council and for the making and disallowance of laws, are made for settled Colonies as well as those acquired by other means.

Unauthorized Settlements. The situation at common law in British settlements which have been neither previously authorized nor subsequently recognized by the Crown is of considerable interest. Chitty, in his *Prerogatives of the Crown*,[1] implies that settlers have no right to make laws unless empowered by the Crown to do so. If that is so, what is the situation in a settled Colony in an uninhabited country which has never been given a constitution by the Sovereign? In British Honduras the settlers had their legislative body which made laws for many years before a dilatory government in the United Kingdom granted them Colonial status in 1862. The inhabitants of Pitcairn Island, with the assistance of visiting naval officers, maintained law-making bodies without any authorization from the Crown during the greater part of the history of the Island. The people of Tristan da Cunha had a constitution of a sort and ran their own affairs without any authorization from the Crown until as late as 1938. Were all the laws made by these communities legally worthless? Did those who enforced them lay themselves open to civil or criminal proceedings?

British subjects in an uninhabited country remain in the allegiance and under the protection of the Sovereign, and they cannot lawfully set themselves up as an independent State. They acquire sovereignty, if at all, on behalf of the Crown, but this involves a conflict with the doctrine that no addition can be made to the Crown's dominions without the Crown's consent—unless one regards the settlers as securing sovereignty without dominion and the occupied country as being comparable with a protectorate. The settlers must carry with them English law as in force at the time of settlement, otherwise they have no law at all. If the home Government is indifferent or inactive, has the common law nothing to say? Are the settlers unable to change or amplify the law they take with them to meet their own needs? It can be asserted, not without a fair degree of confidence, that in such circumstances settlers have a common law right to establish a body to make such laws as they require and Courts to enforce them. This view is admittedly not supported by the broad general principles enunciated in works dealing with colonial constitutional law, but since the exceptional cases with which we are concerned are not discussed, it is permissible to assume, without any reflection on the authors, that they had had no occasion to consider the problem. The alternative is a situation which the strain of common sense and natural justice running through the common law can be relied upon to avoid. The validity of laws made by these home-made legislatures seems never to have been challenged, and since one would be on fairly reliable ground in contending for the recognition of customs gradually

[1] pp. 33-36.

developed by the people and regarded by themselves as binding, it would indeed be incongruous if rules deliberately laid down by their representatives were not accorded like recognition. And, since settlers take English law and, in general, their privileges as British subjects with them, does not this include the right, in case of need, to appoint or elect representatives to make laws for them, a right which would be theirs if they remained in the mother country? It is a pity that in *The Attorney-General of British Honduras* v *Bristowe*[1] the decision of the Judicial Committee made it unnecessary for them to discuss the rules made by the early settlers, but the case does lend a little support for my thesis.

It should, and can without any weakening of the argument, be conceded that a body established by settlers themselves, in exercise of a common law right, is not a regularly constituted legislature. The right of self-government must be provisional and temporary in nature; it cannot undermine the Prerogative right of the Crown, when it sees fit to act, to set up a constitution of its own devising; otherwise, the Prerogative might be frustrated before there had been an opportunity for its exercise. Nor can Parliament be regarded as having had the intention to exclude territories with legislatures of this nature from the operation of the British Settlements Act, 1887, when it defined 'British Settlement' for the purposes of the Act in terms which exclude any settlement with a 'legislature constituted' otherwise than by virtue of the Act.

Conquered and Ceded Colonies. For conquered and ceded Colonies, it is established beyond question that the Sovereign has full power under the Prerogative to make laws either in the constituent field or otherwise. Normally that power would be exercised by formal instrument, but the Sovereign may apparently legislate for a conquered territory even by letters from the Secretary of State.[2]

The general broad principle that the Crown possesses full legislative authority in a conquered or ceded Colony was substantially qualified by the decision of the Judicial Committee of the Privy Council in the leading case *Campbell* v *Hall*,[3] the effect of which, briefly, is that if the Crown grants to a conquered Colony a representative legislative body, without reserving to itself the power to legislate, that power no longer exists. This decision seems to have been generally regarded as

[1] (1880) 6 App. Cas. 143.
[2] *R.* v. *Joykissen Mookerjee* 1 Moo. P.C.C. N.S. 272 at p. 296.
[3] Cowp. 204.

extending not only to the general legislative power, but also to the constituent power, but it is very much open to question whether that was the intention of, or a reasonable deduction from, the judgment.

The action was brought by one James Campbell against William Hall, a tax collector, for the return of duty paid upon goods exported from Grenada, a Colony taken from the French by British forces. By a Proclamation of 1763 and Letters Patent of 1764, the Governor was authorized to establish a Legislature. By later Letters Patent, made before the Legislature was brought into being, the King imposed a duty upon produce shipped from the Island. The question at issue was whether these Letters Patent were valid; whether, having granted a constitution, the King still had power to make a law imposing tax. No question arose regarding the constituent power. It is important to bear in mind that, in at least one other context, the common law recognizes a distinct difference between the constituent power and the ordinary legislative power, namely, that the former is, and the latter is not, exercisable in respect of a settled Colony. It was held by the Privy Council that before the Letters Patent were made imposing the tax, the King had precluded himself from the exercise of legislative authority over the Island of Grenada. It is, to say the least, arguable that this was a reference only to the ordinary legislative power and not the constituent power. It was said in the judgment that 'the King had immediately and irrecoverably granted . . . that the subordinate legislation over the island should be exercised by an assembly with the consent of the governor and council'. The reference to 'subordinate legislation' seems obviously to have been a reference to ordinary laws and not those of a constitutional nature. The words 'irrecoverably granted' must admittedly mean that the power to make laws conferred upon the inhabitants could not be withdrawn and that, to this extent, the constitution could not be taken away by the Crown; but it does not follow that the Sovereign could not amend the constitution, or even revoke it, so long as the grant of legislative authority was preserved. In any case the dictum was *obiter*, since the constituent power was not in issue.

The decision in *Campbell* v *Hall* cannot be regarded as depriving the Crown of all legislative power which is not reserved. I have already referred to the Colonies where the general legislative authority has been lost, for which Letters Patent are made dealing with the office of Governor, some of his powers, the Executive Council and, in certain respects, the Legislature. It is most unlikely that power to make provisions of this sort has always been expressly reserved, but it has never been called in question.

Subsequent cases are not inconsistent with the view I am advancing. The judgment in *re the Lord Bishop of Natal*[1] contains the words 'after a Colony or Settlement has received legislative institutions, the Crown . . . stands in the same relation to that Colony or Settlement as it does to the United Kingdom'; but this passage is *obiter* and it is plainly incorrect. The decision in *Abeyesekera v Jayatilake*[2] amounts to no more than the obvious: that if power to amend a constitution has been reserved by the Crown, it can be freely exercised; and passages in the judgment which might possibly be construed as implying that *Campbell v Hall* affects the constituent power,[3] are not only *obiter* but also, in my respectful submission, obscure.

In the latest case of *Sammut v Strickland*,[4] the Judicial Committee closely considered the effect of *Campbell v Hall*. Their Lordships said they were unable to agree with the statement by the Court of Appeal in Malta 'that it is an established constitutional principle based on *Campbell v Hall* that the grant of representative institutions once made, the Crown is immediately and irrevocably deprived of its right to legislate by Letters Patent or Orders in Council unless there is an express reservation of a right to that effect'. The judgment continued: 'The true proposition is that, as a general rule, such a grant without the reservation of a power of concurrent legislation precludes the exercise of the prerogative while the legislative institutions continue to exist. Nor is it in doubt that a power of revoking the grant must be reserved or it will not exist.' There is no apparent reason to construe the words 'concurrent legislation' in this extract from the judgment as including laws amending the constitution as well as ordinary laws; and the Judicial Committee, though stating that the power of revocation must be reserved if it is to exist, said nothing whatever about the power to amend the constitution.

In brief, it seems that there is, to say the least, a strong case for arguing that *Campbell v Hall* and subsequent cases mean only: (*a*) that, unless there is an express reservation, the Crown does not possess a concurrent power to make ordinary laws so long as legislative institutions continue in the Colony; (*b*) that the grant of legislative institutions cannot be revoked unless the power of revocation is reserved; (*c*) that amendment of the constitution, not amounting to revocation of the grant, remains within the Prerogative rights of the

---

[1] 3 Moo. P.C.C. N.S. 115, 148. [2] [1932] A.C. 260.
[3] Pp. 264, 266. [4] [1938] A.C. 678.

Crown. This last proposition has the support of Chitty in his *Prerogatives of the Crown*.[1] He, however, makes an exception for constitutions founded on local law, and it may well be that the Sovereign's power of amendment extends only to constitutional instruments made by the Crown.

Prerogative and Foreign Jurisdiction. For the exercise of powers and jurisdiction in Protectorates and other dependent territories outside Her Majesty's dominions, the ample powers of the Foreign Jurisdiction Act, 1890, are always invoked, and the question discussed by Hall, in his *Foreign Powers and Jurisdiction of the British Crown*,[2] whether additional or alternative powers are available under the Prerogative, may have little or no importance nowadays. Moreover, in my submission the question cannot arise, because the principal Orders made under the Foreign Jurisdiction Act, 1890,—those made in reliance upon section one—are themselves Prerogative Orders. Before the passing of the first Foreign Jurisdiction Act (in 1843), jurisdiction was exercised and its only possible basis in English law was the Prerogative. As the preamble to the Act shows, it was passed to remove doubts, not as to whether it was lawful for Her Majesty to exercise jurisdiction acquired abroad, but as to how far the exercise of the powers of the Crown was controlled by, and dependent upon, the laws and customs of the Realm. For this purpose it is enacted, now in section 1 of the Act of 1890, that it shall be lawful for the Queen to exercise Her jurisdiction 'within a foreign country in the same and as ample a manner as if Her Majesty had acquired that jurisdiction by the cession or conquest of territory'. The Sovereign's jurisdiction in ceded and conquered territory is exercised under the Prerogative. Unlike other sections of the Act, section 1 does not in terms confer authority to make Orders in Council or any other instruments. It did not create a power; it removed doubts regarding the operation of one branch of the already existing Prerogative rights of the Crown. If that is a correct appreciation of the effect of the section, then, when an instrument is made by virtue of section 1, it is not made simply *under* the Act; it is made under the Prerogative as explained by the Act.

GENERAL ACTS OF PARLIAMENT

So much for Prerogative rights of legislation. The only two important Acts of Parliament of wide general application are the British Settlements Acts and the Foreign Jurisdiction Acts.

[1] P. 33.   [2] P. 10, cf. pp. 222-3.

The British Settlements Acts 1887 and 1945.[1] The principal purpose and effect of the British Settlements Acts was to alter the common law rule that, in a Colony acquired by settlement, though the Crown can, under the Prerogative, legislate in the constituent field, it cannot make laws of other kinds.

The only problem of considerable interest is the combined effect of sections 2 and 3 in their original form; and the interest is not merely academic. The question is not easy to explain unless you know the sections well, but for those who do not I will try to simplify them.

Section 2 enables Her Majesty to make Orders in Council and thereby 'establish laws and institutions' for a British Settlement. Section 3 (now amended) originally empowered the Queen to make Letters Patent and by them to delegate any of her powers under the Act exercisable by Orders in Council to 'three or more persons within the Settlement', i.e. she could establish a local law-making body. The problem is this: could she, notwithstanding this express provision in section 3 for delegation of law-making powers to three or more persons in the Settlement, set up some other kind of legislature under section 2?

The question has been important because delegation to three or more persons within the Settlement may be inappropriate or even impossible in three types of cases: first, where special legislative authority is required to be conferred upon the Queen's representative alone; secondly, where a legislature is to be established for a territory only part of which was a British Settlement; and thirdly, where power has to be vested in a central authority to make laws for a small or remote territory, such as a Pacific island, which happens to be a British Settlement.

The difficulty no longer exists because the British Settlements Act, 1945, solved it by substituting for the reference in section 3 to three or more persons within the settlement a reference to any specified person or authority. But was the amendment necessary? And were Orders in Council previously made under section 2 conferring law-making powers valid or not? Section 2 empowers Her Majesty in Council to establish laws and institutions. There is no apparent reason why, if that section had stood alone, a legislative body, composed of such persons and sitting in such place as Her Majesty thought fit, should not be established by Order in Council under the section. An Order in Council constituting a legislature is a 'law'; and a legislature is an 'institution'.

[1] 50 & 51 V., c. 54; 9 G. 6, c. 7.

But it cannot be denied that the express provision in section 3, for delegation to a particular kind of legislature, by implication excludes delegation to a different kind of legislature under section 2. Here we encounter conflicting canons of interpretation. Acts of Parliament should normally be given their natural meaning and in its natural meaning section 2 enables a legislature to be constituted. On the other hand, some effect must, if possible, be given to every part of an Act of Parliament, and at first sight it appears that, if section 2 gives wide power to establish a legislature, the limited power of delegation in section 3 is otiose. There is, however, an answer to this. First, whatever the effect of section 2, section 3 is not otiose because it enables the Queen to delegate any of her powers under the Act exercisable by Orders in Council, including those of sections 4 and 5. Secondly the powers of section 2 are exercisable by Order in Council; those of section 3 by Letters Patent. This cannot be merely brushed aside as a matter of no consequence. An Order in Council is made at a meeting of the Privy Council and references to Her Majesty are in the third person; Letters Patent (though in practice approved in draft by Order in Council) are made by the Queen herself, reference to Her Majesty being in the first person, and the Great Seal is affixed under the authority of a warrant bearing her signature.

Furthermore, section 4, which enables jurisdiction in a British Settlement to be conferred on a Court elsewhere, demonstrates that Parliament was aware that the local resources of the Settlement might be limited and it would be surprising if Parliament provided a way out of consequent difficulties in the administration of Justice but not in the making of laws. It may therefore be argued that Parliament's intention was that a normal type of legislature, consisting of local inhabitants, could be established by Her Majesty by Letters Patent under section 3; but that any other, abnormal legislative body, should be constituted by Order of Her Majesty in Council. Though it cannot be said that this argument is sufficiently cogent to justify a confident assertion that it is correct, it can at least be claimed that there is no room for dogmatic assertion by an advocate for the contrary view.

There is plenty of evidence for all to see that this difficulty has had its practical consequences.

British Settlements in the Pacific. The Western Pacific Order in Council, 1893,[1] constituted the office of High Commissioner for the Western Pacific and gave him authority over an extensive area con-

---

[1] S.R.O. & S.I. 1948, Vol. VIII, p. 597.

taining hundreds of islands. It would have been manifestly absurd, even if it had been possible, to establish separate legislatures for, *and in*, every island which happened to be a British Settlement within the meaning of the Act. One can assume that the difficulty created by section 3 of the Act was, at least in part, responsible for the exceptional form of this Order in Council. It provides, for the whole of the High Commissioner's area of jurisdiction, an elaborate code of laws. Since the Order could not cater for all eventualities, it conferred, by Article 108, a wide power on the High Commissioner, sitting in Fiji, to make regulations on various specified subjects.

Now any law can properly provide for the making of subordinate legislation and the thought behind Article 108 was probably that it would pass as doing no more than that. But many of the purposes specified in the Article do not sufficiently relate to the contents of the Order to be accepted as no more than machinery for the enactment of subordinate legislation, and if plenary legislative power could not be conferred under the British Settlements Act on an individual not within the settlement, then regulations under Article 108 which were not really subordinate legislation must have been invalid in so far as they purported to have effect in British settlements. Doubts on this score were responsible for the Pacific Islands Regulations (Validation) Act, 1916,[1] which validated, as respects British Settlements, any regulations already made. This Act poses two questions which I cannot answer satisfactorily: first, why did it not take the form of an Act, like that of 1945, to amend the British Settlements Act by removing for good a useless hindrance to efficient government; or, alternatively, why did it not at least go so far as to remove all doubts as to the *vires* of Article 108 instead of merely validating regulations already made? This is just one example of the niggling, *ad hoc* Acts of Parliament which are the bugbear of the Colonial constitutional lawyer.

Even if Article 108 was invalid as an exercise of the powers of the British Settlements Act, it is far from clear that it could not be supported as an exercise of the Prerogative. I greatly regret that I have not time at present to justify this assertion, but study of the British Settlements Acts shows that the intention of Parliament was to extend, rather than supersede, the Sovereign's existing prerogative powers.

The Ross Dependency. When in 1923 the Ross Dependency was placed

[1] 6 G. 5, c. 9.

under the authority of the Government of New Zealand, legal opinion must have been that a legislature, consisting of one person not within the settlement, could be established under section 2 of the British Settlements Act. The Dependency is a sector of the Antarctic, British title to which rests on discovery plus occupation by small parties of scientists. An Order in Council[1] invoking the British Settlements Act conferred legislative powers on the Governor-General of New Zealand. Professor Berriedale Keith[2] challenged the validity of this Order and he appears to have claimed credit for the Pacific Islands Regulations (Validation) Act, 1916. He does not seem to have considered whether there was room for a view different from his.

The original *vires* of the Order can be supported on three grounds. The first two are the same as in the case of Article 108 of the Pacific Order in Council: that under the British Settlements Act legislative power can be given to a single person not within the settlement, and that the Order in Council may be treated as an exercise of the Prerogative. The third raises a new question on the interpetation of the British Settlements Act which affects only the Ross Dependency and any other similar territory. It may be argued that such a tract of land is not a British Settlement for the purposes of the Act, in which case one can rely upon the Prerogative. The Dependency is within the plain meaning of the definition of 'British Settlement' in section 6 of the Act because it was not ceded or conquered; but an interpretation not in accordance with the plain meaning of the words is permissible if it is required to carry out the stated purposes of the Act. The purpose of the British Settlements Act, 1887, according to the long title, was to provide for the government of possessions 'acquired by settlement'; places, the preamble tells us, to which Her Majesty's subjects have resorted and in which they have settled. A handful of scientists spending a few chilly months in the Antarctic may be said to 'resort to' the place, but they certainly cannot be said to have settled, and by no stretch of language can they be called settlers. There can be no room for doubt that, in passing the Act in 1887, Parliament had not in contemplation territories like the Ross Dependency.

The legal problem is of general interest; but, so far as the Ross Dependency is concerned, it seems now to be academic. The territory has been the subject of New Zealand legislation which is not likely to be successfully called in question in any Court.

[1] S.R.O. 1923, p. 712.
[2] *Responsible Government in the Dominions*, Vol. I, p. xviii. Vol. 2, pp. 792, 1039-40.

West Africa. One final shot at the poor drafting of this Act. It was plainly meant to apply to British territories in West Africa.[1] Yet most of them seem to have been excluded from the Act by the definition. The Colony of Nigeria was undoubtedly acquired by cession; the Colonies of Sierra Leone and Gambia are doubtful cases; Ashanti was conquered. The only West African territory clearly acquired by settlement was the Gold Coast Colony. So I feel some confidence in suggesting that the definition is not to be taken too seriously.

The Foreign Jurisdiction Act, 1890. This Act is of great importance for it is invariably relied upon for the exercise of jurisdiction outside Her Majesty's dominions. I must, however, restrict myself to four points of particular interest.

First, there is the well known principle that, if jurisdiction has in fact been exercised, it cannot be challenged in the Courts. Until recently, the authorities do not seem to have been altogether clear, but in *Nyali Ltd.* v *Attorney-General,*[2] Denning L. J., as he then was, stated the rule in terms of the utmost clarity.

I have already mentioned my second point: that section 1 of the Act of 1890 applies the Prerogative itself; apparently with the result that Orders made by virtue of section 1 are Prerogative Orders and not Statutory Orders.

This leads me to my third point. Section 1 applies in their entirety the extensive Prerogative powers applicable to conquered and ceded Colonies, and it does not in terms provide for the making of Orders in Council. From this it seems inevitably to follow that, although Orders in Council have always, or nearly always, been used, foreign jurisdiction, like jurisdiction in conquered or ceded territory, may lawfully be exercised by means of Letters Patent.

My fourth point is merely one of nomenclature. The early Foreign Jurisdiction Acts referred to countries outside Her Majesty's dominions. The draftsmen of the Act of 1890, for the sake of brevity, used and defined the shorter expression 'foreign countries'. The term is still in frequent use, but even if it was appropriate in 1890, which I doubt, it is now an absurdity as regards the great majority of the countries concerned and its perpetuation, particularly in Acts of Parliament, is, I suggest, not only unfortunate but unnecessary.

---

[1] Ridges, *Constitutional Law*, 8th edn., p. 479; Hood Phillips, *Constitutional Law*, 2nd edn., p. 613; Anson, *Law and Custom of the Constitution*, 4th edn. Vol. 2, Pt. 2, p. 64.

[2] [1956] 1 Q.B. 1.

SPECIAL ACTS OF PARLIAMENT

So much for general Acts. There are many special Acts, concerned with only one country or a limited area. I propose to do no more than pick out curiosities. There are only three of them.

First, there is that relic of the past, the Government of India Act, 1833.[1] Nothing remains except section 112, which has nothing to do with India but is preserved because it is the constitutional foundation of the Island of St Helena.

My next oddity is the West Indian Prisons Act, 1838.[2] It is remarkable for two reasons. First, in the middle of the twentieth century, an Act securing Parliamentary supervision of prison rules made in the West Indies is a preposterous anachronism. Secondly, the drafting is almost incredibly bad, even for an early nineteenth century statute. It would shame a pupil in Lincoln's Inn Chambers or an articled clerk.

Finally, there is the Jamaica Act, 1866.[3] The necessity for some of the nineteenth century Acts dealing with the West Indies is doubtful, but not this one. It confirmed two Jamaica Acts. By the first the legislature of Jamaica abolished itself; in the second the non-existing legislature proceeded to give Her Majesty constituent powers. It was not unnatural that someone thought that something required confirmation.

LIMITATIONS ON THE SOVEREIGN'S LEGISLATIVE POWER

Much has been written about the limitations of the powers of Colonial local legislatures but very little about the extent to which the legislative authority of the Crown is similarly restricted. In general, the same principles seem to apply.

First, there is repugnancy to Act of Parliament. It invalidates Orders in Council because the Colonial Laws Validity Act and the Foreign Jurisdiction Act say so. I decline to believe that Letters Patent and other instruments are not subject to the same rule. Secondly, there is the question of extra-territoriality. The extent to which laws made in a dependent territory may have extra-territorial operation is uncertain, but, whatever the true position may be, there is no apparent reason why the same general principles should not govern all legislatures for dependent countries, of which the Sovereign, or the Sovereign in Council, is one. There is, however, this important distinction; that the Queen can make a law for two or more territories which could not

[1] 3 & 4 W. 4, c. 85.   [2] 1 & 2 V., c. 67.   [3] 29 & 30 V., c. 12.

be made by any one of them because it would then purport to operate extra-territorially.

Thirdly, to what extent is it permissible for Her Majesty to delegate her legislative powers? It is abundantly clear that when she establishes a Legislature she must necessarily delegate or create power to make laws; indeed, the delegation is so complete that a Prerogative Order in Council making an ordinary law (as distinct from a constitution) can be amended by local legislation. But how far can she authorize a legislature to amend a constitutional instrument? If the instrument is under the British Settlements Acts there is express authority to delegate. The only broad question upon which there seems to be room for reasonable argument is whether an Order in Council made by virtue of section 1 of the Foreign Jurisdiction Act can authorize a local legislature to amend its provisions. Complex arguments can be extracted from the terms of the Act, but the answer appears to be this: there is no rule of law to hinder Her Majesty from giving the local legislature power to amend a constitutional instrument made under the Prerogative; and as section 1 of the Foreign Jurisdiction Act imports the Prerogative, the Sovereign is equally free to delegate power to amend.

Fourth, it is a well known rule that subordinate legislation cannot normally be given retrospective operation. It has been suggested that this rule applies to instruments made for overseas territories by virtue of general legislative powers conferred by Act of Parliament, but this notion betrays a misunderstanding. The rule relates to subordinate legislation properly so-called—regulations and like instruments made to supplement or give effect to the Act under which they are made. Laws made by virtue of plenary constituent or general legislative authority conferred by Act of Parliament are not subordinate legislation at all, except in an entirely different sense, and the rule has no application. It has been held[1] that a Colonial Legislature may make laws with retrospective operation; and the Crown, from whom most of them obtain their powers, must be at least equally competent.

CONTROL OF LOCAL LEGISLATION

One of the most important branches of my subject is the means by which control is exercised over legislation made in dependent territories and I wish I had more space to discuss it.

The official majority in the legislature need not detain me for it is

[1] *Phillips* v *Eyre* (1870) L.R., 6 Q.B. 1.

almost as dead as the dodo. The Royal assent can, of course, be withheld by a Governor, acting on instructions or otherwise; and if he has assented, then the law can be disallowed provided the power has not been deliberately abandoned. I am careful not to say provided it is expressly conferred, because the power of disallowance exists at common law whether it is reserved or not, a fact which has not always been appreciated. In recent years, however, resort has rarely been had to either the so-called 'veto' or the power of disallowance.

Not so much in danger of becoming rusty from disuse is the reservation of Bills for Her Majesty's pleasure, because constitutional instruments still regularly require Bills of certain kinds to be reserved. It is, I think, worth while to mention the danger of confusion in procedure between disallowance and reserved Bills. Only a law can be disallowed; a Bill cannot. A reserved Bill, if it is to become a law, must receive the Queen's assent. I should not be greatly surprised if some-one were to discover a Bill reserved for Her Majesty's pleasure which everyone thought had been satisfactorily converted into a law by signification that it was Her Majesty's pleasure not to disallow it. If that has happened, then the document is not a law, for no one has assented. As the Bill has been reserved, the Governor has not given the Royal assent: nor has the Sovereign in merely deciding not to exercise a power which does not exist—power to disallow a Bill. Perhaps I am being too fanciful in imagining a Government administering what they think is a law but which has no more effect in law than a piece of blank paper. I know that there has been this confusion, but I have no reason to think that it has ever led anyone right up the garden path.

Lastly, there is the Governor's so-called reserved power, sometimes referred to as the power of 'certification'—incorrectly, because there is no certificate. The Governor makes a declaration to the effect that, notwithstanding the rejection of a Bill by the local legislative House or Houses, it shall take effect as if they had passed it. This device was invented when unofficial majorities first superseded official majorities, and it is surprising how rarely in its lifetime of about 40 years it has been used. Does this demonstrate that the principal value of legal safeguards of this sort is that they encourage resort to compromise, mutual understanding and common sense in order to overcome differences of opinion?

2

SURVEY OF CONSTITUTIONS DRAFTED AT THE COLONIAL OFFICE SINCE 1944

J. C. MCPETRIE

*Legal Adviser to the Secretary of State
for the Colonies*

The last fifteen years or so have been a time of general constitutional advance in the territories for which the Secretary of State for the Colonies is responsible and in that period a number of them have attained independence. The process has naturally involved the making of a great number of new constitutions, which in turn have had to be amended or replaced—indeed, some territories have outgrown two or three constitutions on their way to independence.

These constitutions have not taken the form of Acts of Parliament. They are usually contained in Orders of Her Majesty in Council supplemented by Royal Instructions, though sometimes there are also Letters Patent establishing the office of Governor and defining certain of the Governor's powers.[1] Most of the Orders in Council are made in the exercise of the Royal Prerogative or of the powers conferred on Her Majesty by the British Settlements Acts, 1887 and 1945 or the Foreign Jurisdiction Act, 1890. Some are made under special Acts, such as the Jamaica Act, 1862. Where I refer to a particular Order in Council as the instrument containing a constitution, it is to be understood that this is the main instrument. There may also be amending or supplementary Orders, Letters Patent and Royal Instructions.

When the policy for a constitution has been settled, the preparation of the instruments is normally the responsibility of the legal staff of the Colonial Office. I do not know how many constitutional instruments have been drafted in the Colonial Office during this time but, as an illustration of what the output can amount to during a period of exceptional activity, between June 15, 1959 and June 23, 1960, no less than ninety-two constitutional instruments of one kind or another

[1] An exception was the Malta Constitution of 1947 which was contained in prerogative Letters Patent and Royal Instructions, with no Order in Council.

(including amending instruments) were produced, amounting to about 500 printed pages.

I propose in this paper to survey constitutions drafted at the Colonial Office since 1944. In the time available I cannot look at every constitution. On the other hand a detailed examination of one or perhaps two important constitutions would not give a proper picture of the range and variety of the work that has been done, or form the basis for conclusions about general trends in the field of constitutional development. I have, therefore, chosen to steer a middle course. I propose to examine a fair number of constitutions, but to confine my examination to their basic political structure. For my selection of constitutions I merely claim that it is reasonably satisfactory for purposes of illustration and comparison. Someone else might have selected differently, and the fact that I do not mention a particular constitution does not mean that I think it uninteresting or unimportant.

It will help if, before embarking on my survey, I define one or two terms and give one or two general explanations.

Where I refer to a member of a legislative or executive body as an 'unofficial' member, this convenient though inelegant piece of jargon indicates that the person in question is not a civil servant, while the label 'official' means that he is.

The statement that a Governor has 'reserved legislative powers' means that he has power in certain circumstances to make a declaration that a Bill which the legislature has failed to pass shall be deemed to have been passed; but the exercise of this power where it exists is, of course, very exceptional.

Where I speak of the Crown's power of disallowance I refer to a power in the Crown to disallow a law that has been passed by the legislative chamber and assented to by the Governor—although I do not recollect a single instance of the use of this power in the period under review.

When I say that a Governor has 'reserved executive authority' I mean that the constitution obliges him generally to act in accordance with the advice of his Executive Council (or equivalent body) but that he has authority in exceptional circumstances (often only with the concurrence of the Secretary of State) to act against their advice. I should also explain that under such a constitution there are usually a number of particular powers (which there is not space to enumerate) in the exercise of which the Governor is not obliged to consult the Executive Council, and which he can exercise either in his personal discretion or on the advice of some other person or authority, such as the Premier or a Commission. (In less advanced constitutions a Governor has a general authority to act contrary to the advice of the Executive Council and consequently no question of reserved executive authority arises.)

I shall also be referring to a Public Service Commission and a Judicial Service Commission.[1] The former advises a Governor on the appointment, discipline and dismissal of civil servants and the latter on the appointment of judges. I shall refer to such a Commission as 'executive' or 'advisory' according to whether its recommendations are or are not binding on the Governor.

I shall not be referring in the context of any individual constitution to the power of the Governor of a dependent territory to assent to a Bill passed by the legislative chamber. The position varies. At one end of the scale a Governor has a discretionary power to assent or to refuse assent to a Bill or to reserve it for the signification of Her Majesty's pleasure. At the other end, for example under the Constitution of Jamaica, a Governor exercises his power of assent on Ministerial advice except that, unless he has the authority of the Secretary of State to assent, he is required to reserve certain categories of Bill affecting matters, such as foreign affairs, in which Her Majesty's Government has a direct interest.

Finally, I would say this: many people think of a 'typical Crown Colony constitution' as a constitution in which the Governor is advised by an Executive Council on which there is a majority of Official Members, and makes laws with the advice and consent of a legislative chamber where Official Members are also in the majority. By the beginning of the period which I propose to examine, however, some territories had already advanced beyond that stage; others, for historical reasons, had never had such a constitution.

1944—1947

I have chosen to begin this survey with 1944, because, although general activity in the Colonial constitutional field did not begin until 1946, the constitution granted to Jamaica in 1944[2] really belongs to the general movement which got under way after the war. This constitution established a bicameral legislature consisting of an appointed Legislative Council with a majority of Unofficial Members

[1] In some cases this is a Judicial and Legal Service Commission with power to advise on legal as well as judicial appointments.
[2] Jamaica (Constitution) Order in Council, 1944 (S.R. & O. 1944, No. 1215).

and a wholly elected House of Representatives. In the event of disagreement between the two Chambers, the Legislative Council could delay the passage of a Bill into law for a year, and it is interesting to note that for this purpose no distinction was made between money Bills and other Bills. The Governor had reserved legislative powers, but he could not exercise them without the approval of the Executive Council and of the Secretary of State. The Crown retained a power of disallowance. The Governor was advised by an Executive Council with an unofficial majority, which contained members elected by the House of Representatives from among their own number. The latter could be removed from the Council by the vote of two-thirds of the House of Representatives—a device adopted in later constitutions elsewhere. It was expressly provided that the Governor would consult the Council in the formulation of policy, and he was given reserved executive authority.

An old body styled the Privy Council was kept in existence to advise the Governor on discipline and the exercise of the prerogative of mercy.

In 1946 a new constitution was conferred on Ceylon[1] which established a bicameral legislature, half the members of the Senate being elected and half of them appointed, while the House of Representatives was wholly elected. The Governor had no reserved legislative powers, though power was reserved to the Crown to legislate by Order in Council on defence and foreign affairs. On the executive side, a Cabinet of Ministers responsible to the Parliament of the island was charged with the general direction and control of government. The constitution also established Public Service and Judicial Service Commissions. These were executive. The Judicial Service Commission was given no powers in respect of Judges of the Supreme Court, who were appointed by the Governor in his discretion and were removable by the Governor only on an address from the Senate and the House of Representatives. When Ceylon attained independence in 1947, the 1946 constitution was amended in the way that one might expect, namely, by the removal of the discretionary powers formerly vested in the Governor, the replacement of the Governor by a Governor-General required to act in accordance with constitutional convention and the elimination of all elements of subordination to the United Kingdom.

The year 1946 was an important year for the Far East for it saw new constitutions for Malaya, Singapore, Sarawak and North Borneo

[1] Ceylon (Constitution) Order in Council, 1946.

—the last two having been ceded to the Crown in that year. I shall not spend time on the constitution of the Malayan Union, for it lasted less than two years. The Singapore (Colony) Order in Council, 1946[1] established a Legislative Council with equal numbers of Officials and Unofficials—assuming the maximum permissible number to have been appointed or elected in each category. The Governor had reserved legislative powers and the Crown a power of disallowance. The Executive Council had an official majority and the Governor had general authority to act contrary to its advice.

In 1946 new constitutions were also given to the Gold Coast[2] and to Nigeria.[3] In both territories there was a Legislative Council with an unofficial majority. The Governor had reserved legislative powers and the Crown a power of disallowance. On the executive side the Governor was advised by an Executive Council consisting of certain prescribed Officials and an unstipulated number of other members who might be Officials or Unofficials; the Governor had a general authority to act against the advice of the Council. The Unofficial majority in the Nigerian Legislative Council consisted mainly of persons chosen from among the members of the Provincial Houses established by the Order. These Houses were not legislative bodies. Their main functions were to consider and make recommendations with respect to estimates of revenue and expenditure and Bills affecting their respective regions, before these were discussed in the Legislative Council.

The year 1947 saw the establishment of joint institutions for the three East African territories of Kenya, Uganda and Tanganyika.[4] These were, on the executive side, a High Commission comprising the Governors of the three territories, and on the legislative side a central Legislative Assembly with an unofficial majority, the High Commission being the authority empowered to assent to Bills passed by the Assembly. The High Commission was given reserved legislative powers corresponding to those of a Governor, and the Crown a power of disallowance. The executive and legislative authority of these central institutions extend to such matters of common interest as

[1] S.R. & O. 1946, No. 464.
[2] Gold Coast Colony and Ashanti Letters Patent, 1946; Gold Coast Colony and Ashanti (Legislative Council) Order in Council, 1946 (S.R. & O. 1946, No. 353).
[3] Nigeria Letters Patent, 1946; Nigeria (Legislative Council) Order in Council, 1946 (S.R. & O. 1946, No. 1370).
[4] East Africa (High Commission) Order in Council, 1947 (S.R. & O. 1947, No. 2863).

defence, civil aviation, posts and telegraphs, railways, harbours and inland water transport.

In 1947 a system of Ministerial Government was restored to Malta.[1] The constitution was in the form of a diarchy, that is to say the field of government was divided into reserved matters (roughly defence and foreign affairs) and non-reserved matters. On the reserved side the Governor was empowered to enact Ordinances and in the exercise of this function, as well as in the exercise of his executive authority on the reserved side, he was advised by a Nominated Council of Officials. On the non-reserved side laws were made by the Governor with the advice and consent of a wholly elected Legislative Assembly. The Governor had no reserved legislative powers, though the Crown had a power of disallowance. On the non-reserved side the Governor was advised in executive matters by an Executive Council consisting of Ministers appointed from among the members of the Legislative Assembly.

1948—1953

In 1948, by an Agreement between the Crown and the Rulers of the Malay States, provision was made for a federation of those States and the Settlements of Penang and Malacca; and the unitary constitution of 1946 was revoked. The Agreement contained the constitution of the Federation and in addition certain provisions with regard to the constitutions of the States and Settlements; it was given the force of law by the Federation of Malaya Order in Council, 1948.[2] This Order was the Crown's final exercise of the full powers that had been granted to it by the Rulers in 1945 and thereafter the Crown retained jurisdiction in the Malay States only in respect of defence and foreign affairs. The federal constitution made provision for a High Commissioner to be appointed by the Crown, whose advice the Rulers undertook to accept in matters connected with the government of the Federation. Federal authority extended to a long list of important matters; and federal laws were passed by a Legislative Council, which contained an unofficial majority, and assented to by the High Commissioner and the Rulers. Power to disallow federal laws was vested in the Crown and, in the event of the exercise of that power, the Rulers could withdraw their assent to the law in question.

[1] Malta (Constitution) Letters Patent, 1947, and the Malta (Office of Governor) Letters Patent, 1947.
[2] S.I. 1948, No. 108.

The numbers of Officials and Unofficials in the federal Executive Council were equal, assuming the maximum permissible number in each class to have been appointed. The High Commissioner had a general authority to act in opposition to the advice of the Council.

In 1950 there were new constitutions for Trinidad[1] and the Gold Coast.[2] The Legislative Council established for Trinidad contained only three official members. Of the remainder eighteen were elected and five nominated. The Governor had reserved legislative powers but could not exercise them without the agreement of the Executive Council or, if that was not forthcoming, the authority of the Secretary of State. The Crown retained a power of disallowance. In the Executive Council there was an unofficial majority. All but one of the Unofficial Members were elected to the Executive Council by the Legislative Council from among its own members and could be removed by a vote of two-thirds of the Legislative Council—a device clearly designed, in the absence of a well defined party system, to secure an executive government that had the support of the legislature. The Governor had reserved executive authority. Members of the Executive Council could be charged with responsibility for departments and any member charged with such responsibility was to be styled a Minister. An advisory Public Service Commission was also established and provision was made for a special committee of the Executive Council to advise the Governor on the exercise of the prerogative of mercy in capital cases.

The Gold Coast Constitution provided for a Legislative Assembly with a large elected majority and an unofficial majority in the Executive Council. The Governor's reserved legislative powers and executive authority were on the same lines as in Trinidad. Unofficial members of the Executive Council could be removed not only by a vote of the Assembly, as in Trinidad, but also by the Governor with the approval of the Executive Council, on the ground that the member in question had failed to carry out the policy of the Council: a recognition of the principle of collective responsibility for government policy. Provision was also made for an advisory Public Service Commission and, as in Trinidad, for members of the Executive Council to be given responsibility for departments with the style of Minister.

In 1951 the new constitution granted to Nigeria[3] was the first step

[1] Trinidad and Tobago (Constitution) Order in Council, 1950 (S.I. 1950, No. 510).
[2] Gold Coast (Constitution) Order in Council, 1950 (S.I. 1950, No. 2094).
[3] Nigeria (Constitution) Order in Council, 1951 (S.I. 1951, No. 1172).

towards federation. The constitution established a central legislature and a central executive for the whole country and a legislature and executive for each of the three Regions. This constitution, however, fell short of true federal government in view of the unrestricted authority of the Centre and its powers of control over the Regions.

Sierra Leone also received a new constitution in 1951,[1] the Legislative Council containing a majority of elected members and membership of the Executive Council being equally divided between Officials and Unofficials.

The year 1953 saw the grant of a new constitution to British Guiana[2] and the creation of the Federation of Rhodesia and Nyasaland.[3] The British Guiana Constitution established a bicameral legislature comprising a House of Assembly and a State Council. Except for the Speaker and three official members, the House of Assembly consisted of elected members, while the State Council consisted of nine members appointed by various procedures. The Governor was given reserved legislative powers similar to those contained in the Trinidad Constitution of the previous year and the Crown retained a power of disallowance. It is interesting to note that alternative methods were provided for resolving a conflict of views on a Bill between the two chambers. The Bill if passed by the House of Assembly in two successive sessions and rejected by the State Council could be presented for assent. Alternatively, the Governor could summon the two chambers to meet in joint session and vote on the Bill. On the executive side the Governor was advised by an Executive Council containing three Officials and seven Ministers. The Governor had reserved executive authority.

The constitution of the Federation of Rhodesia and Nyasaland does not strictly come within the scope of my survey, but I would like to mention two of its features. The federal principle is applied in the manner found in Australia, that is to say the legislative and executive powers of the Centre extend to matters set out in a Federal and a Concurrent Legislative List; subject to the overriding authority of the Centre, the Territories are given powers over matters in the Concurrent Legislative List; and matters in neither list are exclusively the concern of the Territories. An institutional safeguard against

[1] Sierra Leone (Legislative Council) Order in Council, 1951 (S.I. 1951, No. 611).
[2] British Guiana (Constitution) Order in Council, 1953 (S.I. 1953, No. 586).
[3] Federation of Rhodesia and Nyasaland (Constitution) Order in Council, 1953 (S.I. 1953, No. 1199).

discriminatory legislation is established, namely the African Affairs Board—a committee of the federal legislative House with power to cause a Bill to which it objects to be reserved for the signification of Her Majesty's pleasure.

1954—1957

In 1954 Nigeria entered upon a system of true federal government. This constitution,[1] which sets out the arrangements for both the Centre and the Regions, lasted until Nigeria attained independence on October 1, 1960. It did not, however, remain static, for the years from 1954 to 1960 were years of steady constitutional advance and the original constitution of 1954 was during that period amended, sometimes very extensively, no less than fourteen times. It will, I hope, be instructive to look at this constitution in its original form and then follow up the more important of the amendments that were made to it.

In this federation, too, the division of powers is according to the principle applied in Australia. The central legislature is unicameral and the legislative chamber (the House of Representatives) contains only three Officials. The Northern and Western Regions have bicameral legislatures, the chambers being a House of Chiefs and a House of Assembly, the Northern House of Assembly containing four official members and the Western House none. The legislature of the Eastern Region is unicameral, the chamber being a House of Assembly which, like that of the West, contains no Officials.

The Governor-General and the regional Governors have reserved legislative powers and the Crown retains a power of disallowance.

On the executive side a federal Council of Ministers is presided over by the Governor-General and, except for three Officials, consists of Ministers appointed from the House of Representatives. At regional level there is an Executive Council presided over by the Governor, and only in the Northern Region does it contain Officials. Each regional Council contains a Premier, on whose recommendations the other Ministers are appointed. Both the Governor-General and the Governors have reserved executive authority. Control of criminal prosecutions is not within the portfolio of any Minister but is assigned at central and regional level to civil service Attorneys-General.

There are advisory Public Service Commissions at both federal and regional level; and the Governor-General and each regional Governor

[1] Nigeria (Constitution) Order in Council, 1954 (S.I. 1954, No. 1146).

has a Privy Council to advise him on the exercise of the prerogative of mercy.

The amendments to this constitution between 1954 and independence were mainly directed to the attainment of what was referred to as 'internal self-government'. The Western and Eastern Regions attained that status first. 'Internal self-government' is not an exact expression, but in the context of a Nigerian Region it involved the following changes—the Governor's reserved legislative powers disappeared; his reserved executive authority was restricted to matters for which Her Majesty's Government had a special responsibility; the Premier replaced the Governor as president of the Executive Council; the Crown's power of disallowance was restricted to a few special categories of law which involved matters of special concern to Her Majesty's Government; the Public Service Commission became 'executive', and an 'executive' Judicial Service Commission was established; the Attorney-General ceased to be a civil servant and a special office of Director of Public Prosecutions was created, the holder of which was not responsible to Ministers.

Other important changes made during this period included the addition of a second chamber to the legislature of the Eastern Region and to the federal legislature; provision to secure that a Judge of the Superior Courts could be removed from office only if the Judicial Committee of the Privy Council recommended his removal on grounds of inability or misbehaviour; and the inclusion of a long and elaborate list of fundamental rights enforceable in the courts.

The Gold Coast also got a new constitution in 1954.[1] The Legislative Assembly became wholly elected. The Governor retained reserved legislative powers. These were exercisable only with the agreement of the Cabinet or, failing that, the agreement of the Secretary of State. The Crown retained a power of disallowance. On the executive side there was a Cabinet of Ministers in which the Governor was replaced as president by a Prime Minister. Certain subjects, however, (roughly defence and external affairs) were the personal responsibility of the Governor. The Public Service Commission, initially 'advisory', was to become 'executive' after a certain period.

1955 saw a new constitution conferred on Singapore by the Singapore Colony Order in Council, 1955.[2] The former Legislative Council was replaced by a Legislative Assembly with an unofficial

[1] Gold Coast (Constitution) Order in Council, 1954 (S.I. 1954, No. 551).
[2] S.I. 1955, No. 187.

majority, mainly elected. The Governor retained reserved legislative powers and the Crown a power of disallowance. On the executive side there was a Council of Ministers containing only three Officials. The Governor had reserved executive authority.

In 1957 Ghana (formerly the Gold Coast) and the Federation of Malaya became independent. The Ghana constitution was contained in the Ghana (Constitution) Order in Council, 1957,[1] and that of Malaya was scheduled to the Federation of Malaya Independence Order in Council, 1957.[2] The latter is not strictly within the scope of this survey, for the draft was prepared by a Constitutional Commission.[3] Having concerned myself so much with the stages of constitutional development in these territories, I have time to say very little about the end result, i.e. the independence constitutions themselves. In both Ghana and Malaya the system of government established on independence was a Cabinet system with Ministers appointed from, and responsible to, the legislature, which was unicameral in Ghana and bicameral in Malaya. Both constitutions provided for executive Public Service and Judicial Service Commissions and the constitution of Malaya made express provision for the protection of fundamental liberties, though less elaborately than in Nigeria. In Ghana judges were removable only on an address from the legislature; in Malaya they were removable only on the recommendation of a special tribunal composed of judges or former judges.

In the same year the Federation of the West Indies was established by the West Indies (Federation) Order in Council, 1957,[4] which was amended in 1958, 1959, 1960 and 1961. The division of powers was again on Australian lines, i.e. residual powers rested with the Territories. There was a bicameral legislature consisting of an appointed Senate and elected House of Representatives, neither of which contained Officials. The Governor-General had no reserved legislative powers, but power was reserved to Her Majesty to legislate by Order in Council on defence and external affairs. On the executive side there was a Cabinet presided over by a Prime Minister. (Originally this was styled a Council of State and was presided over by the Governor-General.) The Governor-General had reserved executive authority in relation to defence and external affairs. The Public Service Commission became 'executive' in 1960, when a Judicial Service Commission, also 'executive', was introduced. This constitution was the first to provide that judges should be removable

[1] S.I. 1957, No. 277.   [2] S.I. 1957, No. 1533.
[3] Col. No. 330.   [4] S.I. 1957, No. 1364.

only on the recommendation of the Judicial Committee of the Privy Council.

1958—1961

In 1958 Kenya[1] and Singapore[2] were given new constitutions.

Under the Kenya Constitution, as amended in 1959 and 1960, there is a Legislative Council with a majority of elected members; the Governor has reserved legislative powers and the Crown a power of disallowance. There is a Council of Ministers not exceeding twelve in number, of whom no less than four must be Officials. The Governor has special authority to act contrary to the advice of the Council. A Council of State is also established as a safeguard against legislation which discriminates unfairly against the members of any racial or religious community. This body can delay the passage of a Bill or may cause a Bill that has been passed to be reserved for the signification of Her Majesty's pleasure. The constitution also contains a long list of fundamental rights enforceable in the courts. (This was inserted by the amendment of 1960.)

Under the constitution of Singapore Her Majesty's representative in Singapore is not styled Governor but Yang di-Pertuan Negara, and must be a person born in Singapore or Malaya. The Legislative Assembly is entirely elected; there are no reserved legislative powers and the Crown's power of disallowance is restricted to certain laws affecting Singapore Government stock. On the executive side there is a Cabinet presided over by a Prime Minister. The Yang di-Pertuan Negara has no reserved executive authority. Provision is also made for a United Kingdom Commissioner who is the representative in Singapore of the United Kingdom Government. Responsibility for defence and external affairs is expressly reserved to the Government of the United Kingdom and special provision is made to enable that Government to discharge those responsibilities. There is a special council, on which the Governments of the United Kingdom, Malaya and Singapore are represented, to deal with questions of internal security. There are executive Public Service and Judicial Service Commissions. The State of Singapore Act[3] terminated the power of Her Majesty to make Orders in Council for Singapore under the British Settlements Acts, 1887 and 1945, and the Straits Settlements (Repeal) Act, 1946; but the constitution reserves to Her Majesty, on

---

[1] Kenya (Constitution) Order in Council, 1958 (S.I. 1958, No. 600).

[2] Singapore (Constitution) Order in Council, 1958 (S.I. 1958, No. 1956).

[3] 6 & 7 El. 2, c. 59.

the terms set out therein, power to amend, revoke or suspend the constitution by Order in Council.

In 1959 the Jamaica Constitution of 1944, which had been amended in the interval, was replaced. Under the new constitution[1] the legislature remains bicameral and contains no Officials. The Governor has no reserved legislative powers and the Crown's power of disallowance is restricted to certain kinds of law affecting Jamaica Government stock. There is a Cabinet presided over by a Premier and the Governor has no reserved executive authority. There are 'executive' Public Service and Judicial Service Commissions and the Privy Council is retained to advise the Governor on the exercise of the prerogative of mercy in capital cases.

In this year the Malta Constitution of 1947, which had been the subject of amendment in the interval, was revoked and replaced by a less advanced constitution which dispensed with the diarchy.[2]

On October 1, 1960, independence came to Nigeria, the largest country both in area and population for which the Secretary of State for the Colonies had been responsible. Its independence constitution, set out in the Nigeria (Constitution) Order in Council, 1960,[3] was substantially that which had gradually and steadily been evolved between 1954 and early 1960.

Sierra Leone had received a new constitution in 1958[4] and in 1959 that constitution was amended so as to bring Sierra Leone to a stage of constitutional development approaching that achieved by Jamaica in 1959.

In 1961 Sierra Leone became independent and its constitution included provision for the protection of fundamental rights very similar to that in the Nigeria Constitution.

Trinidad[5] and British Guiana[6] also received new constitutions in this year, which brought them to a stage similar to that reached by Jamaica in 1959.

Tanganyika, by an amendment of its existing constitution, attained internal self-government in May, 1961, and became independent in December.[7]

---

[1] Jamaica (Constitution) Order in Council, 1959 (S.I. 1959, No. 862).
[2] Malta (Constitution) Order in Council, 1959.
[3] S.I. 1960, No. 1652.
[4] Sierra Leone (Constitution) Order in Council, 1958 (S.I. 1958, No. 1259).
[5] Trinidad and Tobago (Constitution) Order in Council, 1961 (S.I. 1961, No. 1192).
[6] British Guiana (Constitution) Order in Council, 1961 (S.I. 1961, No. 1188).
[7] S.I. 1961, No. 2274.

CONCLUSION

One is bound to ask oneself whether this survey, incomplete and imperfect though it is, reveals any general trends in constitutional development. It is, of course, obvious that over the last fifteen years there has been a progressive loosening of United Kingdom control over its overseas dependencies at an accelerating pace. This process has culminated in no less than ten instances in complete independence —besides Ceylon, Ghana, Malaya and Nigeria there are Cyprus, Somaliland, Sierra Leone, Tanganyika, Uganda and the Southern Cameroons. As the process of emancipation proceeds, forms of government tend increasingly to resemble those with which we are familiar in this country. There is also a general tendency, with constitutional advance, to adopt institutional safeguards, such as commissions designed to insulate the public service and the judiciary against political influence. There is also a movement, though it could not be described as general, towards the inclusion in constitutions of a list of fundamental liberties protected by the courts of law; and in two cases, the Federation of Rhodesia and Nyasaland and Kenya, special bodies have been established with the object of checking discriminatory measures before they have passed into law.

3

THE LEGAL MACHINERY FOR THE
TRANSITION FROM DEPENDENCE
TO INDEPENDENCE[1]

SIR KENNETH ROBERTS-WRAY

'To propose that Great Britain should voluntarily give up all authority of her Colonies, and leave them to elect their own magistrates, to enact their own laws, and to make peace and war, as they might think proper, would be to propose such a measure as never was, and never will be, adopted by any nation in the World.' Thus wrote Adam Smith in his *Wealth of Nations*. Of course, political vistas are apt to change in two hundred years, but Adam Smith should have realized that and it does not excuse his rash dogmatism. My task now is to describe a nicely adjusted piece of legal machinery, which works overtime giving substance to political designs which for Adam Smith would have been fantasies.

THE NEWLY INDEPENDENT STATES

The machinery started work in 1947 on the creation of the Dominions of India and Pakistan. Ceylon followed in 1948 and there was then a lull until 1957, when the Gold Coast, as the State of Ghana, and the Federation of Malaya achieved their independence. Three years later the machine gathered speed and in under sixteen months helped to deliver no less than four newly independent Commonwealth States —Cyprus on August 16, 1960; Nigeria on October 1, 1960; Sierra Leone on April 27, 1961; and Tanganyika on December 9, 1961.[2] This list is not really complete, for I have not mentioned those countries which, during the same period, became independent and simultaneously left the Commonwealth: Burma, Palestine, and the British Somaliland Protectorate. I might even go back to 1931 when Iraq discarded the status of a mandated territory. But I must limit my subject matter to match the space at my disposal. I propose to concentrate upon transi-

[1] See footnote on p. 11.
[2] Jamaica, Trinidad and Uganda have become independent since this chapter was written.

tion to independence within the Commonwealth. It is, however, of interest to glance at the other recent cases. Burma required an Act of Parliament, the Burma Act, 1947, because most of it was within His Majesty's dominions and, though it cannot in my opinion be regarded as a rule of law, it does seem to be an established constitutional convention that the relinquishment of British title requires Parliamentary consent. Further, British nationality was withdrawn from most Burmese who possessed it; provision was made for abatement of pending appeals to the Privy Council and for the temporary continuation of customs preferences; and references to Burma in a large number of Acts of Parliament had to be amended.

The Palestine Act, 1948, was similarly needed to deal with the operation of Acts of Parliament and Privy Council appeals. It also contained an indemnity for acts done in good faith by persons in His Majesty's service, obviously related in particular to the disturbances. It formally terminated the responsibility of the United Kingdom Goverment for the government of Palestine, a wise precaution; and it determined His Majesty's jurisdiction in Palestine, which was no doubt tidy; but neither appears to have been strictly necessary. Jurisdiction was acquired under international law; under international law it was terminated; and though, in general, international rights and obligations have, *per se*, no validity in our municipal law, if the Crown, in exercise of the Prerogative, acquires jurisdiction by virtue of an international transaction, the fact is recognized by the common law and requires no confirmation. It must surely follow that the common law will also acknowledge a surrender of jurisdiction? The constitutional convention that transfer of British title to territory requires Parliamentary confirmation does not extend to the termination of mere jurisdiction. There was no Act of Parliament to put an end to the British Protectorate in Somaliland. In that case there were no statutes requiring consequential amendment. It was known that the territory intended in due course to join the Republic of Somalia and our constitutional machine was called upon for no more than two documents: first, a Royal Proclamation, dated June 23, 1960, declaring that on June 26th Her Majesty's protection should cease and all treaties and agreements with tribes of the territories and Her Majesty's obligations, functions, powers, rights, authority or jurisdiction should lapse; and secondly an Order in Council[1] providing the territory with a constitution for the period between the date of independence and union with the Republic.

[1] The Somaliland Order in Council 1960 (S.I. 1960, No. 1060).

SCOPE OF THE SUBJECT

Comment upon the attainment of independence by those countries which were founder Members of the British Commonwealth (Canada, Australia, New Zealand, the Union of South Africa, the Irish Free State and Newfoundland) would be out of place. I shall have occasion to refer to them again but they are outside my subject. The gradual progress of the 'Dominions', through Imperial Conferences to the Statute of Westminster, from self-government to independence, is a fascinating study. But, far from claiming any credit for it, the machinery which I have to talk about owes much to those who prepared the way for, and constructed, the Statute of Westminster.

To set the bounds of the primary purpose of this chapter, I must begin by stating the obvious—to give independence means no more and no less than erasing marks of dependence. We must therefore ask why the country is not independent and having found the answer we shall know the essentials of the major operation we have to perform.

First and foremost one has to deal with the relationship between the dependent territory and the country on which it is dependent. The essence of the situation is that in both municipal law and international law a dependent territory is subject to some sort of external control or supervision which limits its freedom of action and its sovereignty. This must be removed.

In my earlier chapter I presented a general picture of the powers exercised by the United Kingdom in respect of dependent territories. I was not concerned with other Members of the Commonwealth who have dependencies. If I limit myself to the procedure for granting independence to territories formerly within the United Kingdom's responsibility I shall in fact cover my subject today, with the exception of Western Samoa, where New Zealand's Trusteeship has just been terminated. I have not yet been able to obtain very much information about the legal steps taken, so I cannot compare the New Zealand procedure with that of the United Kingdom. I am told that Western Samoa does not intend, at least at present, to consider applying for Membership of the Commonwealth, but that there is a Western Samoa Act of 1961 by virtue of which New Zealand law continues to operate in relation to the new State as if it were part of Her Majesty's dominions and a Member of the Commonwealth. I am also informed that the Act confers no special citizenship status on Western Samoan citizens, but exempts them from registration as aliens. In this country the only action taken so far is to add Western Samoa to the countries within the Commonwealth Preference Area.

LEGISLATIVE POWER

Returning to the United Kingdom machinery, the most obvious need is to ensure unlimited legislative freedom. The limits to be removed are threefold. First, under the Colonial Laws Validity Act, 1865, laws passed by the legislature of a Colony are invalid if they are repugnant to United Kingdom legislation and, for reasons which it would be out of place to discuss now, this rule must apply to other dependent territories. That rule has to be abolished. Secondly, the United Kingdom Parliament has an unquestionable right to legislate for a dependent territory and that must be terminated. Thirdly, there is the question of extra-territoriality.

The first two obviously need an Act of Parliament, because the powers of Parliament are themselves affected. Sections 2 and 4 of the Statute of Westminster provide models which have been closely followed in all other cases where they were needed—they will not be found in the Acts which secured the independence of countries outside Her Majesty's dominions, the Federation of Malaya, and Cyprus, a republic.

Repugnancy. Section 2, which deals with repugnancy, is of special importance. Long before the Statute of Westminster, it was an established convention that the United Kingdom Parliament did not legislate for the Dominions without their consent, a convention which would have continued to be observed even if section 4 had not given it statutory form. But no mere political arrangement could get rid of the Colonial Laws Validity Act, 1865, and its restrictions on the powers of Colonial legislatures. Section 2, therefore, provided that that Act should not apply to future Acts of Dominion Parliaments and that no future law made by a Dominion Parliament should be void on the ground of repugnancy to the law of England or to the provisions of any existing or future United Kingdom legislation; and that the Parliament of a Dominion should have power to repeal or amend any such legislation in so far as it is part of the law of the Dominion.

A question which has given rise to some discussion is whether in section 2 the words 'any existing or future Act of Parliament of the United Kingdom' include the Statute of Westminster itself, so that

that Act, in its application to a Dominion, can be amended or repealed by the Parliament of the Dominion. It can be strongly argued that it does, but section 6 (2) of the Indian Independence Act, 1947,[1] avoided any doubt by using the expression 'this or any existing or future Act'. The Ceylon Independence Act, 1947,[2] reverted to the words of the Statute of Westminster as also did the Ghana Independence Act, 1957.[3] The Nigeria Independence Act, 1960,[4] the Sierra Leone Independence Act, 1961,[5] and the Tanganyika Independence Act, 1961,[6] in effect followed the example of the Indian Independence Act by referring to 'any Act of the Parliament of the United Kingdom, including this Act'. These differences in words do not, of course, necessarily mean that there is a difference in operation and in fact the greater part of the Ghana Independence Act has been repealed by Act of the Ghana Parliament.

Powers of United Kingdom Parliament. Section 4 of the Statute of Westminster lays down that no future United Kingdom Act shall extend or be deemed to extend to a Dominion as part of the law of the Dominion unless it is expressly declared in the Act that the Dominion has requested, and consented to, the enactment thereof. It was copied without change in the Ceylon and Ghana Independence Acts. But the Indian Independence Act omitted the reference to request and consent, and substituted the words 'unless it is extended thereto by a law of the Legislature of the Dominion'. In the cases of Nigeria, Sierra Leone and Tanganyika, the request and consent phrase is simply omitted.

The Indian Independence Act also adds that no Order or other instrument made after the appointed day under an existing Act shall extend to either of the new Dominions as part of their law. There is logic in this; but though the point is of little practical importance, this addition might have its disadvantages, for it renders inoperative machinery which might on exceptional occasions be useful. Speaking generally, it has not been the practice at the time of independence to repeal existing Acts of Parliament in their application to the newly independent country—that is a matter for subsequent action by the Government and Parliament of that country themselves if they think fit—and some United Kingdom statutes could in very special circum-

---

[1] 10 & 11 G. 6, c. 30.   [2] 11 & 12 G. 6, c. 7, 1st Sch., para. 1(2).
[3] 5 & 6 El. 2, c. 6, 1st Sch., para. 2.   [4] 8 & 9 El. 2, c. 55, 1st Sch., para. 2.
[5] 9 & 10 El. 2, c. 16, 2nd Sch., para. 2.
[6] 10 El. 2, c. 1, 1st Sch., para. 2.

stances prove helpful, provided political objections to their use were not insuperable. For example, the British Settlements Act might provide a simple method of transferring a territory to the administration of some other Member of the Commonwealth. Or take the case of a citizen of another Commonwealth country, perhaps a member of their armed forces, sentenced to imprisonment in a Colony, who, for some good reason, ought to be transferred to his own country to serve his sentence. The only available means of transferring him would appear to be an Order under the Colonial Prisoners Removal Act, 1884.

Closely, but not exclusively, connected with section 4 of the Statute of Westminster is section 11 which, for subsequent legislation, removed Dominions from the definition of Colony in the Interpretation Act, 1889. This, too, has been copied into Independence Acts.

Extra-territoriality. Following section 3 of the Statute of Westminster, they also deal with the vexed question of extra-territorial legislation. It is questionable whether this is necessary. That the legislature of a dependent territory has some extra-territorial power is clear; only its limits are doubtful. This is recognized in the common form section which declares that the legislature has 'full power', not merely 'power', to make laws having extra-territorial operation. But whatever the true rule may be, the limitations attach only to the legislature of a dependent territory, and it seems to follow that they would be automatically abolished by the grant of independence. The inclusion of this provision in the Statute of Westminster was a different matter. The Act did not make a clean cut between dependence and independence. As a matter of political relationships, it amounted to statutory confirmation of established fact. The Dominions had already, by a gradual process, attained their independence. The Statute could not therefore terminate their dependence by the good resounding declaration, found in Independence Acts, that after the appointed day Her Majesty's Government in the United Kingdom shall have no responsibility for the government of the country concerned, and no one could say that particular marks of dependence had ceased, as a matter of law, to adhere to the older 'Dominions' at a particular time or at all. This declaration in the Independence Acts leaves no room for argument. However, no doubt it is a sensible and harmless precaution to include this provision, if only because it is apt to be regarded as one of the chief monoliths in the Statute of Westminster and its omission might possibly be misunderstood.

EXTERNAL AUTHORITY OVER LOCAL LEGISLATION

So much for securing unrestricted authority to the legislature of a newly independent country. The second need is to remove from its legislative process all means of intervention by the country upon which it has been dependent, such as the reservation of Bills, disallowance of laws, and reserved powers. On this, the Statute of Westminster had nothing to say, except in sections 5 and 6, which deal with two points of detail. They remove United Kingdom control over certain legislation relating to merchant shipping and Courts of Admiralty, and they have their counterpart where necessary in the Independence Acts.

It may seem surprising that in the Statute of Westminster there was no mention of powers of disallowance, which have never been repealed except by the Union of South Africa. But the power has been quite lifeless for a very long time and it is of no consequence that the corpse remains on the statute book.

With the new Members of the Commonwealth, however, all powers of supervision or control by the United Kingdom have been abolished. For India and Pakistan, this was done by the Indian Independence Act. But since, in the great majority of cases, pre-independence constitutions are contained in Orders in Council, Letters Patent and Royal Instructions, the removal of powers of control or intervention does not, in the main, require an Act of Parliament. It is sufficient to amend or replace the existing instruments. In the case of Ceylon, the relevant parts of the Constitution Order in Council were deleted by an amending Order. All the other countries have had entirely new constitutions from which external authority has, of course, been omitted.

There are, however, a few statutory controls which need the attention of Parliament. I have mentioned those disposed of by sections 5 and 6 of the Statute of Westminster. Then there is the matter of Colonial Stock. Even when a dependent territory reaches an advanced stage of self-government, it is necessary, under United Kingdom law, if the Government of the country concerned wish their stock to remain on the list of trustee securities, for them to have placed on record their opinion that legislation which appears to the United Kingdom Government adversely to affect the rights of holders of their stock would properly be disallowed. On the grant of independence that becomes impossible but the difficulty is overcome by extending to newly independent countries the Colonial Stock Act, 1934, which substitutes, for the power of disallowance, an undertaking, confirmed by statute, that legislation adversely affecting the rights of stockholders will not be submitted for assent except after agreement with the United Kingdom Government; and that, if attention is called to such legislation after it has been enacted, the Government of the country concerned will take steps to amend it.

EXECUTIVE POWER

I think I have said all that is required on the subject of legislative authority. Of greater fundamental importance, perhaps, is the executive power. The Government of a dependent territory is the Crown; the Queen is the head of the Executive and if the territory is to remain in the Commonwealth and does not immediately become a republic, she so remains after independence, but with an obvious, though vital, difference. In her government of United Kingdom dependent territories she acts with the advice of United Kingdom Ministers; after independence she will act on the advice of the local Ministers. The product of our constitution-making machine does not say so in so many words; it is not the practice for a legal instrument expressly to require the Sovereign to act in accordance with the advice of anyone. The key to the situation is the common form declaration in Independence Acts, which I have already mentioned, that the United Kingdom Government shall have no responsibility for the government of the newly independent country, from which it follows that the United Kingdom Government cannot advise Her Majesty as Queen of that country. This seems to leave a void, but established conventions are quite sufficient to fill it. The constitution vests the executive power in the Queen. Her Majesty is a constitutional monarch in the United Kingdom and its dependent territories and in other Commonwealth countries which are monarchies, and no one could sensibly suggest that she would be otherwise in a country which has just become independent. She will continue to act on the advice of Ministers; the United Kingdom Government's responsibility having been withdrawn, advice can be tendered only by the Government set up by the new Constitution. It is therefore unnecessary for the Constitution to say more. The Constitutions of Ceylon and Ghana, however, provided that both the Queen and the Governor-General should perform their functions in accordance with United Kingdom constitutional conventions, which clearly imports an obligation to act on the advice of Ministers. Though one cannot, of course, criticize these enactments on the ground of redundancy, there can be little, if any, doubt that they were unnecessary, at any rate so far as the Queen is concerned.

The position may not be quite so obvious in the case of a Governor-General, or the Governor in a Nigerian Region, and the Constitutions of Nigeria, Sierra Leone and Tanganyika lay down that in the exercise of his functions he shall act in accordance with ministerial advice. But even if they did not, there could be no room for reasonable argument. It is expressly provided that the Governor-General or Governor is the representative of Her Majesty, in whom the executive authority is vested, and that that authority is exercisable by him on her behalf. The agent could not exercise personal discretion which would be unconstitutional for his Royal principal.

TWO MACHINES

It is implicit in what I have been saying that, except in the case of India and Pakistan, the legal machinery for creating independent states has operated, and still operates, in two distinct workshops. An Act of Parliament is required to produce some of the essentials of independence, notably those taken from the Statute of Westminster, but in the majority of cases the new constitution itself is embodied in an Order in Council and other constitutional instruments made by Her Majesty in pursuance of some existing Act of Parliament or the Prerogative. It can therefore be made, and is made, before the Independence Act comes into operation. Speaking generally (for there may be exceptions in matters of detail) there is no reason in law why it should not come into operation before the Act, but in practice its operation is suspended until the day appointed for independence.

Professor de Smith, in an article on the Independence of Ghana which was published in the *Modern Law Review* in July 1957, made the point that, though it may appear strange that the Ghana Constitution should be contained in an Order in Council, regarded in some quarters as the legislative symbol of Colonialism, there are sound reasons for preferring an Order to a Parliamentary Bill. He wrote 'An Act of Parliament must go through both Houses; amendments may be moved at the committee and report stages of the Bill; delicately balanced compromises, arrived at after strenuous negotiations, may be upset, and even if the amendments are defeated, the ventilation of every contentious issue may have unfortunate repercussions in the territory concerned'. He gave speed as another advantage of an Order in Council in the Gold Coast situation; but experience has since shewn that whenever a constitutional advance is afoot, if the situation did not in fact call for speed, it would be so exceptional as to be quite remarkable. I am not suggesting that there is anything in the mechanics which necessitates undue haste; the trouble has nearly always been that etymological monstrosity the 'target date'—which no one is ever invited to shoot down. True, it is something to aim at, so perhaps it is to be preferred to its cousin—so popular with the Press—the 'scheduled date', which has never seen the inside of a schedule. The custom is to fix the date so early that to expect Parliament to digest a Bill containing the entire constitution and adhere to the set timetable would be to ask for the impossible. Even those engaged in the preparation of an Order in Council have had good reason to wish desperately that, if they must be driven, the route would occasionally take them through a built-up area. Having myself now been out of the turmoil for some time, I feel I can, without too much diffidence, wonder whether those who devote themselves so unsparingly to the arduous job (I am not speaking only of the legal draftsmen) receive anything like the credit due to them. And I should like to acknowledge what I read as a graceful tribute paid by Professor de Smith in the article which I have just mentioned, where he referred to the 1950 Gold Coast Constitution 'produced by the now philo-progenitive Colonial Office'. The picturesque adjective is deserved, even when a workman operating our machine wearily asks, perhaps at the end of a twelve-hour shift, why, after 100 years or more of dependent status, a few weeks here or there make so much difference in arranging a date for independence. He does not mean to put a rhetorical question; he just does not know the answer.

MEMBERSHIP OF THE COMMONWEALTH

I have given a sketch of internal changes within the country and in its relations with the United Kingdom. We must now look further afield, beginning with the Commonwealth. Independence and Membership of the Commonwealth are by no means the same thing. Independence, its form and timing, are matters for decision and action by the country responsible for the dependent territory in agreement with the territory itself, but for the admission of a new Member of the Commonwealth the agreement of existing Members is required. So far, no country attaining independence and wishing to remain within the Commonwealth has been rejected. I dare say one can assume that the United Kingdom Government would always consult, or at least inform, the other Members of the Commonwealth when it contemplated the creation of another independent state which will become a candidate for Membership, but it appears to me that Professor de Smith, in the same article, went rather too far in saying that it is hardly possible for the concurrence of other Members to be withheld; that in consequence the effective power to determine whether a territory shall be admitted to Membership rests with the United Kingdom; and that foreknowledge of likely opposition by other Members might conceivably inhibit a United Kingdom Government from pressing the constitutional advancement of a dependent territory to a point of no return.

Since transition from dependence to independence normally carries with it the opportunity to acquire Membership of the Commonwealth, a comprehensive appreciation of our machine's functions necessitates at least a glance at what Membership involves. The question can be looked at from two viewpoints. First, what, as a Member of the Commonwealth, will the country concerned acquire which it does not possess in its dependent status? And secondly, what will it lose on independence if it elects to leave the Commonwealth?

The Commonwealth, as such, has no constitution and no written document to describe the relationship of each of its members to all the others. But Membership entails legal and other rights and privileges and informal obligations which are known to Members themselves, and even though, as a matter of jurisprudence, we may have to say that, because most of them import no legal rights and obligations, they are not law, that does not mean that the incidents of Membership are not within the lawyer's province. Some of them involve the use of our legal machinery. Others do not, but to ignore them and deal with those which do would be like taking a continental breakfast without the coffee. So I must wander a little way outside the strict limits of the title of this paper.

If one is asked to describe in one word what Membership affords and requires, 'co-operation' must suffice. It is better to be allowed a little more latitude and use three words, 'consultation and information'; but as they do not quite cover all the possible advantages one should for good measure add 'mutual assistance'. On December 15, 1948, Lord Jowitt, then Lord Chancellor, speaking in the House of Lords, said:

'Surely the great benefit the Commonwealth brings is the joint consultation, alike in matters civil and military, the sharing of information, and the resulting solution of common difficulties . . . I would venture to say that the flow and interchange of communication and information and the sharing of common tasks and common friends, are the hallmark and the importance of the Commonwealth relationship.'

I must at this point take the precaution of saying that Members of the Commonwealth may have different ideas about the rights and obligations of Membership, and I am not in a position to state the views even of the United Kingdom Government. I can profess to do no more than sketch an outline as it appears to me.

There are, however, some primary principles which form the background to what I have suggested should be described as 'co-operation', and which by their nature do not appear to leave much room for difference of opinion.

(*a*) First, the old Members were, and indeed still are, 'united by a common allegiance to the Crown'. The Republics who are now Members of the Commonwealth recognize the Sovereign 'as the symbol of the free association of its independent member nations and as such the Head of the Commonwealth'. I cannot imagine that any country would be admitted to Membership which was not prepared to accept that formula or one very much like it.

(*b*) Secondly, as I have said, a new Member can be admitted only by the decision of existing Members, which has hitherto been unanimous.

(*c*) Thirdly, it is generally agreed that a Member will not normally intervene in, or comment upon, the domestic affairs of another Member; and that when one Member contemplates taking any action which may affect the interests or policies of another Member, the former will consult, or at least inform, the latter in advance.

(*d*) Fourthly, a representative of one Member accredited to another is a High Commissioner, possessing ambassadorial status, and he and his Staff enjoy diplomatic immunity.

(*e*) Fifthly, save in those exceptional cases where there are express agreements (which, naturally, are meant to be carried out) there is no element of specific obligation.

(*f*) Sixthly, there are few, if any, subjects on which there can be said to be definite Commonwealth doctrine or policy.

I have suggested, as a three-word definition, 'consultation and information'. The two go hand in hand. No bounds are set but, for most practical purposes, normal activities fall into four groups: external affairs, defence, finance and economics, and education.

External affairs. Here information and consultation are continuous and of great importance. They cover almost the entire field but it is worth mentioning also that one Government may, at the request of another, undertake to represent the interests of that other in particular foreign countries where the second Government is not itself represented. This is, of course, a service which may sometimes be performed for States which are not Members of the Commonwealth, but it is one which has often been undertaken on behalf of Members who are unable, owing to limited resources, to have wide diplomatic representation of their own.

As a dependent territory advances towards independence, the flow of information from the United Kingdom on international affairs increases; but apart from this, the implications of Membership in external affairs (and in some other important matters of common interest) are clear gain to countries which become Members.

Defence. Lord Jowitt, in the speech from which I have quoted, alluded to a Commonwealth partnership in defence, and, if there is little in peace time to show it in action, that is not very surprising. There are, however, such things as combined exercises, military missions, common systems of training and equipment and attendance at courses provided for the education of officers.

Finance and Economics. It is in this field that co-operation is most continuous and most highly organized. Under the general title of the Commonwealth Economic Consultative Council, Ministers of Finance and their senior officials meet regularly; and there are other meetings from time to time of those responsible for economic affairs. In the United Kingdom, Members of the Commonwealth seeking loans have special access to the London Market, and, provided that the statutory conditions are fulfilled, their Government stock has trustee status. Under the Commonwealth preference system, Members have extended to each other, by a series of bilateral agreements, trade advantages such as duty-free entry of goods or preference margins. Dependent territories can enjoy the benefits of Commonwealth preference, trustee status for their Government stock and access to the London market, but they cannot be taken fully into consultation on economic policy, they are not Members of the Commonwealth Economic Consultative Council and they are represented at various meetings only in an advisory capacity as part of the United Kingdom delegation.

Education. Finally, there is the Commonwealth Education Liaison Committee, which provides a forum for the consideration of ways and means of improving Commonwealth educational co-operation. Dependent territories may share the benefits of schemes of co-operation, but do not enjoy individual membership of the Committee, being represented collectively by a member appointed by the United Kingdom Government.

Meetings of Prime Ministers. At the apex of this edifice of consultation are the meetings of Prime Ministers, which take place about once every two years. I should regard attendance at these meetings, rather than consultation and sharing as suggested by Lord Jowitt, as the hallmark of Membership of the Commonwealth. With the exception of the Federation of Rhodesia and Nyasaland, as the successor to Southern Rhodesia, attendance is strictly confined to Members.

Citizenship. For the individual, one of the most valuable incidents of Membership is Commonwealth citizenship. To Canada goes the credit for initiating the scheme of mutual recognition by Members of each other's citizenship. Ideally, it would secure universal acceptance throughout the Commonwealth of a common status, carrying rights, though not necessarily full citizenship rights, everywhere. Only the United Kingdom has so far gone all the way, giving all the rights of citizenship, including freedom of entry and a right, after twelve months' residence, to acquire citizenship of the United Kingdom and Colonies by registration.[1] Elsewhere, the extent to which Commonwealth citizenship is recognized varies considerably. Only in Ceylon is there no recognition of a common nationality status, though British subjects, as defined in the United Kingdom Act, are not regarded as 'aliens'.

The rights and privileges incident to Membership of the Commonwealth which are dependent upon the legal machine which is the subject of this discussion include nationality, diplomatic immunity, Commonwealth preference, trustee stock and the preparation of any agreements between the United Kingdom and the new Member.

[1] Now modified by the Commonwealth Immigrants Act, 1962, 10 & 11 El. 2, c. 21.

INTERNATIONAL PERSONALITY

Stepping over the frontiers of the Commonwealth, we come to the last essential condition and consequence of transition to full independence. Colonial or protectorate status necessarily leaves responsibility for foreign affairs in the hands of the Mother Country, and a dependent country has no international personality. When a territory is at a stage little short of independence, the conduct of external affairs within specified fields may be entrusted by the United Kingdom to the local Government—this is provided for in the Constitutions of the Federation of Rhodesia and Nyasaland, Singapore and the West Indies.[1] But strictly, the local Government, acting in accordance with such arrangements, must act on an agency footing, because, even though a foreign country will probably be content to negotiate with the Government of a dependent territory, it will in the last resort look to the United Kingdom for the fulfilment of the territory's obligations. On attaining independence, the new state becomes an international person, solely responsible for its own external relations. Its recognition as such is a matter for other countries. Nowadays, for most practical purposes, the determining factor is admission to the United Nations, which will probably take place a few days after the date of independence. It is for the Parliament and the Government of the United Kingdom to create the conditions necessary for recognition, and the machinery I have described is ample so long as established international principles are observed by other countries.

It has occasionally been suggested that agreements concerning defence, made, on the attainment of independence, between the United Kingdom and the country concerned, amount to limitations on independence. That is patently absurd, unless it is equally true of a number of similar international arrangements, such as the stationing of American troops in Europe by agreement between the European countries and the United States, not to mention the distribution of Soviet troops over the countries behind the iron curtain.

Consequent upon the acquisition of international personality is succession to treaty rights and obligations. I need say no more than that in most cases an agreement has been made between the United Kingdom and the new States, providing for the assumption and

---

[1] Federation of Rhodesia and Nyasaland (Constitution) Order in Council, 1953, Art. 36(2) & Sch. 2, para. 1; Singapore (Constitution) Order in Council, 1958, s. 73; West Indies (Federation) Order in Council, 1957, Art. 56 (1) of the Constitution.

enjoyment by the latter of obligations and rights arising from international agreements. Such an agreement is, of course, binding only as between the parties, but for the most part other states appear to be willing to accept the position.

CONSEQUENTIALS

I have mentioned all the essentials but there are consequentials, and some of them are important. I should just mention in passing that an Independence Act makes necessary amendments in the Army and Air Force Acts and the Naval Discipline Act and, in a Schedule which does not affect the law of the country concerned, effects a number of other adaptations of United Kingdom laws. I need not go into details: other points are more interesting.

Territory outside Her Majesty's dominions. Soon after the last war, the process of giving more and more self-government, which would obviously culminate in independence, seemed to present a problem the solution of which it was not easy to predict. The greater part of the aggregate area included in the dependent territories consisted of Protectorates and Protected States. How could they be given independence and remain within the Commonwealth? They are not parts of Her Majesty's dominions; all powers and jurisdiction vested in the Crown depend upon the right and duty to protect, which is incompatible with independence. What would take its place? A Protected State has its own Ruler. What would be the relationship between him, as the Head of an independent State, and the Crown? If a Protectorate is governed with a territory which is a Colony, the rights of the United Kingdom to protect could not be transferred to the Government of the Colony unless the Protectorate were not to share the new status but were to remain a dependency of the territory which had been a Colony. Trust territories presented the same problem as Protectorates. The solution, however, as matters turned out, was simple. The Acts granting independence have, in effect, boldly annexed Protectorates and Trust territories by providing that, on the appointed day, they should become part of Her Majesty's dominions. That was the course adopted for the Northern territories of the Gold Coast, the greater parts of Nigeria and Sierra Leone and the whole of Tanganyika. Malaya was a special case. It consisted of seven Protected States and two small Colonies, Penang and Malacca. The way was paved by the previous recognition, in the case of India and Pakistan, that a Republic could remain within the Commonwealth, the Queen, although replaced by a President as Head of the Executive, still being recognised as the Head of the Commonwealth. There was no substantial difference in recognizing that Malaya, with its own Monarch, could likewise be a Member of the Commonwealth. Penang and Malacca were disposed of by the termination of British sovereignty and they remained, like the States, separate component parts of the Federation.

Not quite so straightforward was the related nationality problem, which, in its Ghana context, was fully discussed in an anonymous article in Volume 1 No. 2 of the Journal of African Law. Most of the inhabitants of Protectorates and Trust territories have the status of British Protected Persons. When a territory ceases to be under Her Majesty's protection and becomes part of Her Majesty's dominions, logic and legal principle require that that status should not continue. But Ghana, at the date of independence, had no citizenship law and the British dislike of statelessness is almost as intense as nature's abhorrence of a vacuum. So Parliament in its wisdom disregarded the technicality and decreed that Ghana's British Protected Persons should continue to be British Protected Persons unless and until they became citizens of Ghana under Ghana law. The same provision is made for Nigeria, Sierra Leone and Tanganyika but, by comparison, it is of little importance, since citizenship laws were enacted as parts of their constitutions.

Amendment of the Constitution. When a country becomes independent, the means by which the constitution may be amended must be prescribed. This is of special importance when there is a communal or minority problem. Machinery probably has to be devised to ensure that safeguards provided for the protection of particular classes of persons cannot easily be removed or prejudiced by the majority.

Experience shows that constitutional devices to protect special interests may not be effective and enduring. Much may depend upon the size and political rights of the community concerned. The classic case of the so-called entrenched clauses in the South Africa Act, 1909, is well known. With the experience of South Africa in mind, the first Schedule to the Ghana Independence Act contained a provision—paragraph 6—to the effect that the existing constitution and any law amending or replacing it should not be repealed or amended otherwise than in such manner as might be specified in the constitution. This has been copied for Nigeria, Sierra Leone and Tanganyika. Amendment of the constitution of Ghana required a two-thirds majority, and, in regard to a number of specified provisions (including safeguards for Regional Assemblies and boundaries, and for Chiefly rights) Regional approval was necessary, and in most cases the House of Chiefs was entitled to be consulted. All this has already disappeared. The whole constitution and the greater part of the Independence Act, including paragraph 6 in the Schedule, have been revoked; and under the new Constitution little remains of the original safeguards.

In the Regions of Nigeria, in Sierra Leone and in Tanganyika, there is a similar two-thirds majority requirement; and in Sierra Leone if any one of a number of entrenched provisions is affected, the Bill has to be passed in two successive sessions separated by a dissolution. Procedure for amendment of the Constitution of the Federation of Nigeria is more complicated and it absorbs twelve subsections. This, briefly, is the position: any amendment requires two-thirds majorities in the Federal Parliament; alteration of entrenchment sections needs, in addition, supporting resolutions in at least two Regions; for establishment of new Regions and the alteration of Regional bound-aries there is special machinery requiring Regional support; and representation in the Federal Parliament cannot be reduced except with Regional consent.

Not all entrenched provisions are framed specially for the protection of particular communities. Detailed 'fundamental rights', now usually based upon the Human Rights Convention, are the order of the day. A Director of Public Prosecutions may have vested in him the entire responsibility for prosecutions, in order to preserve it, so far as practicable, from undue political influence. The method whereby a Judge may be removed from office is laid down. I have discussed this question in detail in another part of this volume. Briefly, the position is that most of the newly independent countries have elected to main-tain the procedure recognized for many years with respect to dependent territories: a judicial enquiry, followed, as a rule, by reference to the Judicial Committee of the Privy Council.

AUTOCHTHONY

Finally, reflecting upon the endurance qualities of the goods produced by our constitution factory, I want to say just a word about autoch-thony. Dr Wheare discusses it in his *Constitutional Structure of the Commonwealth*, and Professor Kenneth Robinson added his contribu-tion in November 1961, in the first number of the *Journal of*

Commonwealth Political Studies. I confess that I do not quite understand the urge to have a new constitution produced in such a way that it can claim to be an entirely local product. It is not as if independence constitutions enacted in the United Kingdom are imposed upon the country. They are always the outcome of full consultation and discussion and in the majority of cases independence constitutions have been preceded by one or more full-scale conferences. It can justly be claimed that the constitution gives the people what they ask for, remembering that by 'the people' one does not necessarily mean only the majority. If safeguards are provided for particular communities or minorities, that, surely, makes the constitution more one which is wanted by the people than if it contained nothing except that which would satisfy a majority? Of course, the original independence constitution may be found by experience to be in need of refashioning to fit it to unforeseen dimensions of independence and, even if it is not, one can understand that pride in the attainment of independence may engender a natural desire to have a constitution made in the country itself and not in the United Kingdom. But if autochthony takes the extreme form of deliberately creating a break in legal continuity—of producing a constitution without legal roots, which does not depend for its enactment upon the procedure laid down in the original independence constitution for amendment and revocation, then I should have thought that any urge in that direction is one which local politicians would be well advised to suppress; for a constitution produced in that way must have an insecure foundation in law. It may be that legal principle must concede that there is, in theory, some method by which a nation can give itself a constitution by a process, so to speak, of spontaneous combustion; but there are many ways in which it might be suggested that that should be done, and who can say what is a permissible method in law? It may be that the obvious procedure is for the Government which happens to be in power to produce a draft, submit it to a referendum and, if approved, adopt it. It was in that way that Ghana provided itself with a constitution, but all the prescribed legal forms were observed, the restrictions on legislative power having been lawfully repealed before a Constituent Assembly was set up by law. But suppose that had not been done. Could one assume that, as a matter of law, the Government in power and not, for example, a coalition of all political parties, would be the right people to prepare and present a draft; and that the franchise upon which the referendum is based would be found acceptable if the validity of the constitution were challenged? There seems no doubt that legal continuity was broken in establishing the 1937 Constitution of what is now the Republic of Ireland; in India the break is not so clear; Pakistan seems to be secure. Whether Dr Wheare's expectation is well-founded (that Members of the Commonwealth will, as a rule, seek to achieve autochthony) and, if so, how far they will go, remains to be seen. In Malaya, the question does not appear to arise. In my opinion their constitution undoubtedly derives its legal force from the States and the Federation as well as from the United Kingdom. Nor should I think it had any relevance for Canada, Australia and New Zealand, unless the majority of the population first autochthonize their blood.

It may be, perhaps I should say it is highly probable, that the Courts would stretch many points to uphold the validity of a constitution which can be said in broad terms to have been made or approved by the people of the country; but, however strong national sentiment may be, for my part I should not have thought it worth while to take the risk.

However, I am not a politician, I am only a lawyer, a retired foreman of a workshop which has performed during the last fifteen years, and is continuing to perform, a valuable service for the Commonwealth; and, taking the broad, long-term view, a valuable service for the world.

4

THE INDEPENDENCE OF THE JUDICIARY
IN COMMONWEALTH COUNTRIES[1]

SIR KENNETH ROBERTS-WRAY

To the question how the independence of the Judiciary is preserved, I suggest a fourfold answer: first, by appropriate machinery for appointment of Judges; secondly, by giving Judges security of tenure of office; thirdly, by such general acceptance of, and respect for, judicial independence that the members of the Judiciary can rest assured that it is not likely to be challenged and has not continually to be fought for; fourthly, by the terms of service of members of the Judiciary. First, a few words about the last of these.

TERMS OF SERVICE

Here, I am more than content to quote Sir Albert Napier, Permanent Secretary to the Lord Chancellor from 1944 till 1954. In a paper written for the British Council, on the Structure of the Judicial System in Overseas Territories, he emphasized that a Judge ought to have a high salary and an adequate pension. This is not only because of the heavy responsibilities of his office. The financial reward must be sufficient to induce a successful advocate to relinquish not only his private practice but many of his outside activities as well, and to compensate him for lifelong limitations on the additional sources of income available to him. For example, directorships in companies, which are open to many men in salaried occupations, are denied to a Judge; and when he retires he should be precluded from returning to the Bar. Pensions cannot be calculated in the same way as those of other public officers, since preferment to the Bench comes comparatively late in life. Sir Albert mentioned two ways of meeting that situation—addition of years to actual years of service in calculating pension; or a rule that (as in England) a Judge can earn a maximum pension in, say, fifteen years.

I must, however, suggest a qualification. It is apparent that Sir

[1] See footnote on p. 11.

63

Albert Napier had particularly in mind Judges appointed from a local Bar. In United Kingdom dependent territories the Judiciary has for many years been primarily recruited from the ranks of a Service offering a career for life, not radically different in quality as a career from that of a Civil Servant. Many of the Judges and magistrates are expatriates, and any rule limiting their activities after retirement from the Bench would appear to have little validity on their retirement to their country of origin. In general, therefore, the ordinary Civil Service salary pattern and pension laws are not unsuitable. But they have long been insufficiently attractive for leading members of local Bars, and in one or two cases special pensions have been provided.

PUBLIC SUPPORT

The third of my ingredients for judicial independence is its general acceptance. On this there is little to say except that it depends very largely upon the support of public opinion, without which the independence of the Judiciary must inevitably be in grave danger. With one exception (of which, for obvious reasons, I am not prepared to give details) I have never heard it suggested that there is, or is likely to be, any ground for apprehension in any part of the Commonwealth.

The layman, as much as the lawyer, knows full well that, to quote Sir Winston Churchill, 'the principle of the complete independence of the Judiciary from the Executive is the foundation of many things in our island life. It has been widely imitated in varying degrees throughout the free world. It is perhaps one of the deepest gulfs between us and all forms of totalitarian rule ... The British Judiciary, with its traditions and record, is one of the greatest living assets of our race and people and the independence of the Judiciary is a part of our message to the evergrowing world which is rising so swiftly around us'.[1]

In the United Kingdom, public opinion is given a lead by the rule observed by Parliament that, unless discussion is based on a substantive motion, drawn in proper terms, reflection must not be cast in debate upon the conduct of Judges, either individually or generally.[2]

[1] Hansard, March 23, 1954, Vol. 525, Cols. 1061, 1063.
[2] Erskine May, *Parliamentary Practice*, 16th edn. pp. 380, 457-8. See also the Speaker's ruling regarding the Chief Justice of Seychelles in Hansard, July 30, 1956, Vol. 557, Cols. 925 to 932.

A similar rule is observed in other parts of the Commonwealth. It has been made statutory in some constitutions.[1]

METHOD OF APPOINTMENT

I must now deal with the method of appointment of Judges, which should insulate the choice of candidates from political motives so far as that is possible. Beginning at home, one must confess that, at any rate to the purist, the position is not altogether satisfactory. Appointments of High Court Judges are made by the Queen on the advice of the Lord Chancellor; but the Lord Chief Justice, the Master of the Rolls, the President of the Probate, Divorce and Admiralty Division, the Lords Justices and the Lords of Appeal in Ordinary are appointed by the Queen on the advice of the Prime Minister.

The Lord Chancellor, who figures so largely in the system, is identified politically with the Party in power; but constitutional conventions and traditions have ensured recognition of the dual nature of his office and confidence that he can be relied upon to make good, non-political recommendations; and he is in an exceptionally good position to pick the best men. It cannot be doubted, however, that the office of Lord Chancellor is one which can hardly be copied elsewhere. Though, despite his political shadow, criticism cannot, therefore, reasonably be levelled against the vesting of the Lord Chancellor with so much responsibility, those who have been hyper-critical of the position of Judges in dependent territories should, if they are to be logical, agitate for the elimination of the Prime Minister from his influence in the appointment of Judges in England. I am not myself suggesting that he should be eliminated. As Professor de Smith remarked, in a broadcast talk on November 6, 1958, it is arguable that the principle of distrusting the Executive may be carried too far and that it would be wrong for the Government of the day to be denied any effective voice in judicial appointments.

In the older independent Commonwealth countries, Judges are likewise appointed by the head of the Executive, and the Ministers whose duty it is to advise have not the advantage of a Lord Chancellor among them. Appointments of Judges of the Supreme Court of Canada and the High Court of Australia are made by the Governor-

---

[1] See, e.g., s. 127 of the Constitution of the Federation of Malaya, Sch. I to Agreement annexed to the Federation of Malaya Independence Order in Council, 1957, S.I. 1957, No. 1533; s. 60 of the Singapore Order in Council, 1958, S.I. 1958, No. 1956.

General in Council. In New Zealand and the Canadian Provinces the power is vested in the Governor-General *simpliciter*. In some Australian States it resides in the Governor; in others in the Governor in Council or, in Victoria, the Governor with the advice of the Executive Council, which presumably means the same thing. In the Federation of Rhodesia and Nyasaland appointments are likewise made by the Governor-General, acting in accordance with the advice of the Executive Council.

Among the Members of the Commonwealth who have become independent since the war there is interesting diversity. The Constitutions of India and Pakistan make express provision for the President to consult Chief Justices and other members of the Judiciary, except in the case of the appointment of the Chief Justice in Pakistan.

Before Ceylon obtained her independence in 1947, the device of a Judicial Service Commission had been invented, but under the Constitution it is concerned only with the lower ranks of the Judiciary; the Judges are appointed by the Governor-General acting on the advice of Ministers.

In more recent constitutions, of both independent Commonwealth countries and advanced dependent territories, the functions of the Judicial Service Commissions, established by their constitutions, have extended to the appointment of Puisne Judges. Since in every case the Judicial Service Commission includes a majority of serving or retired Judges there is effective insulation of appointments from political pressure, provided that it does not come in at a later stage—in particular, if appointments have to be made by the Head of the Executive in accordance with the Commission's advice.

But the Judicial Service Commissions are not concerned with the appointment of the Chief Justice. This is inevitable, since a body which makes recommendations for the appointment of persons to any public office cannot properly include persons who may be candidates; whereas it is the essence of a Judicial Service Commission that it should include Puisne Judges, and it may also include the Attorney-General. It is, therefore, not practicable, in a country possessing full internal self-government, to avoid placing responsibility for appointing a Chief Justice in political hands; though the person responsible may be obliged, as in India and Pakistan, to consult some Judge or Judges.

Under the Ghana Constitution of 1957, the Chief Justice and Justices of Appeal were appointed by the Governor-General on the advice of the Prime Minister (after consultation with the Chief Justice in the case of the Justices of Appeal) and Puisne Judges were appointed by the Governor-General on the advice of the Judicial Service Commission. But the present Ghana Constitution provides simply that all the Judges are to be appointed by the President.

In the Federation of Malaya, judicial appointments are in the hands of the Yang di-Pertuan Agong (the Head of State) acting on the advice of the Prime Minister, after consulting the Conference of Rulers and (except for the appointment of the Chief Justice) considering the Chief Justice's advice.

In Nigeria, Sierra Leone and Tanganyika there are Judicial Service Commissions upon whose recommendation appointments are made, except in the case of the Chief Justices, who are appointed by the Governor-General on the advice of the Prime Minister or, in the case of the Regions in Nigeria, by the Governor on the advice of the Premier.

In Cyprus the Judges of the Supreme Constitutional Court and of the High Court are appointed jointly by the President and Vice-President of the Republic. In default of agreement in the appointment of a Greek Judge or Turkish Judge, the proposal of the President or the Vice-President to whose community the Judge to be appointed belongs is to prevail.

In dependent territories, fifteen years ago, the almost invariable practice was for Judges to be appointed by the Governor in accordance with instructions received from the Sovereign through the Secretary of State, and this procedure still obtains in less advanced countries. Control is thus in the hands of the Executive—the Colonial Office—but when Judges are part of a unified legal and judicial service, embracing a large number of territories between which there are frequent transfers, there is no practicable alternative.

Under the heading 'method of appointment' it is convenient to say a few words about the system of furnishing confidential reports on Judges in dependent territories, which has now and then come under fire. Reports are made on Puisne Judges by the Chief Justice and forwarded to the Secretary of State through the Governor, who adds comments if he wishes to do so. If there is a separate Court of Appeal a further report by the President of that Court is included. In the case of a Chief Justice, only the Governor signs the report.

Now it cannot be denied that the furnishing of reports by the Governor is, in principle, out of harmony with judicial independence; but it is unavoidable and, in making reports, Governors are careful to observe the bounds of propriety. Responsibility for making recommendations to the Queen for the appointment of Judges, including their promotion or transfer from one judicial post to another, rests with the Secretary of State. He obviously cannot perform this duty unless he has reports on possible candidates from those in a position to give them. The reports on a Puisne Judge which really matter are those from the Chief Justice and the President of the Court of Appeal if there is one, particularly, but not exclusively, on questions of judicial competence. In the great majority of cases the Governor adds nothing, though he may briefly intimate his concurrence; and if he comments on a Puisne Judge he shows the report to the Chief Justice. If the suggestion that a Governor should not report at all were adopted, the Secretary of State might, and sometimes certainly would, be without information which ought to be in his possession, for there are some matters on which the Governor is in the best position to report. The Judges rightly expect the importance and status of their office to be recognized. On the other side of the scale the Judges have obligations—to maintain the dignity of their position and (particularly in the case of Chief Justices) to play their proper part in public life, especially on formal occasions. Those who are not prepared to do this are not the best suited for the highest judicial office. Further, there are some matters in which Judges can shew themselves helpful towards the Executive (or otherwise) in matters in which their independence cannot possibly be prejudiced.

TENURE OF OFFICE

By far the largest and thorniest branch of my subject, and one which has several times been publicly aired in recent years, is the tenure of office of Judges in dependent territories. But that is only part of a much wider subject, namely, the extent to which, and the means whereby, the independence of the Judiciary is safeguarded in Commonwealth countries, by protecting them from interference and, at the same time, providing a method whereby, for adequate reasons, a Judge may be dismissed. For a full appreciation of the picture as it now presents itself it is necessary to go some way back in history and trace developments in chronological order.

THE UNITED KINGDOM

Introduction. It is only fair to the Stuart Kings to recognize that, in England, the acute controversy may be said to have been due in part to an element of novelty in the views of Sir Edward Coke. We must remember that in Norman times Judges were virtually indistinguishable from Civil Servants, that until the time of William III they were, as a rule, appointed during the King's pleasure and were frequently dismissed for political reasons and that there was no change in the law until the Act of Settlement. Nevertheless, the prime cause of the conflict leading up to that Act seems clearly to have been that the Stuart Kings departed from existing practice for their own ends. It is not to be wondered at that a redoubtable fighter, as Coke proved himself to be, reacted by claiming judicial independence in a more extreme form than seems to have been previously recognized.

This is not the place to say much about that particular decisive battle of the world; but one feature of the campaign which should, I think, be stressed is that Coke succeeded despite not only the pusillanimity of his brother Judges but also the antagonism of two occupants of the Woolsack: Ellesmere, who pronounced that the King was the law speaking, and Bacon, who uttered the famous dictum that the Judges 'must be lions, but yet lions under the Throne, being circumspect that they did not check or oppose any points of sovereignty'.

Now let us consider the effect of the series of Acts of Parliament for which Coke must take the indirect credit. Students of law or political science have probably been taught that in England a Judge can be removed from office only for misbehaviour on an address to the Sovereign by both Houses of Parliament; but there is ample authority for maintaining that that is not the law, and that the true position is that a Judge is removable by other means for misbehaviour, and on an address from both Houses of Parliament for that or any other reason.[1] I have nowhere seen the opposing views discussed or even explained, but the question seems to be a fairly straightforward matter of statute interpretation.

Act of Settlement.[2] Section 3 of this Act provided that 'Judges Commission be made *quamdiu se bene gesserint* and their salaries ascertained and established; *but* upon the address of both Houses of Parliament it may be lawful to remove them'.

[1] Todd, *Parliamentary Government in England*, Vol. II, pp. 726-9; the following books on Constitution Law: Ridges, 8th edn., p. 336; Hood Phillips, 2nd edn., p. 557; Anson, 4th edn., Vol. 2, Pt. I, p. 234; *Shell Co. of Australia* v *Federal Commr. of Taxation* [1931], A.C. 275 at p. 280: Cf. Chitty, *Prerogatives of the Crown*, p. 83; Keir & Lawson, *Cases on Constitutional Law*, 4th edn., Rev., p. 199; Dicey, *Law of the Constitution*, 10th edn., p. 410.

[2] 12 & 13 W. 3, c. 2.

The crucial word is 'but'. It gives what follows the effect of a proviso—a qualification on that which precedes it. A free paraphrase might read: the Judges hold office during good behaviour: provided that they may nevertheless be removed on a Parliamentary address. Surely the intention is clear?—that an address might be presented for the removal of a Judge for any reason which Parliament regarded as sufficient but that, unless Parliament moved in the matter, he could be removed by other means only for misbehaviour.

This construction is fortified, in my submission to the point of impregnability, when it is remembered that an appointment during good behaviour is at common law an appointment for life but imports a liability to removal for misbehaviour by proceedings begun by *scire facias*.[1] If, after that, any doubt remains, it is removed by Act 1 George III, Cap. 23. Section 1 enacted that Judges' Commissions should continue in force during good behaviour notwithstanding the demise of the Crown; and section 2, which enabled the King to remove a Judge upon the address of both Houses of Parliament began with the words 'Provided always'. In short, as Alpheus Todd, writing in 1869, explained in his *Parliamentary Government in England*,[2] the liability to removal on Parliamentary address was 'in fact, a qualification of, or exception from, the words creating a tenure during good behaviour, and not an incident or legal consequence thereof'.

Bill of 1692. It may not be generally known that the Act of Settlement was not Parliament's first attempt to deal with the danger of challenge by the Crown to judicial independence. In February 1692, a Bill[3] entitled the Judges' Commissions and Salaries Bill was passed by the Houses of Parliament; but William III refused his assent for a reason which must command our sympathy: the Bill charged the Judges' salaries on the Crown's hereditary revenues. The Bill provided that every Judge should by virtue of the Act hold his place or office 'so long as he shall well behave himself therein, unless he shall voluntary surrender or resign the same'. It said nothing about the nature of procedure for removal, but an amendment was moved in the House of Lords that 'if any Judge comes to be tried, he may be tried by all the Judges, and so to come hither by writ of error'. The indication is clear that judicial proceedings were in contemplation.

---

[1] Todd, *supra*, p. 727; Ridges, *supra*, p. 336.   [2] P. 729.
[3] Historical Manuscripts Commission, 14th Report, 1894, Pt. VI, pp. 76 to 79.

Judicature Act, 1873.[1] This was Parliament's next offer. It never came into operation but it has an interest peculiar to itself. Section 9 provided that Judges were to hold office for life, subject to a power of removal by Her Majesty on an address presented to Her Majesty by both Houses of Parliament. This is substantially in the same terms as the later Acts with the notable exception that 'for life' appears instead of 'during good behaviour'. Since there is no reference to good behaviour, it would have been very difficult indeed to contend under this Act that Parliament could not have presented an address for the removal of a Judge on any grounds whatever. It is perhaps surprising that section 13 of the Judicature (Ireland) Act 1877,[2] still in force in Northern Ireland, is in the same terms as the Act of 1873.

Present law. The Supreme Court of Judicature (1873) Amendment Act, 1875[3] repealed section 9 of the Act of 1873 and provided, in section 5, that Judges should hold their office during good behaviour, subject to a power of removal by Her Majesty, on an address presented to Her Majesty by both Houses of Parliament. Section 12(1) of the Supreme Court of Judicature (Consolidation) Act, 1925,[4] follows the Act of 1875 verbatim and section 6 of the Appellate Jurisdiction Act, 1875,[5] makes the same provision for Lords of Appeal in Ordinary.

The later Acts are not quite so free from ambiguity as the Act of Settlement but in my submission their effect is the same. There is no 'but'. On the other hand, the word 'only' could have been inserted in the phrase relating to Parliamentary address, but it was not; the common law rule that holders of office during good behaviour may be removed by *scire facias* has not been abrogated; and, in any case, the words 'subject to', like 'but' in the Act of Settlement, import a qualification on a general rule. As I have said, there can be no doubt whatever about the meaning of the Act of Settlement and the Act of 1760, and if Parliament had in a subsequent Act intended to change the law, it would assuredly have done so in perfectly clear terms. The right conclusion, therefore, seems clearly to be that the effect of the present Act is the same as the Act of Settlement; that Parliament may present an address for the removal of a Judge for any cause; and that he may also be removed by other means for misbehaviour. The other means suggested by various writers are, in addition to proceedings commenced by *scire facias*, criminal information, impeachment

---

[1] 36 & 37 V., c. 66.　　　　[2] 40 & 41 V., c. 57.
[3] 38 & 39 V., c. 77.　　　　[4] 15 & 16 G. 5, c. 49.
　　　　[5] 39 & 40 V., c. 59.

or the exercise of the inquisitorial and judicial jurisdiction of the House of Lords.

Comment on Act of Settlement. It may be asked why Parliament, having laid down the principle that a Judge holds office during good behaviour, should take to itself an unqualified power of removal. In 1700 Parliament had had its own quarrel with the Crown but it was not hand in glove with the Judges; and, as Coke's experience shows, the Judges were not to be trusted to maintain their own independence. So, though I do not know the answer to the question, it may be that Parliament was content to leave the removal of a Judge for provable acts of misconduct to judicial process but reserved to itself, and no one else, an overriding power to get rid of a Judge who had lost its confidence.

Comment on present law. I now have another question to ask; and, this time, I do know the answer. Ignoring what is practical and probable (as critics of the position of overseas Judges are apt to do) and considering the strict law and factual possibilities, however remote, is this safeguard for judicial independence in England entirely satisfactory? No; it is not. It is said that Judges are independent. Independent of whom? Not of Parliament which can secure their dismissal. Not of the Executive, in the shape of the Government of the day, which can control the decisions of Parliament. Of course, this is theory. The conflicts between the legislature and the judiciary during the eighteenth and nineteenth centuries have established a healthy tradition of mutual respect for each other's rights; and if today an address for the removal of a Judge were to be proposed, one could be confident that there would be no question of putting on the Party Whips.

But what form would the proceedings take? Todd[1] throws light on this question. The precedents which he describes leave little room for reasonable doubt that the Judge would be fully informed of the complaints against him; that, if he asked for permission to appear by himself or by Counsel in his defence, he would be allowed to do so; and that witnesses would be examined and liable to cross-examination. But Parliament is master of its own procedure and the Judge would in law have no rights. Nor, so far as I am aware, would there be anything to prevent any member of the Lords or Commons from exercising his right to speak and, in so doing, to testify to the facts,

[1] *Loc cit.*, pp. 729-44.

from his own knowledge or even from hearsay. In any case the judges of fact, law and penalty (if any) would be the House as a whole. The presence of Judges in the House of Lords would, of course, be a valuable safeguard, but surely the best tribunal would be one consisting of Judges alone, particularly if the charge was one of judicial misconduct?

However that may be, the origin of the procedure by Parliamentary address has no relevance to twentieth-century conditions; and as it is unlikely that anyone will ever be able to say I am wrong, I am prepared to venture the opinion that it would commend itself to few if the whole matter were to be considered *de novo* today; and, moreover, that, if a case were to occur, Parliamentary procedure might well meet the same fate as that other comatose anachronism which surprisingly awoke about thirty years ago—trial by the House of Lords of a Peer charged with a felony.

DEPENDENT TERRITORIES

Early history. The independence of the Judiciary in dependent territories has been the subject of controversy, not without important misunderstanding and misstatement. In 1870, the whole question of the removal and suspension of a Colonial Judge was referred to the Privy Council. In a memorandum[1] setting forth their views, three forms of process for removing a Colonial Judge were examined.

(*a*) *Burke's Act.* This Act, more correctly called the Colonial Leave of Absence Act, 1782,[2] provides that, if any person holding a Patent office misbehaves, he may be 'amoved' by the 'Governor and Council' subject to an appeal to the Queen in Council.

(*b*) *Suspension.* Under his Instructions and Commission a Governor had power to suspend a public officer, and when a suspension was confirmed by the Queen it was converted to dismissal. This applied to Judges, but in their case it was the usual, though not invariable, practice to refer the matter to the Judicial Committee.

(*c*) *Petition.* A Colonial Assembly might bring charges against a Judge by petition to the Queen for his removal, in which case the Privy Council exercised an original jurisdiction and tried the issue themselves.

The memorandum began with a general statement in the following terms: 'It is obvious that some effectual means ought to exist for the

[1] 6 Moo N.S. Appendix following p. 368; & C—139.   [2] 22 G. 3, c. 75.

removal of Colonial Judges charged with grave misconduct, and that these means ought to be less cumbrous than those existing for the removal of one of Her Majesty's Judges in this country. The mode of procedure ought to be such as to protect Judges against the party and personal feelings which sometimes sway Colonial Legislatures, and to ensure to the accused party a full and fair hearing before an impartial and elevated tribunal'. The memorandum deprecated procedure by way of address from Colonial Assemblies, explaining at some length the fairly obvious objections to the exercise of original jurisdiction by the Privy Council. Their Lordships favoured proceedings by the Governor, subject to review in England either by the Secretary of State or the Privy Council, except that, where the misconduct charged was purely judicial, the maintenance of the independence of Judges required 'that judicial acts should only be brought into question before some tribunal of weight and wisdom enough to pronounce definitively upon them', and this function appertained with peculiar fitness to the Privy Council.

The response of the Secretary of State to the memorandum is apparent from a circular despatch sent to Colonial Governors on July 26, 1929, in which he stated that it had been the practice since 1870 to refer to the Judicial Committee any proposals to dismiss a Colonial Judge and that any such proposal to dismiss a Judge of a Supreme Court or High Court, whatever the charges, would, as a matter of course, be specially referred to the Judicial Committee. Thus, though technically most Judges continued to hold office during pleasure, it was well known that they would never be dismissed without reference to the Judicial Committee and no one suggested that their independence was not secure.

Terrell v *Secretary of State.* In 1953, however, a stir was caused in legal circles in this country (though there was very little reaction among the overseas Judges themselves) by the Judgment of Lord Goddard, C.J., in the case of *Terrell* v *Secretary of State for the Colonies.*[1] Mr a'Beckett Terrell was a Judge in Singapore. At the time of the Japanese invasion he happened to be on leave in Australia and he could not, of course, continue to perform the duties of his office. No other suitable office in the Colonial Legal Service could be found for him, he was within two years of the normal retiring age, and he was required by the Secretary of State to retire. He challenged the right of the Crown to terminate his appointment in this manner, but

[1] [1953] 2 Q.B., 482.

74

the Lord Chief Justice ruled that he held office at pleasure and that the Secretary of State, acting on behalf of the Crown, had an unfettered discretion in the matter. Whether it might have been wiser or more seemly to dispose of the problem of Mr Justice Terrell in some other way I am not prepared to argue, but I do contend that his case has been used to support implications which it will not bear. To say he was 'dismissed' conveys an impression at variance with the facts; his compulsory retirement, in circumstances which were wholly exceptional, had no relevance to his independence as a Judge. Nothing had been done or said to modify or prejudice the principles accepted at least since 1870 and reaffirmed in the circular despatch of 1929. That despatch was sufficient assurance to anyone awake to the facts of political life; but an extra safeguard was provided shortly afterwards by an amendment of Colonial Regulations,[1] laying down that dismissal or compulsory premature retirement of a Judge would require the setting up of a local Judicial Commission and that any question of inflicting punishment or of compulsory retirement would be referred to the Judicial Committee of the Privy Council.

Pamphlet 'British Colonial Judges'. In 1956, the Inns of Court Conservative and Unionist Society produced a pamphlet entitled *British Colonial Judges*. It may be thought unnecessary, or even inappropriate, to make more than a passing reference to a document of this nature; but as it has occasionally been referred to as an authority, without any apparent appreciation of a number of defects, I feel it incumbent upon me to point out some of them.

(*a*) First, it stated categorically that under the Act of Settlement and the Supreme Court of Judicature (Consolidation) Act, 1925, an address by both Houses of Parliament was, and is, required before a Judge can be removed. The authors entirely ignored the authority to the contrary.[2]

(*b*) Secondly, the pamphlet found difficulty in the construction of Colonial Regulation 63,[3] which governed the application of various regulations to the Judiciary. The suggestion in the pamphlet was that it was not clear that a Judge could not, without reference to the Judicial Committee, be compulsorily retired under Regulation 76 (which provided for retirement on grounds which cannot be dealt with by specific charges). Since Regulation 63 stated expressly that

---

[1] See now Colonial No. 322, Pt. 1, Reg. 55.   [2] pp. 5 & 8.

[3] p. 16.

Regulation 76 applied to a Judge subject to certain qualifications, one of which was that the question of his retirement under Regulation 76 would be referred to the Judicial Committee, I cannot see how there could be the faintest room for doubt.

(c) Thirdly, there is a clear implication[1] that Colonial Judges serving in territories where the safeguards have not been made statutory, have 'no security of tenure', and that the Executive can dismiss them at will. No great exception could be taken to this if it had been explained that the passage in question was dealing only with the strict legal position. But there was no such explanation and it appears that the statement was meant to be literally true, for the pamphlet claimed dogmatically that 'it is no answer to say that the type of man appointed Secretary of State for the Colonies would not in fact use his power in such a way, or that the Executive branch of the Oversea Service or the Colonial Office itself would be unlikely to request or advise it. Much less is it an answer to say (if it be true) that the power has never been so abused in the past'. To imply, as this does, that Colonial Regulations, a Circular Despatch and public statements would be ignored or even that a Secretary of State would wish to ignore them, and that if he were to do so he could get away with it, displays a surprisingly unrealistic attitude.

(d) Fourthly, among the recommendations in the pamphlet is that an Act of the 'Imperial' Parliament should create an Oversea Judicial Service and that it should forbid any reduction in the salary attached to any Colonial Judicial Office during tenure of that office by any person.[2] The opinion expressed by the authors, that this should not be regarded as encroachment upon the domain of Colonial Legislatures, shewed little awareness of Colonial politics.

(e) Fifthly, another recommendation is that a Judge should be liable to be dismissed by the Crown, on grounds of misbehaviour or incapacity, after a hearing before, and upon the recommendation of, a Judicial Commission, though he should have a right of appeal to the Judicial Committee.[3] The pamphlet does not, in so many words, suggest that this would be preferable to the established procedure, under which no decision for the dismissal of a Judge can ever be taken except after reference to the Judicial Committee, but that seems to be the implication. It is not easy even to guess the reason, but it is extremely unlikely that the Judges themselves would agree.

(f) Finally, it is recommended that, if a Colonial Judge became unemployed owing to the abolition of his office, his salary should be

[1] p. 18.   [2] pp. 20-21.   [3] p. 21.

borne by the consolidated fund of the United Kingdom; that pensions of all Judges overseas should be charged to that fund; and that the Judges should have a legal right to pension, a right which Judges in England do not enjoy. This was, of course, intended as part of a design to secure judicial independence; but the fact remains that other public servants would have their own good grounds for claiming that their salaries and pensions should be likewise secured, and claims of this sort to exceptional, preferential treatment for Judges would be more likely to cause justifiable resentment than to meet with success.

Other passages in the pamphlet are open to criticism but I think I have said sufficient to justify my opinion that the views put forward are not so balanced, objective and informed as one would have hoped in a document from such a quarter, which was doubtless intended to make a helpful contribution to an important discussion.

Commonwealth and Empire Law Conference. A Paper on the tenure and qualifications of Colonial Judges was considered by a Committee of the Commonwealth and Empire Law Conference held in London in July 1955. Only 11 delegates attended and, as there was no one present who was in a position to answer the critics, discussion was somewhat one-sided. The Committee passed a resolution expressing the opinion that 'Supreme Court and High Court Judges of the Colonial Territories should be appointed to hold office during good behaviour and not during the pleasure of the Crown'; but it was not put to, or adopted by, the Conference as such. In fact, Judges do hold office during good behaviour, except that there is a prescribed retiring age and, as in the case of a County Court Judge in England and High Court Judges elsewhere, the appointment of a Colonial Judge can be terminated on grounds of inability as well as misbehaviour.

Modern Statutory Procedure. Now, however, controversy on this subject is well on the way to becoming academic. Political leaders in overseas countries were alert to see in the parliamentary procedure an historical accident which was no model for a mid-twentieth century constitution, particularly in a country which could not have the advantage of political and judicial traditions built up through centuries. They preferred to preserve and enshrine in their constitutions the accepted procedure for removing a Judge in a dependent territory.

The first in the field was the West Indies, and the Federal Constitution of 1957 laid down the main principle—that a Judge should be removed only on the recommendation of the Judicial Committee.

Soon afterwards, in the Constitutions of Nigeria and Singapore, we find sections setting out the procedure in greater detail. I take as my example the Federal Supreme Court of Nigeria.

If the Prime Minister represents to the Governor-General that the question of the removal of a Judge ought to be investigated, the Governor-General appoints a tribunal consisting of serving or retired Judges. The tribunal reports on the facts and recommends to the Governor-General whether he should request that the question of the removal of the Judge should be referred by Her Majesty to the Judicial Committee, and the Governor-General must make such a request if the tribunal so recommends. If the Judicial Committee advises that the Judge ought to be removed the Governor-General is required to act accordingly.

On the attainment of independence, the Federation of Malaya followed, with a modification consequent upon its unique position as the only Commonwealth Country with a Monarch who is not the Queen: the reference to the Judicial Committee is eliminated and the Judicial Commission itself makes recommendations to the Head of State.

The Judicial Committee procedure has now been embodied in a large number of constitutions, including those of independent Sierra Leone and Tanganyika, and it requires no inside knowledge or prophetic insight to foretell that the process will continue.

One point of interest in the normal procedure is that members of the tribunal may be Judges of Courts in any part of the Commonwealth. The reason for this is perhaps obvious—that in a country with a comparatively small Bench, Judges might find it embarrassing to be called upon to adjudicate on charges against one of their own brother Judges.

In Cyprus, Judges may be retired for incapacity or infirmity or dismissed for misconduct, and the procedure is judicial. In the case of a Judge of the Supreme Constitutional Court, the President and Vice-President are obliged to act in accordance with the decision of a Council consisting of Judges of the High Court. The constitution makes the same provision for Judges of the High Court, except that the tribunal consists of the Judges of the Supreme Constitutional Court.

OLDER MEMBERS OF THE COMMONWEALTH

I have deliberately left to this point an important geographical gap, representing the Members of the Commonwealth other than those which have become independent during the last year or two. My reason for doing so is that, with both the English anachronism and the more enlightened procedure in mind, a comparative study is most illuminating. Let us start with the cases where English law has been closely followed. In Canada the wording is substantially the same as that in the Act of Settlement. In Western Australia it takes the same form as the present English Act. One may reasonably assume an intention to follow English law; and on that assumption it is abundantly clear that in New South Wales, Victoria and Queensland it was realized that the procedure by way of Parliamentary address was not exclusive but was only a qualification on the principle that a Judge holds office during good behaviour, because in each case the provision for Parliamentary address, like that in the Act of 1760, is in the form of a proviso introduced by the words 'provided that' or 'nevertheless'. In New Zealand and South Australia there is not the same degree of clarity but the effect appears to be the same: there are two independent sections, the first stating that a Judge holds office during good behaviour, the second providing for removal by Parliamentary procedure, without any restriction on the grounds upon which an address may be presented.

On the other hand, in the Commonwealth of Australia, India, Pakistan (Supreme Court), Ceylon, Ghana and Tasmania, it is expressly laid down that Judges cannot be removed from office except on an address from Parliament. In India, however, a two-thirds majority is required and in Australia and India the grounds for removal are *proved* misbehaviour or incapacity. In Pakistan the law is the same as in India (except that 'infirmity' is substituted for 'incapacity') and Parliament is empowered to prescribe the procedure for proof. In Ghana, too, there is a stipulated majority but this safeguard seems to be offset by the use of the somewhat ambiguous word 'stated', instead of 'proved', before 'misbehaviour or infirmity'.

In two cases the procedure is judicial. In Canada the removal of a Judge on grounds of incapacity requires an enquiry before a tribunal of Judges; and a Judge of a High Court in Pakistan can be removed only if the Supreme Court, on reference by the President, reports that he ought to be removed.

To complete the picture we should, I think, remember that under the Government of India Act, 1935, a Judge of the Federal Court or a High Court could be removed only if the Judicial Committee of the Privy Council reported that he ought to be removed. The Act is, of course, no longer in force.

The terms of Acts of Parliament in other Commonwealth countries may be of limited value in interpreting English Law, but in fact many of them seem to show quite clearly that those responsible for their contents were not under the impression that a Judge in England may be removed only on an address from Parliament.

It may be fairly asked why many of these countries followed the English Parliamentary pattern, and, moreover, without some of its saving grace; for where it is expressly provided that it is only upon a Parliamentary address that a Judge can be removed, there can, of course, be no question of judicial process. And in none of these countries is there the safeguard afforded by Judges sitting in the Legislature. It is doubtful whether any research would enable one to give an answer with confidence; but it is, I think, fair to assume that some or all of the following explanations are correct, at any rate in most cases:

  (i) that the main purpose in view was not to provide a method of removing Judges but rather to safeguard them against removal;
  (ii) that no thought was given to the objections to the Parliamentary process;
  (iii) that the obvious course in devising constitutions is to follow the law of the mother country; and,
  (iv) that no one suggested an alternative.

Summary. That completes my review of the means whereby judicial independence may be secured. It remains only for me to suggest a brief summary of the position. Under at least two of my four headings, appointment and tenure of office, the legalistic sophist can find material for his hypercritical faculties if he wants to do so. But it is preferable, even on a matter of such supreme importance as judicial independence, to scrutinize strict law under the twin spotlights of fact, past and present, and common sense. If we do that, I for one do not believe we need have much cause for misgivings.

5

FUNDAMENTAL RIGHTS

PROFESSOR A. GLEDHILL

Professor of Oriental Laws in the
University of London

SCOPE AND CONTENTS

You doubtless know the story of the new recruit to the armed forces, coming from a world in which, to a considerable extent, he could eat and drink when and what he liked, rise and go to bed when he liked, employ his leisure as he liked and, if he was dissatisfied with his pay or conditions of service, go on strike. After a few days in the army, chafing at the new restrictions imposed upon him, he asked an old soldier if there was any escape from this tyranny and was told, 'They can do anything with you except put you in the family way'. The veteran at least conceded that a soldier had a fundamental right not to be put in the family way and this will do as an indication of what a fundamental right is. It is a restriction on sovereignty for the benefit of the individual.

The scope of the liberties which have been given general recognition has differed from time to time but there are some today to which almost all civilized countries pay at least lip service. Peaslee's *Constitutions of the World* sets out the constitutions of eighty-nine countries, in all of which there is some recognition of some of the fourteen rights I am about to mention. Eight-four countries recognize the rights to personal liberty, fair legal process and freedom of expression. Eighty-three recognize freedom of conscience and religion. Eighty-one recognize freedom of assembly and association and the inviolability of correspondence and domicile. Eighty recognize the right to property; seventy-nine the right to freedom of education; seventy-seven the right to equality before the law; seventy-six the right to freedom of labour; sixty-three the right to petition government authorities; sixty to certain rights relating to health and motherhood; fifty-nine the right to social security; fifty-six the right of free movement within the nation; and forty-nine protection against retroactive legislation.

The classification I have given is apt to mislead, except as to the kind of restriction to which the peoples of the world have given formal recognition. There is a wide variety in the scope of the formulae defining the recognized rights. In some countries one or more of these rights may be so generally recognized that there is no point in declaring them: the right to petition, for instance, in the Commonwealth. Then the eighty-nine constitutions in Peaslee's book fall into three different classes. There are the normative constitutions of the politically mature countries, for example the Scandinavian countries, in which the Supreme Court interprets the constitution and the executive and legislature abide by the interpretation; the formal constitutions found, for instance in South America, only partially enforced in practice but which it is hoped will be normative constitutions when political maturity is achieved. And there are constitutions devised to throw dust in the eyes of observers while the ruling clique or party does as it likes; here the Fundamental Rights, like bikinis, are important only for what they conceal. Again, some constitutions provide effective legal process for enforcing Fundamental Rights: India, for instance, makes the right to effective judicial process a Fundamental Right itself; other constitutions are silent on the point; but there may nevertheless be a judicial remedy for infringement, and this may be speedy or not. There may be effective protection by convention, as in this country, where it would be impracticable to initiate legislation permitting detention without trial in the interests of public safety except in time of war, legislation expropriating without compensation and legislation to suppress an effective political opposition. On the other hand there may be no effective protection of fundamental rights. The degree to which any particular liberty is enjoyed in a particular country depends on a large number of factors, of which a constitutional provision is but one.

MAGNA CARTA

Now it is one thing to say that a particular legislative or executive act is unjust; it is quite another thing to put into writing principles to inhibit it—and, if we are to take a brief glance at the various attempts which have been made to formulate such principles, we might well begin with Magna Carta. Some of its provisions are found in earlier charters, including the Assize of Jerusalem of 1099, but we cannot ignore the famous declaration 'No free man shall be deprived of life or liberty, save by judgment of his peers or the law of the land'. There are other provisions designed to ensure access to the courts and speedy justice, and the prohibition of arbitrary taxation and arbitrary seizure of property by royal officials. The main object was to ensure the rights of the nobles; but the charter demanded freedom of movement for merchants within the realm and required all men, in their relations with subordinates, to observe the same rules as the King had undertaken to abide by in dealing with his subjects. What is often forgotten is that the English barons of the thirteenth century were well aware of the necessity of providing Fundamental Rights with teeth. Magna Carta provided for the election of a council of twenty-five barons; if any breach of the charter was brought to the notice of any four of them and they, being satisfied of the truth of the complaint, besought the King to right the wrong and he failed to do so within forty days, the council could make war upon the King and seize all the royal property.

THE U.S.A.

Whatever the thirteenth century English nobles intended, Magna Carta established the right to personal liberty for all Englishmen, and the charter is probably regarded with more respect in the United States than in this country. Nonetheless, the American Declaration of Independence of 1776 developed the concept of fundamental rights in declaring all men equal, with inalienable rights to life, liberty and the pursuit of happiness, to secure which government is instituted with the consent of the governed; if the government violates these rights, the people have the right to abolish it and establish a new government. If, after this, we find the American Bill of Rights somewhat prosaic and question the right to pursue happiness, we can see in later formulations of human rights the fruits of this concept in restrictions on sovereignty designed to remove some of the causes of human misery. And we have now reached the stage in the world's constitutional history when the main beneficiaries of constitution-making are not the nobles but the bourgeoisie.

The Founding Fathers of the United States had enough on their hands to reconcile the people to the Constitution of 1787 without encumbering themselves with a Bill of Rights; and the amendments of 1791 consists, for the most part, of restrictions on the federal power. It is Congress that is prohibited from establishing a religion or prohibiting its free exercise, of abridging freedom of speech and assembly, or infringing the right of the people to bear arms. Billeting of soldiers in peace-time is forbidden. The right of the people to be secure in their persons, houses, papers and effects must not be violated. Warrants may only issue if supported by oath and affirmation, and must specify the place to be searched and the thing to be searched for. No person may be tried for a heinous crime except on indictment by a grand jury; no person shall be subject to double jeopardy, or be compelled to be a witness against himself; and an accused is entitled to trial by an impartial jury from the district in which the offence is alleged to have been committed, to be informed of the nature of the charge, to be confronted with the prosecution witnesses, to compulsory process for his own witnesses and to be defended by counsel. No person may be deprived of life, liberty or property except by due process of law; property may not be taken for public use except on payment of just compensation; excessive bail and fines, and cruel and unusual punishments, are forbidden. It was not until 1868, after the War of Secession, that slavery was forbidden, and three years later the States were forbidden to abridge the immunities of citizens, to deprive persons of life, liberty or property without due process, or to deny equal protection of the laws—Congress being empowered to make laws to enforce these rights. The right of rebellion, recognized in Magna Carta and the Declaration of Independence, was, in effect, negatived by a provision that no State should finance rebellion against the United States.

FRANCE

Turning back to Europe, 1791 saw the promulgation of the Rights of Man and the Citizen, embodied in the French Constitution of 1793, and the constitution of the third year of the new republican era; they found no place in the Napoleonic constitutions, but they are reproduced in the constitution of 1946. Though these are mainly concerned with personal and political liberty and property rights, they have a philosophic flavour, claiming that all men are born equal; sovereignty resides in the nation; nobody can exercise authority not expressly emanating from it; and every public servant is liable to be called to account. The purpose of all political rights is to preserve the natural rights of man: liberty, property, security and resistance to oppression. No society in which these rights are not guaranteed can be said to have a constitution. Liberty is the power to do anything which does not injure another. Freedom of opinion is one of the most precious rights and no person should be punished for his opinions unless their manifestation affects public order. Property is an inviolable right; no person may be deprived of it, except for declared and obviously essential public necessity and on payment of just and predetermined compensation. Taxation must be agreed by the representatives of the people and its incidence distributed in accordance with means. No man shall be accused, arrested or detained save in accordance with law and prescribed procedure; every man is presumed innocent until proved guilty. If it is necessary to detain him, his detention must not be more rigorous than is necessary to ensure his appearance for trial. The law may only forbid conduct injurious to society and only provide punishments which are obviously necessary; no person may be convicted under a retroactive law.

The American Bill of Rights and the French Declaration of the Rights of Man influenced most constitutions which have since been promulgated, but they enshrine bourgeois ideals. In the latter part of the nineteenth century and in the present century, the proletariat began to take an increasing interest in politics. Nevertheless the new constitutions of the early part of the twentieth century, particularly those of the period after the Kaiser's War, generally regarded the same rights as fundamental. Unfortunately, the constitutional history of Europe generally, between the two wars, was the subversion of popular liberties and the establishment of dictatorship. It is therefore hardly surprising to find the report of the Simon Commission in 1930 rejecting the Indian demand for the insertion of a Bill of Rights in the new Constitution Act on the ground that they would be useless without the will and means to enforce them.[1] The Joint Select Committee on the Bill which became the Government of India Act, 1935, went further, saying that the recent history of Europe suggested that the most effective way of subverting human rights was to embody them in a constitution, where they must prove either of no practical value or impediments to effective legislation.[2] This argument would, of course, receive a more sympathetic hearing from an Englishman, for whom there is no clear distinction between constitutional and other laws and who believes that his laws do and should guarantee human liberties, than from an Indian about to discard the fetters of colonial rule.

JAPAN

But before considering the Indian constitution, I should like to say a word about the American-made Japanese constitution of 1946, and

[1] 1 Cmd. 3569 (1930), pp. 22-3.   [2] H.L. 6, H.C. 5, 1933-4, p. 216.

the U.N. Declaration of 1948. The former guarantees the right of life, liberty and the pursuit of happiness to the extent that it does not interfere with public welfare.[1] All people are equal under the law and there shall be no discrimination on grounds of race, creed, sex, social status or family origin.[2] There shall be universal suffrage and secret ballot, and no person shall be answerable for the way he has voted.[3] Every person has the right to petition for redress for injury, illegal acts of officials and for the amendment of legislation.[4] No person shall be held in bondage. Freedom of thought, conscience, religion, and assembly are guaranteed.[5] Every person may choose his residence and occupation so far as this does not interfere with the public welfare; any person may leave the country and renounce his nationality.[6] Academic freedom is guaranteed. All people have the right to equal education correspondent to their ability.[7] Marriage must be based on consent of the parties, and the law governing the property of the marriage must be based on equality between the sexes.[8] All people have the right to maintain the minimum standard of wholesome and cultured living and the State must endeavour to promote social welfare and security and public health.[9] All people have the right and obligation to work. Workers have the right to organize and bargain collectively. Service conditions must be fixed by law and children must not be exploited.[10] Property rights must be defined by law in conformity with public welfare; private property may only be taken for public use on payment of just compensation.[11] No person shall be deprived of life or liberty except according to procedure established by law.[12] No person shall be arrested except while committing an offence or on a warrant specifying the offence; he may not be detained without being informed of the charge or without immediate privilege of counsel.[13] The right to be secure in one's house, papers and effects shall not be impaired except on warrant issued for adequate cause and giving adequate particulars.[14] Torture and cruel punishments are forbidden.[15] The accused at a criminal trial has the right to examine all witnesses and to be represented by competent counsel at State expense, if he cannot provide it himself.[16] No person shall be compelled to testify against himself, nor shall he be convicted solely on his own

---

[1] Constitution of Japan, 1946, Art. 13.   [2] *Ibid.*, Art. 14.   [3] *Ibid.*, Art. 15.
[4] *Ibid.*, Art. 16.   [5] *Ibid.*, Arts. 17, 18, 19, 20.   [6] *Ibid.*, Art. 22.
[7] *Ibid.*, Arts. 23, 26.   [8] *Ibid.*, Art. 24.   [9] *Ibid.*, Art. 25.
[10] *Ibid.*, Arts. 27, 28.   [11] *Ibid.*, Art. 29.   [12] *Ibid.*, Art. 31.
[13] *Ibid.*, Art. 33.   [14] *Ibid.*, Art. 35.   [15] *Ibid.*, Art. 36.
[16] *Ibid.*, Art. 37.

confession.[1] No person may be placed in double jeopardy, or convicted under a retroactive law.[2] An acquitted accused may sue the State for redress.[3]

THE U.N. DECLARATION

The Universal Declaration of Human Rights was adopted by the General Assembly of the United Nations in 1948. The rights there declared, though regarded as basic principles rather than rules of law, are expressly declared to be subject to restrictions to secure due recognition of the rights of others, or in the interests of morality, public order, the general welfare of a democratic society and the principles of the United Nations.[4] The individual is, however, guaranteed effective remedies against violation of his rights,[5] which include the right to public trial before an independent tribunal at which he is presumed innocent.[6] Torture, cruel punishments and conviction under a retroactive law are forbidden.[7] Equality before the law, freedom of conscience and religion, freedom of expression, assembly and association, and the right to property, are guaranteed.[8]

You will observe that, in the Japanese Bill of Rights, the protection given to the right of personal liberty shows no great change but property rights are not so sacrosanct. It is true that the right to compensation for expropriation is unimpaired, but what property may be acquired, enjoyed and dealt with is now subject to control by law. A new concept, the Welfare State, with the right to work, the right to a minimum standard of decent living and the right to be educated according to one's capacity, has been introduced. In the bourgeois world, these were by-products of the right to acquire and enjoy property.

But the U.N. Declaration goes on to claim the right to participate in government, the right to work, the right of a parent to determine a child's education and the right to free education in the elementary stages. It also demands freedom to choose one's spouse.[9] The rights in the U.N. Declaration, with the notable exception of freedom to marry, are reproduced almost word for word in the Indonesian Constitution; but the Supreme Court may only declare unconstitutional legislation of the provincial legislatures, and the Federal

---

[1] Constitution of Japan, 1946, Art. 38.   [2] *Ibid.*, Art. 39.   [3] *Ibid.*, Art. 40.
[4] United Nations Declaration of Human Rights, Arts. 29, 30.
[5] *Ibid.*, Art. 8.   [6] *Ibid.*, Arts. 10, 11.   [7] *Ibid.*, Arts. 8, 11.
[8] *Ibid.*, Arts. 6, 7, 15, 20, 17.   [9] *Ibid.*, Arts. 21, 23, 26, 16.

Legislature may give directions to the provinces on restrictions to the Fundamental Rights.[1]

INDIA

Turning now to the Indian Constitution (which has been followed, in so far as it deals with basic human liberties, in the Burma Constitution, the Pakistan Constitution of 1956 and the Malayan Constitution) we notice that the older bourgeois rights, to personal liberty, property, equality, expression, association, assembly, movement and freedom to choose one's avocation, are in one part and the new rights of the welfare state are in a separate chapter. The former are protected by a guarantee of adequate judicial remedy, while the latter, described as Directive Principles, are not—a device borrowed from the Constitution of Eire. The political philosophy behind the Fundamental Rights is liberal, that behind the Directive Principles is socialistic; and the conflict between the two ideologies soon became evident in India in regard to property rights. It became necessary to amend the right to acquire, hold and dispose of property,[2] and the right to follow an avocation,[3] which, as originally constituted, could be reasonably restricted in the general public interest so as to render immune from attack legislation nationalising industries. It was necessary, in other words, to bring these Fundamental Rights in line with the Directive Principle that the economic system does not result in the concentration of wealth and means of production to the common detriment.[4] Then the right to compensation for expropriation[5]— which, as originally constituted and interpreted, gave the expropriated owner the market value, irrespective of the mode of deprivation— was amended so that he only gets what the Legislature says he may have, and only if the title passes to the State or a state-owned corporation. Many of the Indian rights can be reasonably restricted in the interest of the general public; and the courts have held that legislation following a Directive Principle must necessarily be so regarded.

Moreover, no less than twenty statutes, most of them designed to break up the large agricultural estates into small holdings—a policy which, it might be argued, is not necessarily in the best interests of

[1] Indonesian Constitution, Arts. 156 and 32(2).
[2] Indian Constitution, Art. 19(1) (f) and (6), amended by Constitution (First Amendment) Act, 1951.
[3] *Ibid.*, Art. 19(1) (g).   [4] *Ibid.*, Art. 39(b).
[5] *Ibid.*, Art. 31, amended by Constitution (Fourth Amendment) Act, 1955.

Indian agriculture—have been given constitutional immunity against being invalidated for repugnancy to the fundamental rights,[1] and other constitutional provisions[2] have been added which protect a wide variety of expropriatory legislation. I would say that, notwithstanding the elaborate provisions for protection of the Fundamental Rights, the Directive Principles are the more potent.

Another feature of the Indian Constitution is that, while the protection of the person accused of a crime is comprehensive and effective, discretionary detention of political agitators is permitted even in peace time.[3] Under the Rome Convention this is only permitted in times of emergency. It is true that the detenu has a right to be informed of the grounds of his detention and to make a representation; in the event of prolonged detention, he also has a right of recourse to an advisory board but this right may be restricted by ordinary legislation. Just as the old property rights have had to give way to the demands of the welfare state, so the right of individual liberty has had to yield to the demands of the national state. Not only has the right of rebellion been rejected, but the political agitator may be deprived of personal liberty without conviction by fair trial for a defined offence. It must be recognized that, with the improved technique of revolution, something of this kind is a necessary weapon of government—not only in India but in other parts of the world. But if we concede so much, we must recognize the necessity of devising methods of protecting the individual against its abuse.

The Indian Fundamental Rights can only be pleaded against laws; this includes statutes, *jus non scriptum* and delegated legislation, but they cannot be pleaded against administrative rules which have no statutory basis. For instance, if Government lays down rules in the exercise of its executive power, without reference to a statute, governing admission to an educational institution which offend against the right of equality of opportunity, they cannot be impugned as repugnant to this right.[4]

The Indian Constitution distinguishes between rights available to all persons, which include the right of personal liberty, the right to compensation for expropriation and the right to practice religion,[5] and rights available only to citizens, which include most of the others. This is an important point which seems to have been overlooked in many constitutions. In an ideal world, there should be no need of this

---

[1] Indian Constitution, 9th Schedule.   [2] *Ibid.*, Arts. 31A, 31B.
[3] *Ibid.*, Art. 22.   [4] *Ramchandra* v *State*, A.I.R., 1961, M.P.247
[5] Indian Constitution, Arts. 20, 21, 31, 25.

distinction; but in the world around us today, it seems impracticable for many countries to allow to foreigners the same liberties as they accord to their own nationals.

The Indian Constitution provides for a Proclamation of Emergency by the President in face of a threat of external aggression or internal disturbance. This *ipso facto* puts into eclipse the rights[1] of freedom of expression, association and assembly, the right of free movement in India, the right to hold property and the right to follow an avocation.[2] A consequential order may be made suspending the remedies for the other rights.[3]

Though the language in which the Indian rights are expressed is often borrowed from earlier declarations, much of it is original and, in dealing with many of the rights (those last mentioned, for instance), an endeavour has been made to turn them into a form appropriate to a rule in an Indian statute, rather than to state them as general principles, leaving it to the courts to determine their scope and the limitations which can be imposed on them.

There is now an enormous body of case law on the subject, resort to which is being had in other countries, even when interpreting rights not *in pari materia* with the Indian rights. I think that the way in which the Indian judges have dealt with this very difficult new jurisdiction, with very little precedent to assist—skilfully steering between the Scylla of depriving the rights of effective force and the Charybdis of making them impediments to effective legislation—has converted many an English constitutional lawyer from the view I have mentioned earlier; for the present policy of the United Kingdom Government seems to be to impose Bills of Rights on ex-colonial territories.

THE ROME CONVENTION

In 1950 most European countries west of the iron curtain signed the Rome Convention for the Protection of Human Rights. These are based on the U.N. Declaration of 1948 but are expanded and deliminated in the language of lawyers, not necessarily English lawyers. Though, in general, no distinction is drawn between citizens and foreigners, the right of freedom of expression,[4] of assembly[5] and of freedom from discrimination[6] cannot be pleaded against laws

---

[1] Indian Constitution, Art. 19.   [2] *Ibid.*, Art. 358.   [3] *Ibid.*, Art. 359.
[4] Convention for the Protection of Human Rights, Art. 10.
[5] *Ibid.*, Art. 11.   [6] *Ibid.*, Art. 14.

restricting political activities of aliens.[1] The Convention primarily imposes a duty on the contracting states to secure the rights declared in it.[2] I will deal with remedies for infringement later.

The Rome Convention has been drawn upon by the draftsmen of the Bill of Rights in the Nigerian Constitution, though there are amendments and omissions. The Nigerian Constitution specifically provides that an Act of Parliament may derogate from the rights to life,[3] personal liberty,[4] the rights to a fair and speedy determination of rights and obligations,[5] and the right to freedom from discrimination,[6] in a period of emergency, to the extent reasonably justified for dealing with the situation.[7] Any person complaining of a contravention has a right to move the High Court.[8] Many of the rights are liable to be restricted, in prescribed interests, to the extent that is reasonably justifiable in a democratic society. For instance every person is entitled to respect for his private life; but a law, reasonably justifiable in a democratic society, may interfere with his private life in the interests of defence, public safety, public order, public morality, public health or the economic well-being of the community.[9] One can imagine the difficulties facing a court asked to determine whether prohibition legislation contravenes this right. In Europe the right to drink, if not formally declared, is generally recognized. In a Muslim country it is not. Whereas, in India, a reasonable restriction is determined by the opinion of our old friend in the law of negligence, the reasonable man, under the Rome Convention, as in Nigeria, the standard is different; is it majority world opinion, or majority national opinion, that decides the point?

ENFORCEMENT OF THE RIGHTS

Let us consider for a moment means of enforcing the rights. Many constitutions contain no specific provisions for this purpose. If the rights are not effectively binding on the consciences of legislators or administrators, where there is effective representative government, governmental action repugnant to the rights can often be forestalled or condemned by a legislature sensitive to public opinion. Though we may think judicial review a characteristic feature of American constitutional law, this principle was not in fact accepted until after the War of Secession. In the early years of the American Republic, the

---

[1] Convention for the Protection of Human Rights, Art. 16. [2] *Ibid.*, Art. 1.
[3] Nigerian Constitution s. 17. [4] *Ibid.*, s. 20. [5] *Ibid.*, s. 21.
[6] *Ibid.*, s. 27. [7] *Ibid.*, s. 28. [8] *Ibid.*, s. 31. [9] *Ibid.*, s. 22.

doctrine of the sovereignty of the legislature was so widely held that the device for preventing legislation repugnant to the Bill of Rights, in Pennsylvania and Vermont, was to establish representative bodies with power to draw the attention of the legislatures to such repugnancies; in New York, a council composed of the Governor and State judges had a power of veto, which could be overruled by a two-thirds majority of the legislature; even today in Ohio, North Dakota and Nebraska, a State law can only be struck down if all the judges save one find it unconstitutional.

If a law has been in force for some time and is then struck down, it may have created so many rights and liabilities that the consequences may be disastrous; so there is much to be said for a final revision of enacted laws before promulgation. In Eire, the President may refer any Bill, within four days of its being passed by the legislature, to a council composed of ministers, ex-ministers, judges, ex-judges and not more than seven others appointed by himself, on whose advice he will exercise his power of veto. In Italy questions of constitutionality of legislation are referred to a constitutional court, composed of fifteen judges, all lawyers—one-third appointed by Parliament, one-third by the President and one-third by the higher magistrates and executives. If the law is found unconstitutional, it only becomes void as from the day following the delivery of judgment. The objection to relying exclusively on these methods is that it is impossible to foretell the effect of a law in action and, if Fundamental Rights are intended for the protection of individuals, the individual whom the shoe pinches should be entitled to be heard.

There are, of course, devices to minimize the consequences of legislation being declared repugnant to Fundamental Rights. In the United States, it is possible to hold that certain rights, particularly property rights, have been waived; but India has declined to accept the doctrine of waiver.

The fact is that India has taken the problem of enforcing Fundamental Rights more seriously than any other country and has provided the world with an object-lesson. Despite my admiration of the work the Indian judges have done, I fear that the results, over the past twelve years, do not suggest that it is advisable blindly to follow India's example. The enormous body of legal literature dealing with the scope of the rights has been obtained at a heavy price. In the vast majority of writ petitions, the Union or a State is a respondent. A petitioner has the right to originate his case in the Supreme Court, and, if he starts in a High Court, he can appeal to the Supreme Court.

The Supreme Court usually gives notice, not only to the Attorney-General but also to the Advocates-General of the fourteen States. At the hearing there is often a galaxy of legal talent. The cost of these legal proceedings, if the petitioner succeeds, falls on the public; and very frequently when he does not. The Indian Founding Fathers could hardly have contemplated the spate of litigation which has resulted. Although the majority of the cases filed in the Supreme Court are civil appeals, in the first five months of 1961 pressure of other work prevented a single civil appeal from being heard, for the Indian Constitution requires a bench of five judges to hear any constitutional question. One result of this new jurisdiction is that the courts cannot cope with the volume of work which is put before them and the ordinary litigant, endeavouring to enforce a legal right, finds himself in the queue a long way behind the person claiming protection of a Fundamental Right. And it is noteworthy in this context that one of the rights guaranteed by Magna Carta was speedy justice, for justice delayed may be justice denied.

In contrast to the Indian procedure, let us glance at the procedure in the two first cases of alleged breach of the Rome Convention. In the first a citizen of Eire complained of being detained without trial, in violation of the rights of personal security and to a fair trial,[1] to the European Commission of Human Rights, a majority of which held that the detention was covered by the Article in the Convention which permits measures derogatory to a State's obligations in emergencies.[2] This was transmitted to the Committee of Ministers of those States which are parties to the Convention who, as this was the first case of its kind and the opinion was not unanimous, exercised their right to bring the matter before the European Court of Human Rights within three months of the transmission of the report to them. The court duly upheld the majority opinion, but it also decided that in no case can an individual set the court in motion; that can only be done by a State or the Committee of Ministers.

In the second case a Belgian journalist had been sentenced to life imprisonment, subsequently commuted to seventeen years, for collaboration with the German army of occupation. He was released in 1951 but, under the Belgian Penal Code, he was debarred for ever from following his occupation. He pleaded a violation of the right of freedom of expression.[3] The Commission, having examined the claim, exercised its power to endeavour to achieve a settlement between the

---

[1] Convention for the Protection of Human Rights, Arts. 5 & 6.
[2] *Ibid.*, Art. 15.   [3] *Ibid.*, Art. 10.

petitioner and the Belgian Government. As this failed, the matter was referred to the Court. But, before the hearing commenced, the Belgian Parliament amended the Penal Code so as to enable persons in the petitioner's situation to practice journalism of a non-political character. The Belgian Government then pleaded that the petitioner had no further interest in the pursuit of the application but, on the motion of the Delegate for the Commission, the Court referred the matter back to it. Subsequently the petitioner withdrew his application, but this binds neither the Court nor the Commission; so whether the amended Penal Code offends against the Convention is still an open question.[1]

DISCREPANCIES

If the Indian Constitution is over-generous in the scope afforded to the individual to seek redress for infringement of his Fundamental Rights, the provisions in the Rome Convention may be regarded as too niggardly for imitation in areas outside the European community, in which it may be assumed that the countries concerned will make an honest effort to implement their obligations. There is, however, much to be said for a system ensuring scrutiny of claims for protection of a Fundamental Right before leave is given to agitate them in a court. And one advantage enjoyed by the parties to the Rome Convention is that the countries of Western Europe will have a uniform application of the rights. One difficulty which has to be faced is that, if you define Fundamental Rights, members of the general public are inclined to expect too much of them, having too much regard for their own liberty and too little for the rights of others and the necessities of the State. They regard the court's interpretation as whittling away the right. Equality before the law has a fine sound; but India, in this respect generally following American doctrine, holds that it only prevents discrimination between persons or things similarly situated; similarity of treatment is enough; a law may classify persons or things on a basis reasonably connected with its object and discriminate to achieve that object.[2] Then the general public observes with dismay discrepancies to which a lawyer is habituated. You all know of the unsuccessful prosecution of the publishers of *Lady Chatterley's Lover* in England and it may interest you to know what befell when the Japanese translator of that book appealed to the Supreme Court of Japan[3]

[1] Bulletin of the International Commission of Jurists No. 12, pp. 37-99.
[2] *Bombay v Balsara*, A.I.R. 1951, S.C. 318.
[3] *Kyujiyo Koyama* 'A' case 1713-1953, S.C. of Japan.

from his conviction under the Japanese Penal Code for distributing an obscene book.[1] The Japanese court held that anything which tended to excite sexual desire or injure the normal sense of shame is obscene. On behalf of the translator it was contended that the provision in the Japanese Bill of Rights, 'No censorship shall be maintained,'[2] is an absolute prohibition to which no qualification is attached; but the Supreme Court held that, whether a Fundamental Right was expressly qualified or not, it was subject to the general qualification specified in the Constitution that Fundamental Rights must not be abused and must be exercised for the public welfare.[3] Prohibition of censorship does not mean that distribution of obscene books cannot be prohibited. The conviction was upheld. Strangely enough the right of freedom of expression is not specified in the Japanese Constitution.

In an American case, a dope-pedlar was arrested by a preventive officer. He promptly swallowed the dope which was on his person. The preventive officer rushed him to a hospital, had his stomach pumped and got him convicted on the analyst's report on the contents of his stomach. Relying on the Fundamental Right to freedom from unreasonable searches, he successfully appealed. But when the same problem came before the Indian courts, it was observed that there is no such Fundamental Right in India, so it was pleaded that an accused in such a position was entitled to the benefit of the protection against self-conviction;[4] but this was rejected, on the ground that that right could only be pleaded when the accused has been obliged to co-operate in the production of the incriminating evidence.[5]

You may feel that I have over-stressed the difficulties in defining these rights, in setting boundaries to them, in interpreting them and in enforcing them. You may feel that, in action, they do not amount to very much. But it is not my intention to leave such thoughts in your minds. In many parts of the world today, the history of the period between the two wars seems likely to be repeated. Dictatorship is on the march and it cannot co-exist with Fundamental Rights; its ultimate destination is a slave civilization. The Welfare State, with its new mass-produced benefits, may lull people into an attitude of indifference to the old liberal rights. But it is they, at least as much as the benefits of the Welfare State, which have made it possible for the individual to be the captain of his soul, to fulfil his potentialities and,

[1] Japanese Penal Code, Art. 175. [2] Constitution of Japan, Art. 21.
[3] Ibid., Art. 12. [4] Indian Constitution, Art. 20 (s).
[5] In re Palani Gouden, A.I.R. 1957, Mad. 546.

as a by-product, to experience happiness. If we are to content ourselves with social security, state doctoring and free entertainment, individual initiative, the mainspring of human progress, will be inhibited. Either we study these rights and methods for their enforcement and fight for them, or we shall be condemned to an antcivilization.

6

CONSTITUTIONAL WRITS IN INDIA

SIR ORBY MOOTHAM

Formerly Chief Justice, Allahabad High Court

INTRODUCTORY

I must begin with an apology, for the subject of this paper is not accurately reflected in its title. What I want to discuss are not only writs but also those directions and orders for which provision is made in Articles 32 and 226 of the Constitution of India. The jurisdiction vested by these Articles in the Supreme Court of India and in the High Courts is commonly referred to as the 'writ jurisdiction', and although this again is not strictly accurate it is a compendious and convenient name which I propose to use.

I do not intend to give a summary of the law relating to these constitutional remedies, for that can be obtained from the books. My object is to look briefly at the origin and development of the writ jurisdiction, to examine the importance which this jurisdiction has attained in India, and to consider the suitability of the jurisdiction for the purposes for which it is being used. This is not merely an academic exercise. In 1959 the number of applications made to the High Court in London for orders of *certiorari*, prohibition and *mandamus* was 22. In the same year the number of applications made to one High Court in India—the High Court at Allahabad—for the corresponding writs exceeded 4000. We are therefore considering a jurisdiction to which recourse is freely made, and one of the purposes of our enquiry is to find out why that should be so.

Now a power to issue directions in the nature of *habeas corpus* was possessed by all the Indian High Courts by virtue of s. 491 of the Code of Criminal Procedure. Prior however to January 26, 1950, the date upon which the Constitution of India came into force, the power of the courts to issue writs or orders of the nature of *certiorari*, prohibition, *mandamus* or *quo warranto* was exceedingly limited. Broadly speaking, the writs of *certiorari*, prohibition and *quo warranto*, and an order in the nature of *mandamus*, could be issued only by the High Courts of Calcutta, Bombay and Madras. The writ or order did not run beyond the limits of the ordinary civil jurisdiction of the court concerned, which meant that it could be effective only within the three Presidency Towns[1]—and in the case of *certiorari*, probably the most important of these writs, it could not issue in any matter concerning the revenue or its collection, nor was it generally held to be available against either the Central or a provincial Government.

The Constitution brought about a far reaching change. It declared certain rights to be fundamental; and for the purpose of the speedy enforcement of these rights it conferred on the Supreme Court and the High Courts power to issue directions, orders and writs. And at the same time it conferred on the High Courts a further power to issue such directions, orders and writs 'for any other purpose'— with the object, it has been said, of putting the High Courts substantially in the same position as the Court of Queen's Bench in England.[2]

The Article which confers these new powers on the High Courts is Art. 226, and so far as is material it reads thus:

Notwithstanding anything in Article 32, every High Court shall have power, throughout the territories in relation to which it exercises jurisdiction, to issue to any person or authority, including in appropriate cases any Government, within those territories directions, orders or writs, including writs in the nature of *habeas corpus*, *mandamus*, prohibition, *quo warranto* and *certiorari*, or any of them for the enforcement of any of the rights conferred by Part III and for any other purpose.

Part III of the Constitution is that part which deals with fundamental rights, and it includes Article 32 which guarantees the right to move the Supreme Court for the enforcement of those rights and confers on the Supreme Court the power to issue similar directions, orders and writs for that limited purpose.

Two observations of a general nature on the jurisdiction thus conferred on the Supreme and High Courts of India may be made. In the first place, as you will have noticed, the authority vested in the

---

[1] See *Besant* v *Advocate-General of Madras*, 46 I.A. 129; *Ryots of Garabandho* v *Zamindar of Parlakimedi*, 70 I.A. 129. The issue of an order in the nature of *mandamus* was regulated by Chap. VIII of the Specific Relief Act, 1877.

[2] See *Election Commissioner, India* v *Saka Venkata Subba Rao* [1953] S.C.R. 1144 at 1150.

court is not limited to the issue of the five well-known writs which are mentioned in Articles 32 and 226, for the court may also issue, if in its opinion circumstances so require, directions or orders or even some other form of writ. Secondly, the power of the Supreme Court to grant such relief is restricted to those cases where a fundamental right has been infringed; and a direction, order or writ issued by that Court has effect throughout India. A High Court on the other hand can exercise its power under Article 226 not only for the enforcement of fundamental rights but 'for any other purpose'; but at the same time it can exercise those powers only within the territory over which it exercises jurisdiction, that is to say within the State of which it is the High Court.

The words 'for any other purpose' cause some difficulty. They do of course make it clear that the court's jurisdiction to issue writs is not confined to the enforcement of fundamental rights,[1] but whether they empower the court (as the Nagpur High Court has said) to issue a writ, order or direction for any other object which it considers appropriate[2] may be doubted.[3]

SCOPE AND DEVELOPMENT OF JURISDICTION

The scope of the principal writs in India is, subject to two qualifications, substantially the same as in this country. The two qualifications relate to *mandamus* and *certiorari*. A writ of *mandamus* in India is of wider ambit than an order of *mandamus* in this country. In England *mandamus* is a command emanating from the Queen, and accordingly no order of *mandamus* will lie against the Crown; in India *mandamus* is a constitutional remedy and will lie against a Government or any Governmental authority. In India also a *mandamus* can be issued not only, as in this country, to compel the performance of a duty, but also to forbid the doing of something which would be contrary to a legal duty. For example, in the well-known case of *The State of Bombay* v *The Bombay Education Society and ors.*,[4] the Supreme

---

[1] *Jesingbhai Ishwarlal* v *Emperor:* A.I.R. (1950) Bom. 363; *Carlsbad Mineral Water Manufacturing Co. Ltd.* v *H. M. Jagtiani:* A.I.R. (1952), Cal. 315.

[2] *G. D. Karkare* v *T. L. Shevde:* A.I.R. (1952), Nag. 330.

[3] The Supreme Court has said that the concluding words of Art. 226 'have to be read in the context of what precedes the same. Therefore the existence of the right is the foundation of the existence of jurisdiction of the Court under the Article'. *The State of Orissa* v *Madan Gopal Rungta:* [1952] S.C.R. 28, 33.

[4] [1955] 1 S.C.R. 568.

Court issued a *mandamus* to the Bombay Government commanding it not to enforce an order which it had made that no primary or secondary school should admit to a class where English was the medium of instruction any pupil whose language was not English.

As regards *certiorari*, there has been some hesitation, perhaps even some reluctance, in accepting the view that this writ can properly be used to quash the decision of an inferior tribunal on the ground of error of law on the face of the record; and some doubt may even yet remain. This is a matter of great constitutional importance, for it involves the question whether it is in the public interest that quasi-judicial tribunals should be the ultimate arbiters on questions of law.

The view originally taken by the Supreme Court was that the writ could issue on the ground of an error apparent on the face of the record,[1] but shortly thereafter the Court held, in two cases,[2] that no writ could issue to quash the decision of an inferior court, acting within its jurisdiction, on the ground that the decision was wrong. It is perhaps not surprising that in these circumstances different views were taken by the High Courts, and even by the same High Court at different times, with regard to the grounds upon which the writ could issue; and the doubt remained unresolved until 1955 when the Supreme Court considered[3]—it seems for the first time—the *Northumberland* case,[4] and accepted the view that error apparent on the face of the record is a ground upon which the writ may issue. That acceptance was not however unqualified, for the Court went on to say that the error of law must be a 'manifest' or patent error in contradistinction to a 'mere wrong decision'.[5] The difference between these categories of

[1] *Veerappa Pillay* v *Raman and Raman* [1952] S.C.R. 583.

[2] *Parry and Co. Ltd.* v *Commercial Employees Assn. Ltd.* [1952] S.C.R. 519; *Ebrahim Aboobakar* v *Custodian General of Evacuee Property* [1952] S.C.R. 696.

[3] *Basappa* v *Nagappa* [1955] S.C.R. 250; see also *Sangram Singh* v *Election Tribunal, Kotah* [1955] 2 S.C.R. 1.

[4] *Rex* v *Northumberland Compensation Appeal Tribunal. Ex parte Shaw* [1951] 1 K.B. 177; [1952] 1 K.B. 338 C.A.

[5] This view was not new. In *Batuk Vyas* v *Surat Borough Municipality* (AIR 1953 Bom. 133) Chagla, C.J., observed that 'the mere fact that two views are possible on a question of law does not make the decision of a Tribunal with jurisdiction bad on the ground that it has erred in law and the error is apparent on the face of the record, only that error will be corrected by this Court which is clearly apparent on the face of the record, and which does not become apparent only by a process of examination or argument'. A similar view was taken in *Dholpur Co-operative Transport and Multi-Purpose Union* v *Appellate Authority, Rajasthan and ors.* (A.I.R. 1955 Raj. 19).

error was shortly afterwards considered in another case,[1] but the only conclusion at which the Court then arrived was that an error on the face of the record cannot be defined and 'must be left to be determined judicially on the facts of each case'. Unfortunately, if I may say so with respect, the principles on which it has to be determined were not stated.

It is interesting to speculate, if speculation be permitted, on the reason for the hesitation of the courts in India in accepting the English rule. There is the uncertainty which for some years existed in England prior to the decision of the *Northumberland* case with regard to the scope of the writ, and with this was possibly coupled a desire on the part of the courts in India to place some check on the marked tendency of the public to regard relief by way of writ as an alternative to a remedy by way of a civil suit. It must also, I think, not be overlooked that the decisions of quasi-judicial tribunals in India are almost invariably speaking orders—often speaking, if I may so, at some length—and there seems to have been some apprehension that, if caution were not exercised, *certiorari* might issue 'as the cloak of an appeal in disguise'.[2] It is curious also that when, in 1955, the Supreme Court considered the *Northumberland* case, it appears not to have had brought to its notice that the Divisional Court did examine and construe what Lord Goddard, L.C.J., described as 'this very complicated set of regulations';[3] that is to say the Court by implication negatived the view that the error of law must be 'patent'.

THE USE MADE OF IT

(a) SAFEGUARDING OF FUNDAMENTAL RIGHTS

The writ jurisdiction in India is essentially a new jurisdiction, and I think it is difficult for us in this country to appreciate how wide is the use which is made of it. Primarily it is used as a means of safeguarding the fundamental rights which are guaranteed under the Constitution; and these rights, it should be noted, are not all restricted in their application to citizens of India. The rights, for example, to protection of life and personal liberty, and to profess, practice and propagate religion, are guaranteed to all persons in India irrespective of their nationality. The writ jurisdiction has been used to protect these rights

---

[1] *Hari Vishnu Kamath* v *Syed Ahmed Ishaque and ors.* [1955] 1 S.C.R. 1104.
[2] Per Morris, L. J., in the Northumberland case in a sentence to which attention was pointedly drawn by Mukerji J. in Basappa's case, [1955] 1 S.C.R. 250.
[3] [1951] 1 K.B. 711 at 722. The full judgment of the Divisional Court is reported in [1951] 1 All E.R. 268.

in two ways: by invalidating legislation, and by setting aside, or otherwise making ineffective, administrative orders which infringe them.

Parliament in England is sovereign and no court can question the validity of a statute. That is not the case in India. In India the Constitution is supreme, and there are in consequence constitutional limitations on the legislative powers of the Parliament in Delhi and of the State legislatures. One set of limitations arises from the existence of fundamental rights to which I have referred; another from the fact that the Constitution (as in the case of the Constitutions of Australia and Canada) provides for a division of legislative powers between the Central and State legislatures. If an Act of Parliament or of a State legislature abridges a fundamental right or is in excess of the legislative power of the law-making authority its validity may be challenged in the courts; and the easiest and usual way of doing this is by a petition to the Supreme Court under Article 32 or to a High Court under Article 226. Now in a Welfare State—and India is such a state—a good deal of legislation will be concerned either with the imposition of taxes or other methods of extracting money from the public, either for ordinary revenue purposes or for financing public utility schemes. This kind of legislation is likely to bear most heavily on the more affluent members of society, and this no doubt accounts for the fact that such legislation is very often challenged in the courts. A court is of course slow to invalidate an enactment either wholly or in part; but when it is satisfied that the legislature has exceeded its powers either by infringing a fundamental right or by attempting to legislate outside its own field it will strike down—the American expression has found favour in India—the offending provisions. I must add also, for it is of practical importance, that the court's power to ensure that the laws are not repugnant to the Constitution is not restricted to laws made after the Constitution came into force; Article 13 provides that all laws in force in India prior to the commencement of the Constitution, in so far as they are inconsistent with any of the fundamental rights, shall, to the extent of such inconsistency, be void.

The powers of the court when it has before it a petition challenging the constitutional validity of an enactment are very wide. It can dismiss the petition as disclosing no ground for interference[1] or (as the Supreme Court has done in at least two instances[2]) it may at the same time

---

[1] As in *Attar Singh* v *The State of Uttar Pradesh* [1959] Supp. 1, S.C.R. 928; *Babu Barkya Thakur* v *The State of Bombay* [1961] 1 S.C.R. 128.

[2] *Vishweshwar Rao* v *State of Madhya Pradesh* [1952] S.C.R. 1020; *Raja Suriya Pal Singh* v *State of Uttar Pradesh* [1952] S.C.R. 1056.

declare the impugned Act to be valid in its entirety. It can declare an Act to be void.[1] In a number of cases it has held that particular sections of an Act are invalid, and if these sections are severable the remainder of the Act will stand;[2] and the usual practice in such cases is to issue a writ in the nature of *mandamus* directing the respondant Government to forbear from enforcing the sections found to be invalid.[3] The court may further direct the respondants to do something—as, for example, where goods have been seized under a section of an act subsequently declared to be invalid, it may direct the return of the goods to the petitioner.[4]

Of course if a High Court declares a provision of an act of the Central Legislation to be invalid that declaration will be operative only within the High Court's territorial jurisdiction. The resultant position, whereby a law valid in one State is invalid in another, is unsatisfactory, but in practice it is not likely to last long for almost certainly, in one way or another, the correctness of the High Court's decisions will soon be tested in the Supreme Court.

I am tempted to refer to one other question which, although not strictly germane to the subject of this paper, is of interest to lawyers. If a court holds that a section of an Act is invalid, it will ordinarily issue a *mandamus* or give a direction commanding the person or authority seeking to enforce the provisions of that section to refrain from doing so; and that will dispose of the proceedings before the court. But the question then arises, what is the effect of the court's decision on persons who are not parties to those proceedings? Does it amount to a judgment against the statute which binds everyone, or is it the position (as it is in the United States) that the opinion of the court is merely of persuasive effect and operates only as a precedent for the determination of other similar cases? In the case of *The State of Bombay* v *F. N. Balsara*[5] the Supreme Court held that a provision in the Bombay Prohibition Act of 1949, that no person shall consume or use liquor, was invalid so far as it affected the consumption or use of medicinal or toilet preparations containing alcohol. Three years later

---

[1] A recent example is *The Bullion and Grain Exchange Ltd.* v *State of Punjab* [1961] 1 S.C.R. 668.

[2] *Express Newspapers (Private) Ltd.* v *The Union of India* [1959] S.C.R. 12; *Hamdard Dawakhana (Wakf) Lal Kuari, Delhi* v *Union of India* [1960] 2 S.C.R. 671.

[3] *Mohd. Hanif Quareshi* v *State of Bihar* [1959] S.C.R. 629.

[4] *Hamdard Dawakhana (Wakf) Lal Kuari, Delhi* v *Union of India* [1960] S.C.R. 671.

[5] [1951] S.C.R. 682.

a man called Pesikaka was driving a motor car when he had an accident. When he was arrested his breath smelled of alcohol and in due course he was charged, inter alia, with a breach of the Bombay Prohibition Act. His defence was that he had been ill and had taken a tonic which contained a small percentage of alcohol. The question then was whether he had to establish afresh that the ban imposed by the Prohibition Act on the consumption or use of a medicine containing alcohol was invalid or whether he could successfully contend that as a result of Balsara's case that question had been finally settled. The Supreme Court held that once a law has been declared by it to be unconstitutional it is no longer law and is null and void for all purposes.[1] Now it is to be observed that this was so decided by the Supreme Court on the basis of Art. 141 which lays down that the law declared by that Court shall be binding on all courts in India. Laws can however be invalidated by the High Courts, and to their decisions Art. 141 has no application. Does then a declaration as to the invalidity of a law made by a High Court operate only between the parties or has it a more extensive effect? That question has yet to be answered.

The validity of subsidiary legislation purporting to be made under the authority of an enactment which is itself valid is frequently challenged by writ petitions. If in such a case the court finds that the rule or order is one which could not properly have been made, the usual practice is to issue a writ in the nature of *mandamus* requiring the author of the rule or order to forbear from enforcing it.

The writ jurisdiction has also been successfully invoked to nullify administrative orders. The District Magistrate of Ahmedabad had made an order prohibiting the applicant's entry into the city without a permit. The Bombay High Court, on a petition under Art. 226 directed the District Magistrate not to prevent the applicant entering the city as that was something he was entitled to do in exercise of his right to move freely in India;[2] and the Supreme Court has, by a writ of *mandamus*, directed a State Government to forbear from putting into effect a notification making a reference under the Industrial Disputes Act, 1947, although the order making the reference was purely administrative.[3]

I must not of course be understood to imply that the validity of a legislative act can be challenged only by a petition under Arts 32 or

[1] *Balram Khurshed Pesikaka* v *State of Bombay* [1955] 1 S.C.R. 613.
[2] *Jesingbhai Ishwarlal* v *Emperor*, A.I.R. 1950 Bom. 363.
[3] *State of Bihar* v *D. N. Ganguly*, A.I.R. 1958 S.C. 1018.

266. It can be questioned in a civil action or in crimininal proceedings, and this has been done. The most usual way of attacking an Act is however by a writ petition; and that is the only means of challenging an administrative order.

(b) CONTROL OF SUBORDINATE TRIBUNALS

The second important aspect of the writ jurisdiction is its use as a means of ensuring the supervision of the High Courts over the actions of quasi-judicial and, on occasions, even administrative tribunals. Legislation in India, as in this country, increasingly tends to provide for the determination of questions which affect the rights of citizens by such tribunals; tribunals which may, and often do, consist of a single individual. The court usually exercises its control over quasi-judicial tribunals by means of the writ of *certiorari;* but such a writ can issue only if the tribunal has failed to keep within its jurisdiction, or to follow the rules of natural justice or has committed an error of law discoverable on the record. If the tribunal has no duty to act judicially it is purely an administrative body over whose decisions the court can exercise no control by writ. But the court is not devoid of power, for it can, it has been held, issue a direction setting aside an administrative order if it is made in defiance of a mandatory provision of law[1] or in circumstances which run counter to elementary principles of justice. A licensing authority appointed under a Cloth Control Order had refused to renew a dealer's licence to sell cloth, on the ground that his past conduct had not been above suspicion. The dealer had had no opportunity of being heard before the order was made. The court held that the refusal to renew the licence was an administrative act, but that as the effect of the order was to put the dealer out of business he ought to have had the chance of meeting the allegations against him; and it set aside the order. The court distinguished *Narkuda Ali's* case[2] on the ground that as in India the dealer had a fundamental right under the Constitution to carry on his business the renewal of his permit was more than a mere privilege.[3]

The question whether a tribunal has the duty to act judicially depends on the intention of the legislature to be ascertained from the terms of the act by which the tribunal is constituted;[4] and the tendency

[1] *Ram Charan Lal* v *State of Uttar Pradesh,* A.I.R. 1952 All. 752.
[2] *Narkuda Ali* v *M. F. de S. Jayaratne* [1951] A.C. 66.
[3] *Rameshwar Prasad Kedarnath* v *District Magistrate,* A.I.R. 1954 All. 144.
[4] *Province of Bombay* v *K. S. Advani* [1950] S.C.R. 621.

of the High Courts in India is to lean towards a construction which will enable them to exercise powers of supervision. The number of quasi-judicial tribunals in India is large and increasing, and the matters upon which they are called upon to adjudicate cover a constantly growing field. Some are appointed only for a limited purpose like the Income Tax Commission; others are of a more permanent nature, and their decisions may directly affect the occupations and lives of ordinary citizens. Of these probably the most important is the Board of Revenue. The Board decides questions concerning agricultural tenancy rights and has necessarily to construe the provisions of an intricate tenancy law. Other examples are the authorities vested under the Motor Vehicles Act and the various Rent Acts with the power to grant permits to ply motor vehicles for commercial purposes and to make orders allocating vacant accommodation.

The courts have held that the authority who decides to whom a permit should be given, and that some (but not all) of the authorities constituted under the Rent Acts, are bound to exercise their powers judicially; and as a consequence the courts are able to exercise some measure of control over what they do. The situation in the Uttar Pradesh (United Provinces) provides a good illustration of the practical usefulness of the constitutional remedies embodied in Article 226. The relevant Rent Control Act consists of less than twenty sections not always expressed in very precise language; and the High Court has been able not only to ensure that the Act is properly administered but to explain and clarify what the principles laid down in the Act are.

The courts in India are as reluctant as those in this country to interfere in matters which are usually regarded as the domestic concern of the Universities or educational authorities; but the circumstances in India are such that the courts have felt compelled, in the exercise of their powers under Article 226, to intervene far more frequently than here. The Governor of the Uttar Pradesh in his capacity as Chancellor of Allahabad University, and in the exercise of appellate powers vested in him under the University Act, had made an order that a certain professor had ceased to be a member of the Executive Council. The High Court held that in the exercise of these powers the Chancellor was bound to act judicially, and as his order was erroneous in point of law it was set aside.[1]

The Universities of Gauhati and Calcutta have been ordered by

[1] *Dr Ishwari Prasad* v *The Registrar, University of Allahabad;* 1955 A.L.J. 244; affirmed on appeal.

writ of *mandamus* to declare as having passed their final examinations students whom they, in contravention of their rules, had declared not to have passed;[1] and where the Syndicate of a University, acting beyond its powers, had cancelled the examination of a candidate, it was ordered by *mandamus* to reconsider the matter in accordance with its rules.[2]

Nowhere do examinations play a more important part than in India, and it is perhaps not surprising that some candidates who doubt their ability to satisfy their examiners in the ordinary way resort to more informal means. On such malpractices coming to light, the usual course is for the authority conducting the examination to hold an enquiry and, if the cheating is established, to cancel the examination result and, in some cases, to debar the candidate from sitting again for that examination for one or more years. This is a serious matter for the candidate, and every year a number of petitions are filed in which a candidate seeks to challenge the validity of the order made against him on the ground that the enquiry was held in violation of the rules of natural justice. The Supreme Court has held (thereby going further than the Privy Council was prepared to do in the recent case of *University of Ceylon* v *Fernando*)[3] that it is a requirement of natural justice that the candidate whose conduct is in question must be given an opportunity of being heard before a decision is arrived at.[4]

The utility of the writ jurisdiction is especially noticeable in connection with elections and local government administration. The democratic process of election has a firm hold in India and there are numerous bodies ranging from the Lok Sabha, the equivalent of our House of Commons, to the village panchayat, the members of which are elected by universal suffrage. Disputes, which are not uncommon, with regard to the conduct of an election are ordinarily decided by a tribunal, usually the district judge or the local executive officer; it is only recently that in the case of a dispute arising out of a parliamentary election there is an appeal to the High Court. It is obviously desirable that, if the election tribunal misdirects itself with regard to the law applicable, there should be a speedy remedy: and that is, in fact, provided by the writ jurisdiction.

Elections are not however the only matters about which disputes

[1] *Tapendra Nath Roy* v *University of Calcutta*, 58 C.W.N. 295.
[2] *Maya* v *Principal, Basirhat College*, A.I.R. 1957 Cal. 428.
[3] [1960] 1 All E.R. 631.
[4] *Board of High School and Intermediate Education* v *Gyanshyamdas Gupta*: Civil Appeal No. 132 of 1959 decided on February 6, 1962.

may arise. The Government in most States has a statutory power to remove the chairman or a member of a municipal body if he is guilty of certain malpractices or if, in its opinion, he has so abused his position as to render his continuance as a member detrimental to the public interest. The Government usually has also the power to dissolve or supersede a municipal body if in its opinion the latter has failed in the performance of its duties or has abused its authority.[1] The exercise of these powers is likely to give rise to feelings of resentment, and it is here again that the writ jurisdiction provides a convenient means of challenging and, if necessary, of having set aside an order of the State Government when that order shows that it was made otherwise than in accordance with law.

(c) ENFORCEMENT OF ART. 311 (2) OF THE CONSTITUTION

I have sought to give you some idea of the varied uses which are made of the writ jurisdiction, but the picture will not be complete if I omit a brief reference to yet one more. Every civil servant in India holds his post at the pleasure of the President or of the State governor as the case may be. A clause in the Constitution, Art. 311 (2), provides however that no civil servant 'shall be dismissed, removed or reduced in rank until he has been given a reasonable opportunity of showing cause against the action proposed to be taken in regard to him'.

Now the number of civil servants in India is large, and as the administration expands and the number of concerns run by the state increases, so does the number of civil servants. In addition to the many grades of persons employed in Government offices, the railways are owned by the State and all railway employees hold civil posts under the Central Government; while the employees of the numerous State owned road transport services hold similar posts under the State Governments. The constitutional protection afforded by Art. 311 (2) against arbitrary dismissal or removal or reduction in rank extends therefore to a large number of persons. Many, of course, are in receipt only of a small salary. If a civil servant considers that his services have been terminated, or that he has been reduced in rank, contrary to the provisions of Art. 311 he has a remedy by way of suit for a declaration that the order against which he complains is invalid; but for reasons to which I shall refer shortly this remedy is both expensive and slow, and it is not therefore surprising that recourse should be had to the writ jurisdiction. A large number of petitions are filed alleging a

[1] See, for example, the U.P. Municipalities Act, 1916, ss. 30 and 40.

contravention of Article 311 (2) and, provided the facts are not in dispute, the courts, on the whole, are not likely to refuse to consider the petitioner's complaints on the ground that an alternative remedy exists. The usual order made by the court when it is satisfied that the Article has been infringed is to direct the issue of a writ of *certiorari* quashing the offending order. It should however be observed that the relief so granted by the court does not extend beyond the quashing of the order; the court will not direct that the petitioner be reinstated in the post he formerly held, nor will it direct the payment of any arrears of salary.

POPULARITY OF THE JURISDICTION

In the circumstances it is not surprising that the writ jurisdiction in India immediately found favour. The extent however to which recourse is had to it is, at first sight, astonishing. I have already referred to the number of applications made in one State alone. The number of such applications for the whole of India is not easily obtainable but there can be no doubt that it is very large.[1] For this there are three reasons.

In the first place the writ jurisdiction affords an expeditious remedy. The general rule is well established that a court will not issue a writ, (or an order or direction) if there exists some other remedy which is equally convenient, beneficial and effectual; which means, in England, that an order will ordinarily not issue if there is a remedy by way of a civil action or appeal. In India, and certainly in the State from which I come, local conditions have to be taken into account; and it is unfortunately the case that in many instances the alternative remedy by way of suit is neither equally convenient nor equally effective. This is so because of the volume of ordinary litigation and the multiplicity of appeals. Most civil courts have more business to deal with than they can manage. If the amount at stake is not large—as in the majority of cases—the suit is tried by a munsif or subordinate judge from whose decision an appeal lies to a district judge. From the latter's decision an appeal lies, on a question of law, to a Judge of the High Court from whose judgment, by leave, an appeal lies to a Bench. In the result a great deal of time, measured often in years, may elapse before a final decision is reached. This delay may be calamitous where the matter in dispute is, for example, the legality of an order dismissing

[1] The Indian Law Commission stated, on the basis of figures not entirely complete, the number in 1956 to be over 14,000.

a low-paid railway employee from his job, or refusing a tradesman a licence to purchase a controlled commodity or debarring a student from sitting for an examination. A petition under Art. 226—if the court will entertain it—is heard far more expeditiously; the delay is a matter of weeks or months rather than of years.

The second reason why recourse to the writ jurisdiction is favoured is its comparative cheapness. It is not, I think, very generally realized that in India a court fee is charged on a statement of claim or plaint, usually on an *ad valorem* basis. The amount of the court fee varies from State to State; in all of them it is substantial. In some cases a fixed fee is payable. But whether the fee is fixed or is on an *ad valorem* basis it has to be paid by a plaintiff on the institution of his suit and, be it noted, by the appellant on the filing of an appeal. The amount of the court fees, added to the ordinary costs of litigation, may itself deter a possible suitor from instituting legal proceedings in the ordinary civil courts. The court fee payable on an application for relief under Art. 226 is fixed: it varies considerably from State to State, but generally speaking it is not high.

There is also, I think, a third reason. It is the desire of the ordinary citizen who goes to law to have his case decided by the High Court, and if he can approach that court directly without going through the costly and tedious process of reaching it by way of the lower courts he will take that course.

Experience over the last ten years has shown that the writ jurisdiction is of great value. It provides a speedy means of safeguarding fundamental rights and a relatively inexpensive and effective means of enforcing the constitutional guarantees embodied in Art. 311. It ensures that the courts can exercise an effective supervision over quasi-judicial tribunals and so maintain the rule of law. All in all the development of the writ jurisdiction constitutes, I submit, one of the most important advances in the administration of justice in India since the attainment of independence.

RESTRICTIONS AND LIMITATIONS

The jurisdiction is however subject to certain restrictions and limitations, and the question remains whether they can be removed or reduced.

The first limitation is territorial. I have pointed out that the writ jurisdiction of the Supreme Court extends to the whole of India, but that of a High Court does not reach beyond the boundaries of the

State of which it is the High Court. This limitation has serious practical consequences, for it means that a writ, order or direction addressed to the Central Government, or to a department or officer in Delhi of that Government, can be issued only by one High Court, namely the High Court which includes Delhi within its territorial jurisdiction; and that is the Punjab High Court. A person who lives outside the Punjab—possibly more than a thousand miles away— may well be deterred on the ground of expense from making an application under Art. 226 in that court.

The other limitations, which relate to the writ of *certiorari*, arise out of the nature of the jurisdiction itself. Where relief is sought on the ground that the decision of an inferior tribunal is erroneous the error must be one of law, and it must appear on the record. Further, the court's power of intervention is limited in such cases to quashing the impugned decision; it cannot substitute for that decision the order which it considers the tribunal ought to have made.

Can these limitations be removed or their effects mitigated? Not very much can be done except with regard to the first. Art. 226 could, it is suggested, be altered to enable a High Court to issue a writ, direction or order to any government or governmental official, or to any quasi-judicial tribunal, whether within or without the State. A court does not however issue a writ unless it has the means of enforcing compliance with its order. It would therefore be necessary also to extend to the whole of India the jurisdiction of a High Court to punish for contempt. The other limitations are, broadly speaking, inherent in the nature of the writ jurisdiction, and without altering radically the character of that jurisdiction little can be done. It is impossible to see how the court could examine questions of fact, or how it could substitute its own decision for that of the tribunal, without becoming, in substance, a court of appeal. The requirement that the error of law on which the court is asked to pronounce must appear on the record is not one that is likely to be the cause of much difficulty in India, for the 'record' of the inferior tribunal is ordinarily a complete record containing everything relevant—and possibly a good deal which is irrelevant—to the matter in dispute. So also with the form of the order: it is, I believe, almost the invariable practice in India for a tribunal to state the reasons for its decisions. If difficulty in fact exists the solution would appear to be a simple one: a statutory provision that the tribunal must state in writing the reasons for its decisions.

On the whole, therefore, it seems that not very much can be done to enhance the effectiveness of the writ jurisdiction. The question however does arise whether a new procedure which is without the existing disadvantage might not be substituted for disposing of the matters which are now the subject of proceedings for a writ of *certiorari*. A suggestion was made by Singleton L. J. in the *Northumberland* case that a party aggrieved by the decision of a tribunal on a question of law should have the right to appeal to the High Court, and that suggestion is one which, I suggest, deserves consideration. The number of persons and bodies in India vested with quasi-judicial powers is already large and is likely to grow larger. The matters with which such authorities have to deal affect governments, local authorities and citizens: and for the effective functioning of the administration at its various levels and the upholding of the rights of individuals it is often essential that the authoritative determination of questions of law should be obtained with the minimum of delay. The courts must be the final arbiters on questions of law; in one way or another the decision of the courts has to be ascertained. A right of appeal, limited to a question of law, would seem to be the means of achieving directly what is now secured by a less convenient process. It would—or could —solve the territorial difficulty; technical disputes as to the meaning of 'on the face of the record' or as to the necessity of a speaking order would lose their importance and, above all, the appellate court, when it disagrees with the order of the subordinate tribunal, could in appropriate cases itself make the order which ought to have been made in the first place.

I ought perhaps to conclude by pointing out that the writ jurisdiction has not escaped criticism, and suggestions have been made that it should be curtailed or even abolished. The criticism does not come from the public but from governments and government officials. Departments do not always like their actions to be subjected to too close a scrutiny, and the knowledge that the orders they make can be brought before the courts has made them wary. This, quite understandably, is irksome in a country which until so recently has had a tradition of autocracy. The more serious complaint is that the writ jurisdiction provides too easy a means of challenging the validity of legislation of a progressive nature and is therefore a hindrance in the way of India becoming a welfare state. It is true that legislation is challenged by this means, and that this does at times cause what must be an irritating delay; but social reformers are apt to be impatient and 'to ride rough shod over individuals' rights as matters of little consequence'. The real obstacle however is not really the writ jurisdiction but the existence of fundamental rights. So long as they exist the validity of legislation will be open to challenge, and it is surely better that it be determined by the speedy means of the writ jurisdiction than by the lengthy process of a civil action. The writ jurisdiction has proved its worth; and I do not think that its future is in danger.

7

JUSTICE, EQUITY AND GOOD CONSCIENCE

DR J. DUNCAN M. DERRETT

Reader in Oriental Laws in the University of London

The formula which provides the title of this essay deserves investigation particularly because its meaning is obscure and its function is open to debate. In India, Pakistan and Burma (with the exception of the Original Sides of the former Presidency High Courts of Bombay, Calcutta, and Madras and corresponding jurisdictions of High Courts which have evolved, as it were, from them) the court must decide the case in the absence of a rule from statute, the written sources of the personal laws, custom, or case-law, according to 'justice, equity and good conscience'.[1] This provision can, and occasionally does, produce contradictory results.[2] For example, a claim by, or through, an illegitimate child, in circumstances where the relevant system of law is silent, could be upheld on the ground that natural justice favours claims by natural relations, as opposed, for example, to the claim of the State by escheat[3]; or it could equally be rejected on the ground that to encourage heritable claims that deny the need for legitimacy and valid marriages between parents would be against public policy.[4] In Africa numerous Ordinances provide that a native custom shall be applied provided that it is not repugnant to natural justice, equity and good conscience. It may well be debated whether a particular custom is to be applied, and what criteria must be satisfied if this test is to work. Similarly it is provided that in the absence of distinct provision in the customary law the court must apply 'justice, equity and good conscience'. The Northern Nigeria Sharī'a Court of Appeal Law, 1960 (M. 16 of 1960), s. 15, directs the court to apply 'natural justice, equity and good

[1] Government of India Act, 1915, s. 112. F. B. Tyabji, *Muhammadan Law*, 3rd edn., Bombay, 1940, 28-9.
[2] Bijay K. Acharyya, *Codification in British India*, Calcutta, 1914, 319-20.
[3] *Jagarnath Gir* v *Sher* (1934) 57 All. 85, 100-1.
[4] *Meenakshi* v *Muniandi* A.I.R. 1915 Mad. 63, 67 col. i.

conscience' as a residual category of law. It is therefore a residual source of law, but apparently enacted in embarrassingly vague terms. There is even an instance where, when the method of ascertainment of a personal law is to be determined, the court is directed in case of doubt to ascertain it, or to determine, according to justice, equity and good conscience.[1] Here it serves a more limited purpose, but not necessarily without important effects. In particular both South Asia and Africa are put in a dilemma whether or not to import English or other foreign laws under the cover of this formula. In some quarters there is doubt whether a provision apparently authorizing reference to foreign laws will have the same meaning when judges of foreign nationality eventually leave. And if justice, equity and good conscience may mean something very different after a number of years, why should it bear its present meaning now? In short is there any, and if any what, authority for supposing that a foreign system of law, or foreign systems of law generally, is or are incorporated into the legal system of a country which possesses this obligation (or facility) of reference to that source.

It may be argued at the outset that 'justice, equity and good conscience' is a nice, comfortable formula meaning as much or as little as the judges for the time being care to make it mean. One might confine one's activity to considering how judges have in fact construed the direction to consult it. The results would not be of permanent value, since just as the concept of public policy varies with the years and the venue, so precedents may be of little help where this phrase is called into play. Let us agree at once that study of the judicial applications of the 'residual' or 'repugnancy' references has limitations. Very few cases show a real curiosity as to what the phrase means, many expressions fall *per incuriam*, and consequently are of no authority. But a survey of some representative applications of the formula, and a review of its extraordinary history, may help to place the matter in perspective, showing that it still has a lively part to play in the development of the legal systems of developing countries.

This essay will deal first with the concept as present in the minds of jurists of England in the sixteenth century. For this purpose it will be necessary to enter upon a preface explaining it against the background of Romano-canonical juridical thought of the time. We shall then pass to the problem of sources of law for the administration of justice in Bombay Island, the movement to apply Roman Law there,

[1] Laws of Kenya 1948, p. 1927, cap. 149, s. 11.

and authoritative recognition of the applicability of 'justice, equity and good conscience' in the Island (and shortly afterwards in Madras). The next link in the chain is the re-birth of the principle from the confused antipathies of English legal methods personified in the procedure of the Supreme Court of Calcutta, on the one hand, and the oriental happy-go-lucky judicial administration personified by the courts of the East India Company in Bengal, Bihar and Orissa, on the other. The further story of our formula in South Asia naturally follows. The adoption of the formula in Africa, and its subsequent history in West Africa, in the Sudan, and (to a minute extent) in East Africa forms the last chapter of the story. The part which the Civil Law has played in bringing the formula to India, and the roles it played in the laws of India and Pakistan, deserve treatment at length, and they are sketched somewhat lightly in this article.

THE ROMANO-CANONICAL ORIGINS OF THE FORMULA

It will be news to Indians, Pakistanis, and Africans that 'justice, equity and good conscience' has, in origin and tradition, little to do with English law, still less the Common Law of England. Yet if this had been explained to judges in India between about 1790 and 1870, the great formative period of all branches of Indian law except its modern constitution, it would have received ready acceptance. About 1870–80 the doctrine developed that it was a provision which not only let in English law, and in particular Common Law, but was intended to have that effect. It will be shown in this essay that the views of, for example, Sir James FitzJames Stephen and Sir Frederick Pollock, the most vocal representatives of contemporary juridical reflection,[1] took far too narrow a view of its history and function—a defect particularly regretable in the latter, for he was ranked as a legal historian as well as a jurist. Sir George Rankin was much nearer the truth when he pointed out, as recently as 1941,[2] the fact that 'justice, equity and good conscience' did *not* point to English law, and hinted that the

[1] G. C. Rankin, *Background to Indian Law* (Cambridge, 1946), 119. F. Pollock, *Law of Fraud . . . in British India*, Calcutta 1894, 6-8, 10. The same, *Essays in the Law* (London, 1922), 61. U. C. Sarkar, *Epochs in Hindu Legal History* (Hoshiarpur, 1958), 376-8. A. S. Nataraja Ayyar, *Mīmāṃsā Jurisprudence* (Allahabad, 1952). *Morley's Digest.* W. Stokes, *Anglo-Indian Codes*, I, xvi, xxi, 55. See now Derrett at (1962) 64 Bom. L.R. (J.), 129 ff, 145 ff.

[2] 'The personal law in British India', J.R.S.A., 89, May 1941, 427-441, at 433.

behaviour of judges in India ought not to be explained by facile and unhistorical generalizations. But he was himself quite ignorant of the origin of the phrase, and the function which it was then intended, and fitted, to perform.

It would be a mistake to suggest that the law of Rome supplied the concept. It is not found as a ready-made formula anywhere in Roman, or for that matter Romano-canonical, texts. It arose out of Romano-canonical learning common to the whole continent of Europe as it appeared to English minds of the sixteenth century. All the materials lay ready to hand, and all the parts of the formula still lie scattered profusely in the literature which was the common reading for constitutional lawyers of that period.

It must be recollected that in discussing the nature of justice and the judicial process, the 'office of the judge', and the sources of law to which the judge must apply himself, the contemporary jurists did not rely exclusively upon Roman materials. These served as a useful quarry, and were repeatedly referred to, but the scheme into which they were fitted was one which had been evolved out of the practice of mediaeval Italian cities and states, and the experience of France and Germany, and the great fund of humanistic learning that had been drawn upon with increasing vigour and effect by the jurists of the 'Alciatist' as opposed to the (old-fashioned) 'Bartolist' school. A discussion of the full meaning of the first title of the Digest, *De Iustitia et Iure*, would then start with references to Aristotle,[1] sometimes to his original Greek text, but more often to the translations which were then commonly read all over Europe.[2] We are thus not concerned with what Justinian meant, or what Aristotle himself meant, but with what such sources were believed to imply in practice by the leading authorities of the legal world about 1500. Specialist studies of the concept of *aequum et bonum* or of *ius naturale* as known to Cicero or Ulpian or Tribonian cannot help us.[3] We are concerned with what was said by Giasone da Maino, *alias* Jason, by Budaeus, Tiraquellus, Connanus, Boerius; the views of Grotius, Heineccius, Hunnius and other later writers, not excluding Domat (of whom we shall hear later), are only of value in so far as they evidence

---

[1] *Rhet.* I, 13; *Ethic.* V, 10.

[2] Joachim Perionius (*Aristotelis Stagiritae Tripartitae Philosophiae Opera Omnia*, Basileae, 1563, I, col. 467B; II, col. 89A, 102 A-B).

[3] Moritz Voigt, *Die Lehre vom Jus Naturale, aequum et bonum und ius gentium der Römer*, 4 vols. Leipzig, 1856-76. F. Pringsheim, 'Bonum et aequum', *Z.S.R.*, 52, Rom. Abt., 1932, 78-155.

the continuation into their times of views expressed by their predecessors.

It emerges from the studies of these authors that all law is founded upon the law of nature. Upon that rests the divine law, which is binding upon all Christians. Non-Christian countries and peoples may have the law of nature administered to them so far as it is not abrogated by other sources of law. The natural and divine laws are not relevant, nor need we refer to them, where custom or positive law or the terms of a valid grant or contract provide the rule of decision. Naturally, no such source can be incompatible with natural or divine law—if it were, it would be void. When we come to these applicable sources there are varying, though equally valid, methods of categorizing and cross-classifying them. We are at once in a difficulty in that our vocabulary is not adequate and a few words have to do duty in several different senses. We are by no means bound by the vocabulary of the Romans; but they had like difficulties, and quite distinct sources of law are found both in the writings of classical authors and in the Corpus Iuris passing under a shared name. It is necessary to explain, from time to time, what is meant by a common term, such as *aequitas*, and what connotation is intended in the context.

Aristotle took great pains to explain that τὸ δίκαιον, which is habitually translated *iustitia*, 'justice', needs and presupposes (if it does not comprehend) τὸ ἐπιεικές, which is translated *aequitas*.[1] The function of τὸ ἐπιεικές is to adjust the written statute (of which the Greeks had plenty) to the particular circumstances of the case, and to point out the truly just solution to a problem, for which formal general rules are offered. It may not be just, in short, to apply statute or custom, or maxim or principle, without taking into account factors which place the affair in a special light—factors, such as 'public policy', which make it inexpedient, and so improper, to follow out logically what an over-particular, and necessarily generally expressed, law seems to imply. This fitted admirably into the Romanic propositions that *aequitas* had two functions, (i) to correct, modify, and if necessary amend statute law—in fact to serve as a comrade and interpreter for an otherwise inefficient and unintelligible element

[1] J. Oldendorpius, *Tractatus locorum communium actionum iuris civilis ad usum forensem secundum aequissimas legislatorum sententias* . . . (*Volumen V Tractatuum ex Variis Iuris Interpretibus Collectorum*, Lugduni, 1549) fo. 101 v, nos. 18, 20. Budaeus (cited below) translates τὸ ἐπιεικές *aequum et bonum* (p. 2), ἐπιείκεια *aequitas*.

of law;[1] and (ii) to supplement, make good, and otherwise remove the deficiencies of the written, or otherwise ascertainable, source of law.[2] When we get down to practical details the picture emerges somewhat as follows.

Since *ius est ars boni et aequi*[3] it follows that *all* persons exercising judicial responsibility, whether originally or as delegates, must act so as to produce a result which is both *bonum* and *aequum*.[4] That is to say, an Ordinary, a judge delegate, a court of merchants, an arbiter, or an arbitrator, must give a decision which possesses *benignitas* and *aequitas*. It is only in marginal situations, where all other valid sources of law fail, that *naturalis aequitas*, 'natural equity', the ultimate source, is called upon. But, as we shall see, even in that context the judge must apply his mind to *law* and not to non-legal considerations or rules of his own invention.[5] Contrasted with the office of the judge is the so-called *arbitrium rusticorum*,[6] which seems to have been the Romanic counterpart of 'palm-tree justice', whereby the 'arbitrator' divides the disputed property equally between the two parties: here no juridical activity can be seen—he splits it between them, like the Monkey in Aesop's fable, as the simplest way of quieting the noisier party. It is not even 'rough justice', or 'substantial justice', for no judicial discretion whatever has been used, and where there is no judicial

[1] H. Grotius, *De Aequitate, Indulgentia et Facilitate*, at end of *De Iure Belli et Pacis* (Amstelaedami, 1735) ch. 1; G. Durandus, *Speculum Iudiciale* (Basle, 1563), p. 140; J. Cuiacius, *Recitationes. . . De Iustitia* in I.C., *Operum, Tomus Secundus*, Lugduni, 1606), 135 B-C. R. Zouch, *Quaestionum Juris Civilis Centuria*, 3rd edn. (Oxford, 1682), 5-8.

[2] F. Connanus, *Commentariorum Iuris Civilis* I (Paris, 1553), fos. 44a-45b; Cuiacius, *op. cit.*, coll. 129A, 135C. J. Story, *Commentaries on Equity Jurisprudence* (Boston, 1836) I, 5; 1st Eng. edn. Grigsby (London, 1884), 4.

[3] Celsus, reported by Ulpian, Dig. I, 1, 1, pr.

[4] *Aequum et bonum est lex legum:* T. Hobbes and the author of *Principia Legis* (1753). Oldendorpius, *ubi cit.*, no. 30: *qui rationem atque exercitationem boni et aequi ignorat, is sane . . . maximam iuris partem ignorat.* Connanus, *ubi cit.*, fo. 48a; H. U. Hunnius, *Encycl. Iurius Universi* (Cologne, 1675), p. 3; H. Treutler, *Selectarum Disputationum ad Ius Civile*, ed. Hunnius (Frankfurt, 1624), I, 18, 19f. G. Budaei, Parisiensis, *Annotationes in Libros Pandectarum* (Paris, 1542), pp. 1-5; Cuiacius, *Recitationes . . . De Iustitia* (1606 edn.), col. 94D, 129D.

[4] Bartolus, *Sec. Bart. super Dig. Vet.* (1547) (ff. mandati vel contra, § quaedam), fo. 114 f; Jason, *de Actionibus* (Lugduni, 1540), fo. 24 v, no. 138; Cuiacius (*ubi cit.*, 93C); Oldendorpius, *op. cit.*, fo. 102 r, no. 29. Story (1836 edn., p. 15, 1884 edn., pp. 9-10) cites *Cowper v Cowper (Earl)* (1734) 2 P. Will. 720, 753.

[6] *Prima Bartoli super Digesto Veteri* (Lugduni, 1547) fo. 135 v; *Prima Baldi super Dig. Vet.* (Lugduni, 1547), fo. 195 r.

discretion there is no *ius*, no *iustitia*. In the *arbitrium rusticorum* there is no harm in the 'arbitrator' walking about and waving his arms: a judge, by contrast, must give judgment sitting. Not that mistakes cannot be made sitting, or that if he sits he is exempt from supervision and perhaps punishment: but the first requirement of any judgment is that it shall be delivered with attention to essential and indispensable forms, and this is one of them.

Positive law, which equity modifies or supplements, is made up of *ius scriptum*, the written law, i.e. statutes, constitutions, rescripts, *responsa*, and *ius non scriptum*, the unwritten law which is found out by reference to witnesses or other appropriate sources that tell us what has been taken for law in practice so long as the memory of the people, or class, has run.[1] Custom, *consuetudo*, is the best example of this category, and it is to be applied where there is no repugnancy to natural or divine law, or to the *ius scriptum*. If we see *iustitia* as the correlative of *aequitas*, then *iustitia* consists of positive law, made up of written and unwritten sources, statutes and custom, the applicability of these being determined either by positive law itself, or by the natural equity, that is to say, the natural reason of the case. But in another sense *aequitas* comes *into* this picture of *iustitia*. There can be no *ius* in practice without its twin, the *aequitas* in sense (i) which modifies or amends it to suit circumstances.[2] *Ius strictum*, or *summum ius*, the 'letter of the law', can very seldom, if ever, move without the aid of *aequitas*, 'equity'. Thus, in sense (i) *aequitas* is bound up with *iustitia*, and yet seems to be by definition an addition to it *ab extra*. In the second sense of the term, *aequitas* fills the gaps left by the positive law. It supplements the *ius scriptum sive non scriptum* for cases not covered by statute, for example, or contemplated by custom in so many words. In sense (ii) *aequitas* is a most important source of law, particularly for developing countries. *Aequitas* in this sense is both *scripta* and *non scripta*. A good example of the latter is the rule prohibiting unjust enrichment.[3] Where *ius scriptum* and *aequitas scripta* happen to conflict the latter prevails; where *ius non scriptum* and *aequitas scripta* conflict the latter may prevail; against *ius scriptum* or

[1] Hunnius, *op. cit.*, pp. 27-30.
[2] Bartolus, *Prim. Bartoli super Codicem* (*Bartoli Commentaria in Primam Codicis Partem*, Lugduni, 1547), fo. 33 v, no. 4; Iacobi Cuiacii, *op. cit.*, col. 91B, 1832E.
[3] Baldus on Cod. III, 1, 8; Angelus de Perusio *ad loc.* (*In Codicem Comm.*, Venetiis, 1579, fo. 40 v); Jason de Mayno, *In Primam Codicis Partem Comm.*, Venetiis, 1568, fos. 121 v—122 v. Baldus, *in Sec. Dig. Vet. Partem Comm.* (Venetiis, 1577) fo. 22 v—23 r.

aequitas scripta, aequitas non scripta cannot prevail. The prince alone, or his deputy, can solve difficulties raised where the second-mentioned conflict arises.[1] 'Written' equity lies in the praetorian law embodied and amalgamated with the Civil Law in the Corpus Iuris of Justinian; it is also created by the joint efforts of judges, councils, and jurists in the development of the Romano-canonical system through the ages. 'Unwritten' equity is a complex source, always on the point of turning into 'written' equity.[2] The judge knows that the case is not provided for in the books, he views the law that has a bearing upon the topic and would supply the answer were this not a *casus omissus*, and investigates the 'equitable' rights of the parties.[3] Bartolus, in a short but penetrating analysis of this predicament, shows that the party with a 'natural equity' is at a disadvantage against the party with an equity founded on the civil law; that a party with a general equity is likely to lose the case against the party with a special equity. On the one hand the judge considers the conduct and relationship of the parties, on the other the capacity of the law having a general bearing on the situation to produce an answer suitable to the case. By analogy, and similar well recognized methods of reasoning, he may draw forth, as it were, by unwritten equity, the rule applicable to the case.[4]

So much for *ius strictum, aequitas* (i), and *aequitas* (ii). Throughout we have assumed that traditional forms of law, and traditional courts, have been pursuing the course laid down for ages. The judge is answerable to an established superior, the sources of law are not in doubt, and all the time the judge has written and/or traditional sources upon which he must rely. But there are two classes of cases where, without departing for a moment from his judicial function, he cannot rely upon those sources because they do not help him. In a case where the established political authority is taken away, or is itself in doubt, and in a case which none of his formal sources contemplate, he must fall back upon his duty, his 'office', to give a decision *ex bono et aequo*.[5] This brings us to *aequitas* in a further sense, sense (iii). The ultimate source of law is, of necessity, the most difficult to explain and predict. Often referred to in the Corpus Iuris, little or no help is given us as to how it would work. Moreover, its importance is enhanced by the fact

---

[1] Bartolus, *ubi cit.*, n. 20 above, no. 5; *Prima Bart. sup. Dig. Nov.* (1547) fo. 97 r; *Sec. Bart. sup. Dig. Vet.* fo. 51 r.

[2] Bartolus, *ubi cit.*, no. 20 above, no. 4; Oldendorpius, *ubi cit.*, fo. 102 r, nos. 27f.

[3] *Sec. Bartoli sup. Dig. Vet.* (1547), fo. 109 r.

[4] Bartolus, *ubi cit.*, no. 20 above, no. 5.

[5] See above, p. 119, n. 4.

that, by the time of our jurists, the formal method of judicial administration had been abandoned in favour of decisions *ex bono et aequo* in at least two well-marked contexts. Even in cases where there was little or no doubt as to the nature and identity of the political superior, and the judge's position in the constitution—even in cases where justice and equity provided ample and notorious rules—the law itself provided, by explicit enactment or by long sufferance and tradition, that *aequitas* (iii) was the *primary* source of decision. In cases of widows[1] and orphans, in disputes regarding dowries and certain problems raised by testaments[2], it was as a matter of fact provided that the technical *exceptiones*, 'formal defences', should not be available. In these and certain other contexts the judge was authorized and required to concern himself with the substantial rights of the parties[3] and to be put off by no defences or procedural steps which obscured the truth.[4] The further possibility, that the judge should accept fictions in order to give a just decision, does not seem to have been contemplated by our jurists. Moreover, amongst merchants transactions regularly proceeded upon the faith that disputes would be resolved by experts traditionally invested with judicial authority to act without regard to procedural regulations operative in other *fora*, and to apply laws of international origin, consonant with natural law, and fundamentally expressive of *aequum et bonum*.[5] Moreover, even where the case was not before a court of merchants the civil judge had the duty of deciding *ex aequo et bono*, if statute and equity (i) were silent, equity (ii) were inapplicable, and the equities of the parties were obscure in view of a *lacuna* in their solemn written agreement.[6]

It is evident that decisions *ex bono et aequo* were of the utmost importance in many branches of judicial activity, certainly in western

[1] *Consilia D. Ludovici de Roma (Pontani)* (Venice, 1493), cons. CCCCXXX.

[2] *Iasonis Mayni . . . in Primam Infortiati Partem Comm.* (Venetiis, 1568) fo. 39 v, no. 201.

[3] *Ludovici Pontani . . . in Primam atque Secundam Dig. Nov. Partem Comm.* (Venetiis, 1580), fo. 48, no. 11; *Andreae Alciati . . . Operum*, Tom. III (Frankfurt, 1617), col. 525.

[4] *Sec. Bart. sup. Dig. Vet.* (1547), fo. 114 r.

[5] *Sec. Bart. sup. Dig. Vet.* (1547), fo. 114 r; fo. 115 r. Baldus (*Baldi Ubald. Perusini . . . in Quartum et Quintum Codicis Lib.*, Venetiis, 1572), fo. 117 r. Jason (*in Primam Infortiati Partem Comm.*, 1580), fo. 39 v, no. 204. F. Pollock, *Essays* (cited above), p. 55f.

[6] Inst. III, 25, 5, cited in the gloss on Decretal. Greg. IX, I, 32, 2: *et ubi deficit lex et contractus, iudex facit quod ex bono et aequo sibi videtur.* G. Durandus, *Speculum* (see n. 1, p. 119 above), p. 133, col. i. (*Argumentum Institutionum Imperialium*, Paris, 1519, fo. 189 v).

countries, and in cases where no actual conflict of laws was in question. What did this jurisdiction amount to? Did it mean that the judge followed his nose, and gave judgment according to his fancy? No, these were cases for Judgments of Solomon. It is emphasized again and again that the judge consults analogous provisions of law; juridical maxims, in particular those contained in the Corpus Iuris, even though they have not in fact been applied to such a case in the written sources of law or equity; and the writings of jurists steeped in legal thinking.[1] Let us take three typical cases.

Merchants must decide *ex bono et aequo*. Is it lawful for goods belonging to merchants of country X to be seized at the application of a merchant of country Y as security for payment of a debt owed by another merchant of country X who is outside the jurisdiction of the *forum* and whose own goods cannot be attached for some reason (e.g. they are not available)? This is, practically, a case of reprisal. If reprisals are consistent with the law of nature they are available and the court of merchants can be authorized by the local monarch to grant reprisals in such cases. But reprisals in fact are condemned by Papal rescript and by a well-known royal constitution; theologians more-over are disposed to doubt whether they are consistent with divine law. Yet, since reprisals are a method of enforcing an equity which the defendant ignored or frustrated, and are a means of securing that justice is done, when all simpler methods have been tried in vain, it is proper to hold that reprisals may validly be granted by a properly authorized mercantile court, or at its application.[2]

Widows are, as we have seen, in some places entitled to have their cases tried *ex aequo et bono*. Technical 'exceptions' are thus excluded. Can the exception of prescription, i.e. that the disputed property has been in the *bona fide* possession of the defendant for, say, thirty years, be admitted?[3] Is it consistent with *aequitas* (iii) that a rule of limitation of actions, which is essentially a rule of procedure applicable in the *forum*, should keep the widow from property which she could prove to be hers by right? The answer seems to be that the rule of prescription, which is part and parcel of the civil law of the Romans, whose laws contain so high a proportion of natural equity, is a rule founded

---

[1] *Prima Pars Consiliorum Acutissimi . . . Pauli de Castro* (1522), Cons. VI, fo. 4 v; Hunnius, *op. cit.*, p. 50.

[2] Jacobus a Canibus, *Tractatus Represaliarum* (*Volumen XVII Tractatuum ex Var. Iuris Interp. Coll.*, Lugduni, 1549), fo. 18, no. 19.

[3] See n. 1, p. 122 above. Bartolus, *Sec. Bart. sup. Dig. Vet.*, f. 114 r, glosses. *Consilia D. Ludovici*, fo. 43 v (cons. CXLIX).

upon considerations of much wider import than the defeating of claims by widows. If the defendant was indeed a *bona fide* possessor it is conclusively presumed that the plaintiff has been negligent or incompetent to the degree stigmatized by the law—*dormientibus lex non subvenit*. This represents a maxim of universal application, and is fitted to a court which procedes *ex bono et aequo*.

Finally, in any court a time may come in which the case presented and proved on *either* side is sound. No amount of *iustitia* or *aequitas* (i) or (ii) can help out the judge in such a predicament. A plaintiff sues for restitution and proves that he is entitled and has constructive possession of the property; the defendant proves title and actual possession grounded upon it. What is the judge to do? There are several possibilities. He could sequestrate, to force a concord. Or he could divide the property between them. This would not be a case of *arbitrium rusticorum*, for since the dispute is about possession, and therefore profits pending decision of the main action, no manifest harm will ensue by a division in this fashion since neither party has proved his title to the whole.[1] Or he could decide by the use of the dice, with which all courts should be supplied! Problems of law may often properly be settled by dice.[2] Perhaps this is not one of them, since the problem is essentially not of law but of fact, and doubts regarding fact are not to be settled by recourse to the judicial dice. Perhaps the judge should postpone a decision indefinitely, or say to the parties *Ite cum Deo*, 'Go with God', i.e. 'Good morning'. He can add if he likes, 'One of you is lying but I do not know which of you it is.'[3] Alternatively he can say *Uti possidetis, ita possideatis*, a puzzling decision[4] which, it has rightly been noticed, amounts to *Ite in nomine diaboli*, 'Clear off, the pair of you, and go to the devil!'[5] On balance both the last suggestions are more negations of the judicial office than exercise of judicial discretion, and since equality is equity the equal division between the parties seems most in accordance with *aequum et bonum*, or the basic rule that unless the plaintiff proves his case the defendant wins.

---

[1] Rebuffius, *Commentaria in Constitutiones* . . . , 1613, p. 742; *Decisiones Burdegalenses Nicol. Boerii . . . Collectae* (Lugduni, 1566) Quaestio XLII (p. 86f at pp. 93-4, no. 39 (1520)); Quaest. CCXXXIX (pp. 446-7 (1531)). Baldus, *ad Lib. XXVIII Dig.* (Venetiis, 1577), fo. 84 r (on Dig. XXVIII, 5, 40).

[2] Boerius, Quaest. CCXXXIX, p. 446, col. ii.

[3] Baldus, *ad Lib. VII Cod.*, fo. 49 r.

[4] Boerius, Quaest. CCXXXIX, p. 446, col. ii. G. Durandus, *Speculum* (Basle, 1563), p. 524, no. 32.

[5] Boerius, *ubi cit.*, pp. 93, 447.

We have seen enough to realise that the structure of the jurisdiction of any judge to administer any law was built up, in the minds of the jurists of the period in which we are interested, in this fashion:

iustitia —ius strictum, summum ius	{ ius scriptum ius non scriptum }
aequitas— { aequitas scripta aequitas non scripta }	{ aequitas moderans (i) aequitas supplens (ii) }
bonum et aequum—aequitas (iii), (conscientia)	

One point remains. What was the nature of *conscientia*, 'conscience'? Here is another of these words doing duty for a group of terms which our vocabulary lacks. In one sense *conscientia* is Aristotle's ἐπιεικές. In another it is the judge's juridical knowledge in general, his 'conscience' as a judge.[1] In yet another it is the judge's realization of the true facts of the case, drawn from personal acquaintance with them independently of the pleadings and evidence. The first sense is an embarrassment to us, and must be disregarded. The last must be brushed aside: the judge's conscience as to facts is nowhere proper to the judicial process.[2] The second is relevant. It is to the 'conscience' of the judge that all litigants, not merely those who litigate *ex bono et aequo*, appeal. Now 'conscience' has no meaning where law is clear. But where the law is unclear, or non-existent, or its applicability is challenged, appeals to the judge's conscience are likely, and indeed inevitable.[3] Judged from the judge's seat one party will then have acted consistently with conscience, the other will not. The judge's conscience will decree or reject the suit accordingly. What is done *ex aequo et bono* in an appropriate case (where there is jurisdiction *ex bono et aequo*) is bound to be consistent with the judge's conscience and with the 'good conscience' of the parties. Thus the English translation of *bonum et aequum* was 'conscience', and of *ex bono et aequo* 'according to good conscience'.[4] A Court of Conscience is therefore one which acts *ex bono et aequo*,[5] and it will be evident at once that although

---

[1] *Clarissimi Iuris Utriusque ... Baldi Commentaria super Decretalibus* (Lugduni, 1521), fo. 56 r. *Summae Sylvestrinae* (Antwerp, 1581), II, 70 f.

[2] *Secunda Pars Consiliorum ... Pauli de Castro* (1522), Cons. CCXCIX, no. 4.

[3] Jason *de Actionibus* (1540), fos. 23 v—24 v, no. 138; *Iasonis Mayni in Primam Infortiati Partem Comm.* (1568), fo. 51 v.

[4] Beaver's trans. of Duck, at pp. xxviii, xxix. *iudicandi ex aequo et bono demandata est* = 'judging and determining according to Equity and Good Conscience'.

[5] Sir Thomas Smith, *De Republica Anglorum*, II, 12; trans. J. de Laet (Lug. Bat., 1641), 198-9.

fifteenth-century petitioners of the Chancellor used to affirm that their adversaries had acted *encountre ley et reson et bone conscience*,[1] 'against law and right and good conscience', or words to that effect,[2] the Chancellors gave justice *ex aequo et bono* like all other judges, that is to say where positive law and written law failed, and not otherwise. Thus to call a Chancery court a Court of Conscience is only approximately correct, and may lead to misunderstandings.

Our jurists notice that in matrimonial causes *aequitas* is most particularly to be observed. It is evident in this and in other fields of canon law that the office of the judge is exercised according to equity, and that *ex bono et aequo* he may vary the sentence or determine the issue largely and at his discretion in the interests of peace, the benefit of religion and the church, and the welfare of the parties.[3] Yet even when equitable decisions, based upon the *plenitudo potestatis* of the Pope, most notoriously varied with the importance of the parties and the subject-matter of the dispute, no one suggested that in applying 'public policy'[4] and similar criteria the judge departed from a truly judicial path, or that he gave a judgment in anything but a professional manner upon the basis of legal arguments. The great role played by the Roman civil law in the administration and development of canon law proves that the authorities looked to law, and not to expediency, as the ultimate criterion.

The role of *ex bono et aequo* jurisdiction in modern canon law[5] and international law,[6] as also in modern continental (and Turkish) judicial administration,[7] is beyond the scope of our present study.

JUSTICE, EQUITY AND GOOD CONSCIENCE IN ENGLAND

The common law in its earlier centuries no doubt knew the fundamental bases of judicial decision-making, within which this customary

---

[1] W. P. Baildon, *Select Cases in Chancery* (London, 1896), p. 119, case 121 (1420/2). C. K. Allen, *Law in the Making*, 6th edn. (Oxford, 1958), 390.

[2] W. T. Barbour, *Oxford Studies in Social and Legal History*, ed. Vinogradoff, iv (Oxford, 1914), 182, 212.

[3] Joan. Staphil. Arch. Tragurini, *Super Gratiis* . . . (*Volumen XIIII Tractatuum*, Lugduni, 1549), fo. 29 r, no. 9.

[4] Jason, *de Actionibus* (1540), fo. 24 v; Claudius Cantiuncula, *De Officio Judicis* (1543) (in *Vol. II Tractatuum*, as above), fo. 293 r, no. 6.

[5] C.J.C., c. 144; c. 1500; c. 1929.

[6] L. Oppenheim, *International Law*, ed. H. Lauterpacht (London, etc., 1952) II, p. 68-9. K. Strupp, *Ac. Dr. Int., Receuil des Cours, 1930* (III), (Paris, 1931), pp. 357f, 376, 399.

[7] Z.G.B. §4; B. K. Acharyya, *Codification* (cited above), 35f.

system, this *ius commune*, fitted. But the scope of common law judges was naturally confined to issues that could be solved, grievances that could be remedied, according to that *ius commune* or the statutes, the *ius strictum* (modified, interpreted, and applied according to judicial equity) which supplemented or abrogated the *ius commune*. We have seen that the equitable jurisdiction of the Chancellor completed the picture of *iustitia* and *aequitas*, particularly *aequitas* in sense (ii). Courts of Conscience and Requests came into existence to supplement and rival courts of merchants, and other courts of a civil law origin, such as the Court of the Admiral, which were not bound by common law remedies or common law procedure.

The formal recognition that all law must be based either upon strict law, equity, or good conscience is evidenced during the activity which effected the reformation of the English Church and its separation from Rome. At that time it was necessary to appeal not to the English constitution as such, but to the fundamental sources of law upon which the English constitution itself stood. The Acts of the English Parliament were addressed directly to the English people, but with more than a glance at continental opinion, which would inevitably be guided by continental jurists. The man who took a leading part in putting the ideas of the time into words was Thomas Cromwell, Secretary to King Henry VIII. Cromwell is known to have spent some time studying civil law in Italy,[1] and he put his knowledge to good use. The Supplication of the Commons, which he drafted (1532), reveals a reliance on the Romano-canonical division of sources of law. The Commons were petitioning for relief against taxation and against other alleged inconveniences in the ecclesiastical jurisdiction in England,[2] and the whole was directed to the undoing of papal authority in this country. We note that the word *ius* can as well be translated 'right' as 'law', and that *ius* in this context will tend to mean *ius scriptum*, in particular statute and the common law as administered in the King's courts. We note, too, that reason and in particular natural reason was viewed as synonymous with *ius naturale*: what is reasonable must be *ex bono et aequo*, but reason may be called upon at an earlier stage to supply the rule of equity in sense (ii).

[1] Dict. Nat. Biog; R. B. Merriman, *Life and Letters of Thomas Cromwell* (Oxford, 1902); J. A. Muller, ed., *Letters of Stephen Gardiner* (Cambridge, 1933), 399.
[2] H. Gee and W. J. Hardy, *Documents Illustrative of English Church History* (London, 1896), XLVI, pp. 145f. Merriman, II, 105, 109, 110.

The Commons are made to declare that the rules against which they complain are 'ayenst all equytee right and good conscience'; 'against all justice lawe equite and good conscience'; and 'against all lawes right and good conscience'.[1] What was against conscience was not binding even morally, since granted that what could not be established in a court of law might be established in a court of conscience, what could be established in neither was not binding in any way whatever. Later we are told[2] that a practice 'standeth not with the right order of justice nor good equity (*bona aequitate=ex bono et aequo*)'; 'contrary to right and conscience'. Again, a claim is made, 'it standeth therefore with natural equity and good reason . . .'[3] In the Act of Succession we are told that, notwithstanding positive law on the subject (which is about to be repealed), the succession of the bastard Elizabeth would be against 'all honour, equite, reason, and good conscience'.[4] A statute of Mary declares that Cranmer, as Archbishop, pursued a course 'against all laws, equity and conscience'.[5]

It is evident from these, as from other examples, that the appeal to 'justice, equity and good conscience' is an appeal to sources of law other than English common and statute law. It is an appeal to fundamental laws, recognized universally, though the actual application of any of them might give rise to debate.

The phrase therefore embodied a concept of the Romano-canonical system that was very much alive in the high constitutional thinking of the founders of the Reformation in England, and with the continuation of the controversies into the next two centuries it could hardly slip out of sight. Nor was this likely while the jurisdiction of the courts administering Civil Law, and the character of the law they administered and its advantages over the Common Law, were constantly brought into question. A series of publications intended to enlighten the public, and in particular the Stuart kings, as to the truth of these matters, appeared from the beginning of the seventeenth century,[6] and these went in many cases into a number of editions, so that we can be sure that the subject enjoyed continuous attention.

[1] H. Gee and W. J. Hardy, *Documents Illustrative of English Church History* (London, 1896), XLVI, pp. 145f. Merriman, II, 105, 109, 110.

[2] (1533-4) 25 H. VIII c. 14 (St. of R. 454); (1534) 25 H. VIII c. 21 (Gee and Hardy, LIII, pp. 8, 209f).   [3] Last cited statute (G. and H., p. 211).

[4] (1536) 28 H. VIII c. 7, preamble.

[5] (1553) 1 M. c. 1, st. 2; *H.C.Jo.* 26-28 Oct. 1553.

[6] T. Ridley, *A View of the Civile and Ecclesiastical Law* (London, 1607), 2d. edn. Gregory (Oxford, 1634), repr. 1662, 1664, 1675, 1676; R. Zouch, *Jurisdiction of the Admiralty of England Asserted* (London, 1663, 1686); A. Duck, *De*

The result is that when the East India Company acquired the Island of Bombay, and inherited judicial responsibilities there, a climate of opinion at home favoured the continuance of the Civil Law there (it remained from 1665 to 1672),[1] and was in no doubt but that if there were any deficiency in the laws to be applied it was to be made up by reference to our formula. This position was arrived at along two independent paths. Firstly the convenience of continuing the Portuguese set-up gave considerable weight to the claims of Civil Law, and the theory was current that Civil Law was the only law suitable to be administered to Christians and non-Christians in countries ruled by Christian monarchs.[2] The Civil Law was the best and most suitable source of 'natural equity', and hardly any country, Christian or non-Christian, was envisaged as likely to be ruled so well as by laws derived from that source.[3] It was believed on good authority that even the Ottoman conqueror of Constantinople had called for a Turkish translation of the Greek version of Justinian's *Corpus* in order to guide himself in governing his new empire,[4] and if the Turk respected Justinian it was hard to see how the Mogul and his subordinates and former subjects could object to a similar course being followed. The desire to apply Roman law to India starts with the commencement of English rule in Bombay and ends, after a period of decline (as we shall see), only with the nineteenth century. The second path which let in justice, equity and good conscience was the demands of the East India Company itself for a system of law which could be applied conveniently to the foreigners who traded along the coast, a system of mercantile law which would satisfy the requirements of trade and avoid the notorious inadequacies of the common law, and the frustrating limitations of the English Admiralty court.[5] Bombay was to become a commercial centre; courts might safely administer common law with reference to some crimes (we

Usu et Authoritate Juris Civilis Romanorum in Dominiis Principum Christianorum (Lug. Bat., 1654,.repr., 1679, 1689); J. Beaver, *History of the Roman or Civil Law* (London, 1724) includes a trans. of C. J. Ferriere's work and a partial translation of Duck. D. O. Shilton and R. Holworthy, *High Court of Admiralty Examinations 1637-1638* (N.Y., London, 1932).

[1] Sir Charles Fawcett, *First Century of British Justice in India* (Oxford, 1934), 3, 6, 34, 44, 46.

[2] Duck, *op. cit.*, passim.　　　　　[3] Wiseman, cited below.

[4] Wiseman (cited below, p. 131), pp. 272-3; Duck I, ii, 6, cited in turn by Wood (1704), p. iii.

[5] H. J. Crump, *Colonial Admiralty Jurisdiction in the Seventeenth Century* (London, 1931), pp. 5, 20f, 165f, 177f.

exclude piracy and the peculiar offence of 'interloping') and matters of real property and contract between merchants and non-merchants; but there was the problem of testaments, and much judicial business of importance would be of a maritime character or derived from customary transactions usual between international merchants.

Hence in 1669 the judges appointed under the Company's Laws were 'in all things' to behave themselves 'according to good conscience',[1] and the oath undertakes that the judge will behave himself 'duly and truly towards all according to justice and good conscience . . .'. The demand for a Judge Advocate qualified in Civil Law made in 1670 was refused,[2] but factors who had studied Civil Law and Common Law were sent out to India. Eventually Wilcox, a former clerk in the Prerogative Office, and so acquainted with ecclesiastical procedure, was appointed Judge to administer the law of England in Bombay in 1672.[3] The Judge was expected to act according to law, reason, and equity.[4] How this worked is well shown by the provisions made by the Governor for the apprehension of persons found forestalling, regrating, and engrossing produce.[5] It was known that these crimes were punishable by the laws of England, some said even by the common law, but there was no pretence that English statute law applied to Hindus and Muslims domiciled on Bombay Island, for that had never been applied to them. However it was an offence at natural law, and perhaps, as Coke would have it, at divine law;[6] and therefore the natives were as amenable to it as their colleagues under Portuguese rule were amenable to the natural law in the matter of certain offences over which the Portuguese courts claimed exclusive jurisdiction.

Royal Charters of August 9, 1683, setting up a mercantile and admiralty court at Bombay,[7] and December 30, 1687,[8] setting up a Municipality and Mayor's Court at Madras, reveal awareness of this theory. The Court of Judicature at Bombay is to consist of one person learned in the Civil Law, and two merchants. They are to handle all mercantile and maritime cases whatsoever 'according to the rules of equity and good conscience, and according to the laws and customs of merchants'. The Mayor's Court at Madras is to try and

---

[1] Fawcett, p. 23.   [2] *Ibid.*, 34. Aungier again asked in 1671.

[3] Fawcett, pp. 46, 49, 81, 83.   [4] Fawcett, p. 54.

[5] Fawcett, p. 82.

[6] S. Browne, *Laws against Ingrossing, Forestalling, Regrating and Monopolising*, 2d. edn. (London, 1767), 83-4.

[7] Fawcett, p. 133. J. Shaw, *Charters Relating to the East India Company from 1600 to 1761* (Madras, 1887), 72, 81.

[8] Shaw, cited above, pp. 88, 89.

adjudge 'in a summary way according to equity and good conscience and according to such laws orders and constitutions that we have already made'. This policy carries out with perfect faithfulness the policy advocated with vehemence by Sir Josiah Child, a businessman of great repute and for long the Chairman of the East India Company. In his view, repeatedly published,[1] the English were hampered in their competition with the Dutch by three disadvantages, namely, (i) the high legal rate of interest, (ii) the absence of a law of negotiable instruments, and (iii) the absence of a proper mercantile court to which all merchants, whatever their nationality, could resort in expectation of speedy and inexpensive justice. All the limitations of the English courts, including the Admiralty court, could be avoided by a juris-diction set out in the Charters mentioned above. Child's fancy for the Roman Law itself, of which there is ample evidence (for he himself said that the judge should proceed discreetly according to common equity and good conscience, which is the general rule of the Civil Law . . .),[2] was evidently due to the learned and partisan clamour of Robert Wiseman, D.C.L.,[3] who repeatedly urged that Roman Law was the only residual law to which any court anywhere need look, and to the famous, but now neglected, *Symboleography* of William West. The former says *inter alia* '. . . the civil law is of such large extent, and so vast a comprehension, that nothing can fall out, whereon the ministration of law, equity, or any part of justice may be necessary, which either the words of that law, or the reason thereof will not decide . . .'[4] The spirit of the Roman Law was incorrupt: '. . . as in publick matters, *salus populi* was *suprema lex*, so in private, *quod aequum bonumque fuit*, was that which made up the Law with them; the dispensation of true right and pure equity was thought the most effectual means to preserve the whole.'[5] Again, 'the Roman Civil Law has not the preeminence of other laws in title and denomination onely, but it is thought also, that in the books there are laid up such treasure of human Wisedom, Policy, Justice, Equity, and natural Reason, that

---

[1] J.C., *Brief Observations concerning Trade and Interest of Money* (London, 1668; B.M. 1029.b.1(2)), p. 6, pts. 12, 13; J. Child, *A New Discourse of Trade* . . . (London, 1693), pp. 106-113; 'Philopatris', *A Treatise wherein is Demonstrated I That the East India Trade is the most National of all Foreign Trades* . . . (London, 1681; B.M. 1029.i.30) at p. 35.

[2] Fawcett, pp. 133-4.

[3] *Law of Laws or the Excellency of the Civil Law above all other Humane Laws whatsoever* . . . (London, 1657, 1686).

[4] *Ibid.*, edn. 1686, p. 261.

[5] *Ibid.*, p. 264.

the art of doing equal justice, and the doctrines of true and uncorrupted right, is taught by them onely. *Jus*, said Celsus, *est ars aequi et boni'*,[1] Meanwhile West, who supplies in his *Second Part* numerous forms of documents needed for international commerce and known to the Civil Law, adds a long chapter on the nature of Equity derived exclusively from Romanic sources and intelligible rather to persons trained in that system than in the common law.[2] He has a good section on *conscientia*, relying on Oldendorpius' definition of the function of the judge's conscience in detecting fallacies and administering equity;[3] and yet he shows clearly that though equity works to supply the gaps in law, 'to maintain *aequum et bonum*', conscience has no scope without law, for they 'join hands in the moderation of extremitie' (where any law is to be found on the point).[4]

The history of Dr St. John's period of office as Judge-Advocate and *de facto* judge of the court of judicature in Bombay (1684-7) goes beyond our present enquiry, but it is of interest to see that this protégé of Sir Leoline Jenkins, the well-known English civilian, made the Civil Law unpopular even with the Company, and that the Royal Charters of 1726 and 1753 which regulated the Mayors' Courts in the Presidency Towns, courts which were essentially English courts administering English law, avoid the phrase 'justice, equity and good conscience' or 'equity and good conscience', with its Civil Law flavour and substitute 'justice and right'. The fact that it has been held judicially that the latter formula does not differ in meaning from our own[5] does not obscure the evident fact that the draftsmen of the Charters were perfectly aware of the difference when they drew them.

In our story there appears to be no further reference to the formula from the English side, for the mention of the administration of justice in accordance with equity and good conscience which we find in Ordinance of Gambia No. 13, March 28, 1844, s. 5 may not be purely English in origin, but may well have come to Africa from India.

JUSTICE, EQUITY AND GOOD CONSCIENCE IN BENGAL

From Bombay and Madras in 1687 to Calcutta in 1781 is a long step in space as well as in time. When the formula was re-born in

[1] *Law of Laws or the Excellency of the Civil Law* . . . (cited above), p. 280.
[2] *The Second Part of Symboleography* . . . *whereunto is annexed another Treatise of Equitie* . . . (London, 1611) fo. 173 v; 174 v.
[3] *Ibid.*, fo. 176 v, sect. 13.   [4] *Ibid.*, sect. 12.
[5] *A. D. Narayan* v *Kannamma* (1931) 55 Mad. 727, 746. Shaw, p. 235, 261.

Calcutta the two Charters of the 1680's were almost forgotten, and it is only with difficulty that we can imagine how the phrase can have been revived. Regulations for the Administration of Justice in the Courts of Dewannee Adaulut (i.e. Dīvāni 'Adālat, or civil court) of the provinces of Bengal, Bihar and Orissa passed by the Governor-General (Warren Hastings) and Council of Fort William in Bengal on July 5, 1781[1] included sec. 60, 'That in all cases, within the jurisdiction of the Mofussil Dewannee Adaulut, for which no specific Directions are hereby given, the respective Judges thereof do act according to Justice, Equity and good Conscience', and sec. 93 which makes the same provision for the Judge of the Sudder (i.e. Sadr, or chief, appellate) Dewannee Adaulut. The provisions are obviously procedural, as are most of the provisions in these 'Regulations', and they are intended to set out the law by which the exercise of the judges' office should be judged in all matters (and they were at first very many) wherein the positive law of the Company was silent. This somewhat peculiar way of introducing justice, equity and good conscience gives us a clue to explain the meaning and purpose of its introduction.

The Regulations were nothing more nor less than a draft compiled by Sir Elijah Impey and forwarded to the Council on July 5, 1781. In his letter[2] he explains what were his sources. The Rules, Orders and Regulations of the Sadr and Mufassil Dīvāni 'Adālats, some of which were very recent (in particular those of April 17, 1780 and April 6, 1781), were revised, rearranged and pruned so that repealed elements might be excluded, and he added thereto 'some few new Rules, which I hope may prove conducive to the due Administration of Justice ...' Our rule is one of these, evidently. The Council had on April 6th previously resolved[3] that Impey be requested to carry out this work of revision and compilation but nothing was said about making additions. The request reached him on April 18th and his work was finished by July 5th. This did not leave time for communication with anyone at Bombay or Madras. Impey for his own part acknowledges considerable indebtedness to Mr [Edward] Otto Ives, judge since 1780 of the 'Adālat at the important city of Murshidabad, who favoured him with a 'very laborious and able work'.[4] That it was laborious and able is also certified to us by the Council themselves.

---

[1] India Office Mss. (Records), Beng. Rev. Cons. 50/33 (1 June–13 July 1781), pp. 397, 424; *Regulations in the Revenue and Judicial Departments enacted by the Governor General in Council . . . of Bengal A.D. 1780-1792* (London, 1834), pp. 176, 185.   [2] Beng. Rev. Cons. 50/33, p. 312.
[3] Beng. Rev. Cons. 50/32, p. 451.   [4] Beng. Rev. Cons. 50/33, p. 313.

They saw his work and ordered that their approbation should go to Mr Ives.[1] That both Impey and the Council should express acknowledgement to Ives, when no part of his 'laborious and able work' needed to be referred to where it coincided with existing regulations from which Impey was expected to provide a short digest or code, suggests forcibly that Ives was chiefly responsible for the relevant addition, as for the other elements which were not present in the former regulations and orders.

Before considering why Ives should have made this suggestion and how he came to make it, and with what object Ives, Impey and the Council came to agree in this respect, it is necessary to eliminate one competitor for the honour of inventing the phrase in Bengal, and to examine more closely Impey's own right to that title. Sir John Day, a barrister in no great practice in the Middle Temple,[2] was sent out to India by the East India Company as their Advocate-General in 1777. He had been appointed in the previous year when it was realized that a barrister ought to represent the Company in its cases before the Supreme Court at Calcutta, since conflict between the Court and the Council had very soon emerged, and indeed had not been unexpected ever since the Supreme Court had been set up with the intention of protecting Indians from the 'oppressions' of the Company's servants. William Hickey, whose opinions have always to be taken with a pinch of salt, but whose memory was exceptional, gives us a very poor impression of Day,[3] and indeed Day's account subsequently of his refusal to appear in court to plead the Company's causes agrees much less with the contemporary correspondence than with Hickey's account,[4] though both can be made to agree. In Hickey's view Day was incompetent and lazy, and no great lawyer as well as vain. Day's own Opinions, several of which are extant, as well as his letters, have more than the usual eighteenth-century flavour of pomposity, indirectness, and hypocrisy.[5] Yet Day, as Company's Advocate-

[1] Beng. Rev. Cons. 50/33, p. 432.
[2] Admitted 20 Sep. 1759; called 8 Feb. 1765. He appears to have died in 1795 or 1796.
[3] *Memoirs*, ed. A. Spencer, 4 vols. (London, 1913-25), II, 151; III, 299-301.
[4] I.O. Mss (Rec.) *Home Misc. Ser.* 421, pp. 605-19. Correspondence between Day and Impey at B.M. ADD. MSS. 16, 267 fo. 23 r—26 r = 16, 263, fos. 20-35 (12-13 July 1779).
[5] *Report from the Committee to whom the Petition of John Touchet and John Irving, Agents . . . were severally Referred* ([London] 1781), Gen. App. no. 4, and Cossijurah App. nos. 5, 9, 18, 20. The unpaginated volume is cited below from the inked pagination of the B.M. copy.

JUSTICE, EQUITY AND GOOD CONSCIENCE

General, certainly studied the Company's Charters. The greater part of his work, as he subsequently boasted, was directed to upholding the Company's jurisdiction, such as it was, against the 'pretensions' of the Supreme Court.[1] He even boasted that he went in fear of his freedom, and, prisons being what they were, his life, because of his steady opposition to the Supreme Court's policies;[2] and it was because of his advice that the Council dared, by a stroke that has never ceased to elicit surprise and even indignation, to oppose the execution of the Supreme Court's process in respect of *zamīndārs* by force of arms in the celebrated Cossijurah Case.[3] He could not have done this without knowing the exact footing upon which the Company's courts and other authoritative bodies acted, and this would mean searching through the old Charters. If the Charters of Bombay and Madras would have been of little direct help to him in this work relative to Bengal, it is certain that before he took up his appointment he would have looked into the history of Dr St. John. Not all the papers would have been available to him, but he must have known that even with the royal appointment procured for the learned doctor through Sir Leoline Jenkins he suffered much embarrassment in Bombay and was later repudiated by Child and his employers in London, claiming, at one stage, not to have been paid for his work. Letters Patent were procured for Day giving him precedence over all advocates in Calcutta,[4] but his appointment, properly, lay and remained with the Company itself, with whom he later entered into acrimonious and fruitless controversy regarding a salary Warren Hastings rather idiotically promised him in addition to his regular salary. A desire not to fall into the trap that awaited St. John, and caught many another King's Judge in India, would have urged him to consult the terms on which St. John went out, and to determine the nature of the controversies in which he was embroiled in reliance

[1] *State of Sir J. Day's Claim* (cited above), p. 29.
[2] *Ibid.*, pp. 29-33.
[3] The group of opinions is dated October 17, 1779 to February 23, 1780. He notes at p. 477 the want of positive provisions of law and the defective character of the constitution. Coss. App. no. 26, pp. 507, 508, 510. J. F. Stephen, *Nuncomar* (cited above); B. B. Misra, *Judicial Administration of the East India Company in Bengal, 1765-82* (Patna, 1953); the same, *Central Administration of the East India Company, 1773-1834* (Manchester, 1959), 233f. B. N. Pandey, *Sir Elijah Impey in India, 1774-1783*. Ph.D. Thesis (unpublished), London (1958).
[4] B.M. ADD. MSS. 16263, fo. 18 is a copy. The date: December 5th, 18 Geo. III (1778).

upon his Charter. Moreover, Day was educated at the Bar at a period noted for two phenomena of importance, namely the popularization of Civil Law and, more strongly, Natural Law doctrines amongst barristers, both at the common law and Chancery Bars; and the development of the law merchant as a branch of common law under the influence of Lord Mansfield. In a liberal age, when most barristers (and Day was no exception) were well-read in the humanities, our formula would not fail to have a meaning in theory if not, at any rate on English soil, in practice.

Yet, when Day discusses the Patna case and other problems involving a consideration of the juridical bases of the judicial process as known in the *mufassil* of Bengal, the terms he uses show awareness of our *concept* without any awareness of its terms.[1] The formula is not there. He does not seem ever to have been on good terms with Impey, and though it is unlikely they failed to meet, Impey and Day were opposed in interpretation of the Regulating Act, and probably thought little of each other as professional men. On his return to England in 1785, about three years after Impey had done the like, Day boasted of his opposition to Impey during the quarrels between the Supreme Court and the Council, and this he was unlikely to do when Impey's own danger was past (and long after Impey and Hastings had seen eye-to-eye over the question of the Company's civil courts) unless in fact Impey and Day had been from the first unreconciled. Thus when the Council, who were quick enough to acknowledge Day's help in 1780 in another connexion,[2] ignored him and showed their obligation to Ives, we are entitled to assume that Ives, and not Day, was the source of the additions made by Impey to the old regulations, amongst which our phrase is to be found.

As for Impey's claim to be the author, this is feeble enough. In a collection of charters, rules, orders, and instructions which Impey compiled for his own use and which still survives,[3] the Charters of 1683 and later containing the phrase 'equity and good conscience' do not figure. In the Bill he and all his fellow judges compiled in collaboration with Hastings and his Council in 1776[4] no such conception appears: on the contrary Impey and the rest saw themselves acting as legislators and judges by turns, so that every gap could be filled by reference to the native laws or English law as the case might

---

[1] *Report from the Committee* . . . Gen. App., no. 4, p. 112.
[2] *State of Sir J. Day's Claim*, pp. 17-18—testimonial dated February 29, 1780.
[3] B.M. ADD. MSS. 16, 268-70.
[4] I.O. Mss. (Rec.) *Home Misc. Ser.* 124, fos. 160-177.

be. In his interesting and long judgment in the Patna case, which was concerned with professional misconduct in persons exercising a *de facto* judicial office, he makes it clear that the validity of their acts is not to be judged by English legal standards, but by standards of universal application. This is a reference to the same standards to which justice, equity and good conscience, or strictly good conscience alone, would refer us, but the phrase does not appear. 'Though the observations already made are not narrow or confined to the rules of evidence of any particular system of municipal laws, but what would naturally arise to men of common sense [i.e. natural reason]; yet for the purpose of determining *quo animo* these defendants acted, it will be necessary to examine these proceedings still more liberally than we did when we were enquiring whether their acts were strictly justifiable'.[1] While entering upon the latter question Impey, C.J., said, 'I have no hesitation to say, that I think the whole and every part of Mr Tilghman's argument [*delegatus non potest delegare*] is founded in law, natural justice, and common sense . . . .'.[2] The last phrase, which represents our phrase, shows how far he was from any formulation of the concept in those very terms, only a little over a year before the request to frame the regulations came to him.

We are left, then, with the conclusion that Ives was the author of the notion. Why he should have been so concerned on the subject of the jurisdiction of the country judges is no mystery once we realize that in between the Patna case and the case of *Gora Chund Dutt* v *Hosea*[3] Ives himself had been involved in the very difficulties of which the Company had been complaining at large, and on which Day had been advising them that acts normally done in the *mufassil* could not possibly be defended or 'justified' in the Supreme Court. Ives was a quite exceptionally well-qualified man. From the post of Persian Translator to the Murshidabad Board he had been appointed, in addition to his duties as translator, to the incredibly onerous post of Superintendent (note, not judge) of the Inferior Dīvāni 'Adālat in that city.[4] Here numerous *munsiffs* actually decided the cases, and Ives confirmed their decrees. He showed concern for incorrectly-decided cases,[5] and urged the government repeatedly to improve the establish-

[1] *Report from the Committee* . . ., Patna App. no. 17, pp. 291f (January 17, 1780), p. 305.
[2] *Ibid.*, Patna App., no. 16, p. 289.
[3] See n. 5, p. 138 below. *Home Misc. Ser.* 421, pp. 124-41, 437-40, 511-46. *Report from the Comm.* . . ., Gen. App., no. 4 (pp. 112-5, 116).
[4] I.O. MSS. (Rec.), Fac. Rec. Murshid. 13 (unfoliated), March 27, 1777.
[5] Fac. Rec. Murshid. 16 (unfol.), March 11, 1779.

ment and to make provision for more effective judicial administration.[1] He was a very different type of man from his colleagues who were involved in the unfortunate Patna affair. But on March 23, 1779, a certain Bolanaut Shoam, father of a party to a case that had been pending since 1777, intervened in the hearing before one of Ives' *munsiffs*, saying, 'I plead after the Calcutta manner', relying on all sorts of technicalities unheard of in the *mufassil*, and abusing the *munsiff* for an ignoramus.[2] Summoned to the Cutcherry (Board's office) by Ives he refused to come and claimed that 'Hastings-Fastings' himself could not attach him (in view of the apparent supremacy of the Supreme Court over the Company). Force was applied to him, and he summoned Ives, his *munshi* and a *munsiff* before the Supreme Court to answer to a plea of trespass, assault, and imprisonment. On June 11, 1779, the Council authorized North Naylor, the Company's Attorney, to enter an appearance for Ives and to defend him.[3] About this time the Supreme Court heard the case of Hosea, Ives' colleague in Murshidabad, whose irregularities, in dealing with a suit for an amount above the limit of jurisdiction of Ives' court, gave much pain to Sir John Day when he came to examine the facts.[4] Despite his advice that nothing could be said to justify the conduct of Hosea and his assistants, the Council thought that it would be advantageous to have a decision as to whether a man could be sued as an individual for acts done in his judicial capacity. Rightly, as it turned out, for Impey, C.J., held that in suits instituted before the provincial councils, except in cases of manifest corruption, the court would not enter into the regularity of the proceedings.[5] The Dīvāni 'Adālats, therefore, were courts in the true sense of the word, and though they were not courts known to English law they had, by reference to the residual sources of law, perhaps *iure naturali*, a jurisdiction which the Supreme Court would recognize. Thus undoubtedly Ives had jurisdiction to attach for contempt of court; and we can be sure that in *Bolanaut* v *Ives* judgment was entered for the defendant. But the necessity of investing the *mufassil* courts with their residual jurisdiction, of making them subject to a system of law which, while *not* being English law, provided a fair standard which the Supreme Court could

---

[1] Fac. Rec. Murshid. 14 (unfol.), December 3, 1777; *ibid.* 14, June 1, 1778; *ibid.* 16, August 9, 1779, September 27, 1779.

[2] Fac. Rec. Murshid. 16, May 3, 1779.

[3] *Home Misc. Ser.* 421, pp. 547–86 (June 11, 1779).

[4] Stephen, *Nuncomar*, II, 157-9.

[5] *Ibid.*, 159.

apply to them, giving them at once protection, security, and a measure of subjection to control, as for example for 'manifest corruption', must have been plain to Ives, who was so much involved. His suggestion will have won ready acceptance from Impey, that justice, equity and good conscience was the law by which the judges were bound in the absence of positive regulation.

From whence would a man like Ives obtain the phrase? We may never know. He went to India as a youth with no training in law. If he saw an English law-book while at Murshidabad it is most unlikely that it contained anything that could have led him in this direction. He made a good judicial officer but he was not firmly wedded to law, and was posted to political duties about six years after the event we are discussing. Possibly the phrase was born from a suggestion of North Naylor. He was only an attorney, but he was steeped in the Company's constitutional affairs, was actually imprisoned for contempt in the course of his duties, and died as a result of being so imprisoned.[1] Naylor's views on all this must have been heart-felt: and that he communicated with Ives, whom he had to defend, is more than likely. And there the quest for the author of our formula will have to rest until new evidence appears.

JUSTICE, EQUITY AND GOOD CONSCIENCE IN INDIA AND PAKISTAN

The provisions of the Regulations of 1781 for the judge to apply justice, equity and good conscience were copied from Regulation to Regulation, and from Regulation to Statute, and this residual source of law is now firmly fixed in South Asia. The area in which it can operate is progressively narrowed, but gaps in the personal laws (especially Hindu and Islamic)[2] and gaps left in the interstices between them, where a conflict of personal laws can occur,[3]—gaps, too, in the judge-made, uncodified, topics of private and public law[4]—may still

[1] Coss. App. nos. 21, 23, 26, pp. 480-1: January-March, 1780.

[2] *Radha v Raj Kuar* (1891) 13 All. 573, 575; *Lalla Sheo v Ram* (1894) 22 Cal. 8; *Mancharsha v Kamrunissa* (1868) 5 B.H.C.R. ACJ. 109, 114; *Vithal v Balu* (1936) 60 Bom. 671, 678-9.

[3] *Raj Bahadur* (see below, p. 145); *Sheikh Kudratulla v Mahini* (1869) 4 B.L.R. FBR, 134; *Budansa v Fatima* (1914) 26 M.L.J. 260=22 I.C. 697, 699; *Pavitri v Katheesumma* AIR 1959 Ker. 319; *Robasa v Khodadad* [1948] Bom. 223.

[4] *Ram v Chunder* (1876) 4 I.A. 23, 50-1; *Gokuldoaa v Kriparam* (1873) 13 Ben. L.R. 205, 213 PC; *Akshoy v Bhajagobinda* (1929) 57 Cal. 92; *Chinnaswami Chettiar v P. Sundarammal* (1955) 2 M.L.J. 312; *Satish v Ram* (1920) 48 Cal. 388 SB; *Kotah Transport v Jhalawar Transport* A.I.R. 1960 Raj. 224, 231.

be filled by reference to this source. We realize at once that since 'justice' represents *iustitia*, *ius scriptum* and *ius non scriptum*, there is little occasion for it to be applied where, by definition, *ius* of either sort exists. If a statute or valid custom were available there would be no recourse, under the Regulations, to the principle. But though this seems like an error, in fact it was correctly devised. In, for example, an instance where a code is silent it is proper to fill the gap with equity, namely *aequitas* in sense (ii). The first step will be to see whether the other provisions of the code throw any general light on the problem. This implies an interpretation of *ius scriptum*. But whenever we apply our minds to *ius scriptum* we remember that what we are interpreting is not *summum ius* (for *summum ius summa iniuria*), but *ius* modified and controlled by *aequitas* in sense (i). Thus equity in very many cases involves consultation of law, and so, although that instinct is not false which leads judges constantly to let drop the word 'justice' in the formula or to refer to the formula in the apparently illiterate form 'equity, justice and good conscience',[1] it is proper to have the full phrase even in those cases where we refer to a wide range of legal sources as *residual* sources of law.

We must concern ourselves with the questions, to what law or laws did the judges turn; and with what effects? The story must be viewed period by period. Up to about 1850 reference was made to the written laws of the Hindus and Muslims, particularly in matters of contract and transfer of property—for the laws were rich enough to admit of such reference, jurists were available to interpret them, and though the Regulations did not *oblige* the judges to apply the personal law in such contexts it was only just to apply a system that might, or indeed must, have been within the contemplation of the parties to the dispute.[2] Where the exact provisions of the native laws were not clear, or even where they were clear but their universality and justice were not evident, and the judges needed to be reassured that what they were administering was consistent with justice, equity and good conscience in the broad sense of what was naturally just, 'natural justice' in the wider sense of that term, aid was taken of Roman Law, the laws of continental countries, English law, both common law and statute law,

---

[1] *Aẓiẓ Bano* v *Muhammad* (1925) 47 All. 823; *Chinna* v *Padmanabha* (1920) 44 Mad. 121; *Ramchandra* v *Ramkrishna* (1951) 54 Bom. L.R. 637, 641.

[2] *Sibnarain* v *R. Chunder* (1842) Fulton 36, 66=1 I.D. (O.S.) 683 per Grant, J; *Zohorooddeen* v *Baharoollah* (1864) Gap No. W.R. 185, 186; Baillie, *Digest of Moohummudan Law on the Subjects to which it is usually Applied by the British Courts of Justice in India* (London, 1865), pp. xxi-xxiii.

and finally Natural Law. In the characteristic Slavery Case,[1] to which the writer has referred elsewhere, the judges, after consulting pandits, cite Pufendorf. The early decades of the nineteenth century saw relatively less use of technical English books than books of a decidedly Romanic complexion, such as Colebrooke's work on the law of contract,[2] and books on 'civil law in its natural order'. In this way Domat and Pothier in English translations, side by side with Pufendorf, began to train as well as aid the amateur jurist who sat in the country courts. Nor were the Privy Council, when established as an effective court of appeal from 1833 onwards, differently minded. Reference to the formula by name was rare in those early days. But their Lordships protest that they apply a rule which is naturally just, and more or less universal in civilized countries,[3] and we see again and again that the English rule is allowed to be followed only when it satisfies this fundamental requirement. Consultation of Roman, French, Dutch, German and other laws was fashionable in the Privy Council, in the Sadr Dīvāni 'Adālats, and even in the Supreme Courts where the suitability of application of English law was in doubt, or there was reason to believe that the law in force in the country courts ought to be followed even in the Supreme Court. Almost at the end of the period G. Bowyer, D.C.L., Barrister-at-law, published his *Commentaries on Modern Civil Law*,[4] the last of a long line of works on Civil Law (in fact expurgated Roman Law), with the intention that it should be used in the *mufassil* of India. He dedicated it to the Marquis of Lansdowne, Lord President of the Council, and it was undoubtedly used in India.[5]

But gradually better-trained lawyers found their way into the judicial service of the East India Company. In 1831 the celebrated Raja Rammohun Roy had recommended in an influential book that European judges sent to India should be at least twenty-four years of age, and should have a certificate of proficiency in *English* law.[6] His

---

[1] W. H. Macnaghten, *Principles and Precedents of Hindu Law* (Calcutta, 1828), II, 272-3; 4th edn. of Kennett's trans., 1729.

[2] *Treatise on Obligations and Contracts* (London, 1818). See 24 RabelsZ. 662-3.

[3] (1835) 5 W.R. 98, 99 P.C.=4 I.R. 743; 8 M.J. 69, 73-4=4 I.R. 910, 917-8; 6 M.I.A. 145, 159; 8 M.I.A. 500, 524-5; 10 M.I.A. 123, 145; 13 M.I.A. 467, 473.

[4] London, 1848. See Dict. Nat. Biog. His *Commentaries on Universal Public Law* was used in India: e.g. 14 S.D.A.R., 862 (1858).

[5] *R. A. Roy* v *R. K. Debea* (1856) 12 S.D.A.R. 643=15 I.D. (O.S.) 114.

[6] *Exposition of the Practical Operation of the Judicial and Revenue Systems of India* (London, 1832), 47.

notion, which was eminently sound, was that a judicial outlook and ability were essential in the judges, and that it was more practical to expect those in someone who had been trained in his own native system of law through materials in his own language than in those who picked up the methods of the existing courts by a hotchpotch casual experience of the medley of laws administered there. This was a bold recommendation, but was obviously attractive notwithstanding the unsuitability of the English law of that time for export to foreign countries. The East India College at Haileybury in fact taught English law and the principles of 'universal jurisprudence'. The best legal learning that could be obtained from Germany was made available to the cadets.[1] One result was undoubtedly the increase in consultation of continental laws in India. The celebrated case of Holloway, J., in Madras will be called to mind.[2] Holloway used to cite Latin maxims, passages from the *Digest* of Justinian and the opinions of German jurists from the bench almost as often as he cited English authorities, and he must have been the despair of the Bar. English law was to be administered under this source only if it was right;[3] and the same test was applied to all other candidates for consultation. If Islamic law was offered, as in the case of preemption amongst Hindus, it might be rejected on the ground that preemption was not consistent with the formula, having been abandoned and disapproved in Germany.[4] But apart from this additional stimulus to continental laws, the overall effect of the better training of judges was the more regular application of English rules so far as they were suited to the circumstances. Indeed, almost as a counterblast to Raja Rammohun Roy's recommendation the Bengal Legislature enacted that by 'justice, equity and good conscience' it should not be understood that English or any foreign law was to be introduced into India.[5] The intention in 1832 evidently was that if an English rule was applied this was to be because it happened to be an expression of justice, equity and good conscience.[6] Yet in the

[1] 24 *RabelsZ.* 671 and n. 36.

[2] 24 *Zeits. f. ausl. und intern. Privatr. (RabelsZ.*), 1959, 657f at 670f.

[3] *Madras Railway* v *Zemindar of Carvatenagaram* (1874) 1 I.A. 364, 372; 24 RabelsZ. 673.

[4] *Ibrahim* v *Muni* (1870) 6 M.H.C.R. 26; cf. *Sheikh Kudratulla* v *Mahini* (1869) 4 B.L.R. 134.

[5] Reg. VII of 1832, s.9. Different personal laws. *Morley's Digest*, pp. clxxiii-iv. *Sec. of State* v *Adm. Gen. of Bengal* (1868) 1 B.L.R.O.C. 87, 97.

[6] (1857) 13 S.D.A.R. (Cal.) 1140=16 I.D. (O.S.), 139. Cf. *Gopeekrist* v *Gungapersaud* (1854) 6 M.I.A. 53, 75-6 (English law not applied). *Shapurji* v *Dossabhoy* (1905) 30 Bom. 359, 362.

realms of guardianship, wills and trusts the English chancery rules soon occupied the field,[1] and to this day the formula means nothing but English rules. Between 1850 and 1880 the struggle between English and continental and American rules went on, with English law gradually gaining an ascendancy. An unfortunate decision gave the impression that English law was invariably to be referred to.[2] This emanated from a judge who, working in Bombay, was unduly influenced by the fact that on the Original Side of that High Court English common law, pure and simple, had long been held to be the residual law. His successors were more cautious, but by 1870 the view had gained ground that in practice the phrase meant English law unless there were some element in the case which made the English rule inappropriate.[3] English jurists summing up at that time were impressed by the infiltration of English rules into contract and tort, and overgeneralized from the resulting picture. They were preoccupied with the question of codification, and utilized the undoubted habit of consultation of English law in those fields as an excuse to hasten the codification of Indian law upon English lines subject to local modifications. Where codification took place the further reference to continental laws was sharply cut off, and judicial equity constantly refers to English precedents.

From 1880, or thereabouts, to the present day the formula has meant consultation of various systems of law according to the context. The dictum in the Privy Council which is so often cited,[4] and which leads to the view that English law will first be consulted wherever the formula applies, is just not true. In trusts, guardianship, tort and contract, English law is indeed looked to first. So also in conflict of laws questions (on topics like domicile), and constitutional matters, though American rules frequently compete for attention, if not as frequently as might be desirable. In those contexts where English law is consulted

[1] *Waghela v Sheikh* (1887) 14 I.A. 89, 96; *In the matter of the petition of Kahandas* (1881) 5 Bom. 154, 158; *In the matter of Saithri* (1891) 16 Bom. 307; *V. J. Walter v M. J. Walter* (1927) 55 Cal. 730, 741; *Mollwo v Court of Wards* (1872) I.A. Sup. Vol. 86.

[2] *Dada Honaji v Babaji* (1865) 2 B.H.C.R. 36, 38; *Webbe v Lester* (1865) 2 B.H.C.R. 52, 56.

[3] Cf. *Mehrban* (1930) 57 I.A. 168, 170=11 Lah. 251 with *Muhammad v Abbas* (1932) 59 I.A. 236=7 Luck. 257.

[4] *Waghela v Sheikh* (1887) 14 I.A. 89, 96 (a guardianship case): 'In point of fact, the matter must be decided by equity and good conscience, generally interpreted to mean the rules of English law if found applicable to Indian society and circumstances'. A different tone was taken in *Guthrie v Abool* (1871) 14 M.I.A. 53, 65 cf. *Muhammad v Abbas* (cited at n. 3 above).

as a matter of course, there is no reason to suppose that English common law, as distinct from English law as a whole, ought to be regarded. The suggestion that we have to consider particularly the common law, to the exclusion of statutory amendments,[1] is incorrect: it is to a developed system of law that we must refer, and we cannot ignore the developments which have occurred in the system we choose for first reference. The correct position is explained in the frequently-cited passage from the judgment of Barnes Peacock, C.J., in *Degumbaree Dabee* v *Eshan Chunder Sein:*[2]

'Now, having to administer equity, justice and good conscience, where are we to look for the principles which are to guide us? We must go to other countries where equity and justice are administered upon principles which have been the growth of ages, and see how the courts act under similar circumstances; and if we find that the rules which they have laid down are in accordance with the true principles of equity, we cannot do wrong in following them.'

As Stone, C.J., said in *Sec. of State* v *Rukhminibai:*[3]

'. . . one shall regard the law as it is in England today, and not the law that was part of the law of England yesterday. One cannot take the common law of England divorced from the statute law of England and argue that the former is in accordance with justice, equity and good conscience and that the latter which has modified it is to be ignored.'

In the former case English cases were cited as the latest exponents; in the latter the doctrine of 'common employment' was rejected because it had been abolished in England.

In other fields of law the priority of English rules is by no means admitted. Where the systems of personal law are silent, or where they are inapplicable because the religions of the parties differ, the English law, and indeed other systems of foreign law, seem hardly the obvious choice. In practice analogies are sometimes drawn from the nearest personal law. The effects can be incongruous, but perhaps less harm is done than by the application of a system utterly unconnected with the

---

[1] *Philomena* v *Dara Nussarwanji* [1943] Bom. 428; *Cheriya Varkey* v *Ouseph* A.I.R. 1955 T.C. 255, 257 FB; *Pavitri* v *Katheesumma* A.I.R. 1959 Ker. 319; *Manni* v *Paru* A.I.R. 1960 Ker. 195, 196.
[2] (1868) 9 W.R. 230, 232.
[3] A.I.R. 1937 Nag. 354—followed in *Sm. Mukul* v *Indian Airlines Corp.* A.I.R. 1962 Cal. 311, 320.

parties' contemplation when they entered into the transaction which gave rise to the action. Where there is no possibility of reference to a personal law, reference to no specific law, to a statute, or to the English law as a last resort is found. Instances where the English law has been repudiated as not in accordance with the law usual in civilized countries,[1] as unsuited to India, or to the case,[2] and so not applied there, are not infrequent. In *Raj Bahadur* v *Bishen Dayal*[3] the family were neither Hindus nor Muslims, but the family had followed the Hindu law of inheritance by custom and the Hindu law was applied to them. One of many instances of silent reference to the formula is found in *Chathunni* v *Sankaran*,[4] where a patrilineal man married a matrilineal woman and it was held that natural justice required that the child should inherit patrilineally through his father and matrilineally through his mother, a situation not contemplated by any system of personal law. *Radha* v *Raj Kuar*[5] is perhaps an example of reference to a concept of justice in the judge's mind which has a distinctly liberal tinge, not referable to any particular system of law, and not apparently due to English law. A man lived with a woman of lower caste whom he could not marry and was outcasted. He died, and the woman held property which was acquired by him and died leaving it to her children by him. His brothers, who had remained in caste, sued for this property, claiming that the woman and her illegitimate issue had no right to it. The court held that as the property was not ancestral and the brothers had contributed nothing to its acquisition they were not entitled to it, but that justice, equity and good conscience gave it to the children. In *Jagarnath Gir* v *Sher Bahadur Singh*[6] the formula allowed a mother to succeed to her illegitimate child. In that case analogies from the Anglo-Hindu law were drawn upon. In *Viswanatha Mudali* v *Doraiswami*[7] it was held that dancing-girls, whose customs in many respects differed from the personal law, were to be governed by Hindu law or by analogies drawn from the Hindu law. In *T. Saraswathi Ammal* v *Jagadambal*[8] it was held that propinquity, being a fundamental principle of Hindu law, could be relied on under our principle to enable the dancing-girl daughter and the married daughter of a woman to succeed together to her property in the absence of a customary rule

[1] *Gatha Ram* v *Moohita* (1875) 23 W.R. 179.
[2] *Ramratan Kapali* v *Aswini* (1910) 37 Cal. 559.
[3] (1882) 4 All. 343, 349-51.   [4] (1884) 8 Mad. 238.
[5] (1891) 13 All. 573, 575.   [6] (1934) 57 All. 85.
[7] (1925) 48 Mad. 944; *Venkata* v *Cheekati* (1953) 1 M.L.J. 358.
[8] A.I.R. 1953 S.C. 201, 204 col. i.

to the contrary. In *Sudarshan Singh v Suresh Singh*[1] it was held that the illegitimate son and illegitimate daughter of a Hindu woman share her estate equally, though if Hindu law had been applied by analogy the daughter would have been preferred to the son. In *Iravi Pillai v Mathevan*[2] a problem in the residual law to be applied to matrilineal families was solved by the application of Hindu law, i.e. patrilineal law, a system which had been applied previously to fill gaps in the customary matrilineal systems. In *Pavitri v Katheesumma*[3] a Muslim male had had an illegitimate daughter by a Hindu female. The daughter sued for maintenance out of his estate. This was refused to her on the ground that justice, equity and good conscience, whether one searched the Hindu law or the English common law, was hostile to such claims. In *Robasa v Khodadad*,[4] a case recently followed in Pakistan,[5] a spouse was converted from Zoroastrianism to Islam. It was held that under our principle, which by no means required reference to English law (which in any case provided no helpful analogies), a party to a solemn pact could not bring it to an end by unilateral act, and the marriage did not stand dissolved. It was not possible to apply the Islamic law, which was applicable only where *both* parties were Muslims.

A further use for the formula arises where the doctrines of the personal laws are obscure because of differences of opinion between the native jurists. In *Aẓiẓ Bano v Muhammad Ibrahim*[6] it was held that a choice most consistent with justice, equity and good conscience could be made between the conflicting opinions in Islamic law; and a similar view was evinced with reference to Hindu law in *Rakhalraj v Debendra*.[7]

It remains to discuss a peculiar feature of 'justice, equity and good conscience' as known in South Asia. Repeatedly advocates attempt to argue that a provision of the personal law, or indeed of some statute, is not to be applied in the circumstances because it would be contrary to equity and good conscience so to do. In no case have they succeeded. It is very curious that this argument should be raised, since in *Moonshee Buẓloor Ruheem v Shumsoonnissa Begum*[8] the Privy Council indignantly and with great emphasis repelled the notion that a definite rule of the personal law could be nullified because it did not

---

[1] A.I.R. 1960 Pat. 45. [2] A.I.R. 1955 T.C. 55 FB.
[3] A.I.R. 1959 Ker. 319. [4] [1948] Bom. 223.
[5] *Farooq Leivers v Adelaide* P.L.R. (1958) 2 W.P. 1116.
[6] (1925) 47 All. 823. [7] A.I.R. 1948 Cal. 356.
[8] (1867) 11 M.I.A. 551.

square with the court's notion of justice, equity and good conscience. Sir James W. Colvile said:[1]

'The passages just quoted, if understood in their literal sense, imply that cases of this kind are to be decided without reference to the Mahomedan law, but according to what is termed, "equity and good conscience", i.e. according to that which the judge may think the principles of natural justice require to be done in the particular case. Their Lordships most emphatically dissent from that conclusion. It is, in their opinion, opposed to the whole policy of the law in British India, and particularly to the enactment (Reg. IV of 1793, s.15) . . . which directs, that in suits regarding marriage . . . the Mahomedan laws with respect to Mahomedans . . . are to be considered as the general rules by which Judges are to form their decisions; and they can conceive nothing more likely to give just alarm to the Mahomedan community than to learn by a judicial decision that their law, the application of which has been thus secured to them, is to be overridden upon a question which so materially concerns their domestic relations. The Judges were not dealing with a case in which the Mahomedan law was in plain conflict with the general municipal law, or with the requirements of a more advanced and civilized society—as, for instance, if a Mussulman had insisted on the right to slay his wife taken in adultery. In the reports of our Ecclesiastical Courts there is no lack of cases in which a humane man, judging according to his own sense of what is just and fair, without reference to positive law, would let the wife go free; and yet, the proof falling short of legal cruelty, the Judge has felt constrained to order her to return to her husband.'

This left it open to be supposed that the personal laws could be overridden if they were inconsistent with the requirements of a more advanced and civilized society, and indeed in *Mahomed Kadar* v *Ludden*[2] it was contended that the Islamic institution of *mut'a* (the temporary marriage amongst Shias) was subject to modification disallowing the husband's right to divorce unilaterally. It was however held that what the Privy Council had in mind was inhumanity or barbarity, and that short of these the personal laws could not be impugned. Yet similar attempts are regularly made even in these days. Again and again we find the judges saying that the provision of law is

[1] At p. 614.　　　　　　　　　　　　　　[2] (1886) 14 Cal. 276, 286-7.

not repugnant to those principles[1]—and rightly so, for, as we have seen, there is no ground for supposing that in South Asia the formula operates as a *repugnancy* rule. Where we are concerned with *custom*, no doubt a custom is to be followed if not contrary to *natural justice:* but that is another question entirely. The equity which ancient Roman advocates used to urge upon the court, *aequitas* in sense (i), and the 'equity of the statute' which flourished in England until the eighteenth century, have no place in modern South Asia.

JUSTICE, EQUITY AND GOOD CONSCIENCE IN AFRICA

A complete survey of the scope of the phrase in Africa would be impossible in this already lengthy paper. Moreover, it seems that many valuable decisions are not published. It is clear that reference to some Indian cases has taken place,[2] but that on the whole judges prefer to treat the formula as if it meant 'public policy', 'natural justice', and the like. But an instinct to refer to a developed system of law, and in particular one which is accessible to the practitioners as well as to the court, is well evidenced[3] and is, as we have seen, perfectly sound in principle.

It is no mystery how the formula came to Africa. As soon as it was determined that the administration of African customary law should be integrated with the judicial administration of the Supreme Court of the Gold Coast, a reorganization of the jurisdiction and practice of that court required a definition, in s. 19 of the Supreme Court Ordinance of the Gold Coast, 1876, of the scope within which native laws or customs should be judicially applied. We have already seen that customs were to be enforced if not repugnant to natural justice, equity and good conscience (or ordinances for the time being in force), and that 'in cases where no express rule is applicable to any matter in controversy, the court shall be governed by the principles of justice, equity and good conscience'. Similar provisions are to be found in the laws of Gambia, Sierra Leone, Nigeria and Northern Rhodesia.

Instructions for drawing up the Ordinance were communicated by the Colonial Secretary, Lord Carnarvon, on 16th April 1875.[4] It was then the custom to supply the Queen's Advocate, Mr Chalmers, with

[1] *Km. N. Sp. N. Valliammal* v *J. A. Ramachandra* A.I.R. 1959 Mad. 433; *Revappa* v *Balu* A.I.R. 1939 Bom. 59, 61 Col. i.
[2] H. W. Hayes Redwar, *Comments on some Ordinances of the Gold Coast Colony* (London, 1909), 59, 65.
[3] Views cited by E. Guttman (1957) 6 I.C.L.Q. 401f, at 412.
[4] Despatch no. 55 of that date. P.R.O., C.O. 96/116. Sept. G.C. No. 10, 867, sent September 6, 1875, received October 1, 1875.

copies of Indian statutes on subjects under consideration for legislation.[1] Here was no exception: various 'Laws' were sent out, and Mr Chalmers says, 'I have adopted very numerous provisions from these laws; but not without carefully considering the questions of local suitability which presented themselves in each instance.'[2] Although he did not refer to the [Indian] Punjab Laws Act, Act IV of 1872, it is quite clear that he consulted it.[3] The relevant provisions of that Act are contained in ss. 5-7.

s.5. In questions regarding succession, special property of females, betrothal, marriage, divorce, dower, adoption, guardianship, minority, bastards, family relations, wills, legacies, gifts, partition, or any religious usage or institution, the rule of decision shall be—

(a) Any custom applicable to the parties concerned, which is not contrary to justice, equity or good conscience, and has not been declared to be void by any competent authority;

(b) the Muhammadan law ... and the Hindu law ...

s.6. In cases not otherwise specially provided for, the Judges shall decide according to justice, equity and good conscience.

s.7. All local customs and mercantile usages shall be regarded as valid, unless they are contrary to justice, equity or good conscience, or have ... been declared to be void by any competent authority.

Punjab is somewhat peculiar, in that, in the matters where the personal law normally reigns supreme, local customs for the most part take the place of those laws, and cut across religious denomination. The provision in s. 5 (a) is not at once intelligible. If the formula meant English or any other foreign law it must make nonsense of the basic provision that customary law must be the primary source, for naturally very few of the customs of the Punjab would be likely to agree with foreign laws. It is evidently a piece of incompetent draftsmanship, and what the legislature meant to say was that customs should be binding if they were not repugnant to natural justice, *ius naturale;* and the same comment must be made about s. 7.[4] This is eloquent proof that by the 1870's influential and well-informed men,

---

[1] Same volume, October. Reference to a despatch of March 5, 1876. See also G.C. No. 12, 303, *ibid.*
[2] Covering letter submitted to Governor Strahan, September 4, 1875, ref. as n. 4, p. 148 at para. 3.
[3] J. M. Sarbah, *Fanti Customary Laws* (London, 1897), 18, 30; Hayes Redwar, *op. cit.,* 59.
[4] I.O. MSS. (Rec.) *Home Misc. Ser.* 124, fo. 171.

such as the Law Member of the Viceroy's Council, had totally forgotten what our phrase really meant. Mr Chalmers, faced by this anomaly, tried to improve on its evident solecism by turning 'justice' into 'natural justice'. This did not render it a satisfactory provision, and we must read the repugnancy provision as if it were 'repugnant to natural justice', and treat the following words, 'equity and good conscience' as superfluous.

Very good sense has been shown in the Sudan in dealing with the relevant residual provision there. The Civil Justice Ordinance, 1929, s. 9 provides, for a land singularly short of statutory or case law, that, 'In cases not provided for by this or any other enactment for the time being in force the courts shall act according to justice, equity and good conscience'. Here the borrowing is likely to have been direct from India rather than indirectly from the Gold Coast. There is ample evidence[1] that under our principle the courts of the Sudan apply English law (including English statutory law), Egyptian law, Indian law, or indeed the law of any country the written sources of which are readily available to them, that there is a distinct preference for English law, and that this preference rests upon principles fully recognized. It has been pointed out that the public needs as residual systems of law systems with which the Bar as well as the Bench may be familiar,[2] and that the system with which members of the Bar, law teachers and law students alike are best acquainted, questions of religion apart, is the English law, and that therefore English cases and statutes are most readily to be cited.

The predominance of English law in African territories ruled or once ruled by the British is not therefore surprising. But one may wonder whether, or for how long, it will continue.

CONCLUSION

The effects of the formula in India have been to smooth out discrepancies between systems of law, and to introduce conceptions which strongly resemble the general character of English law. Actual rules of English law are regularly relied upon in some fields.[3] In so far as this has established lines of authority the importation of American

---

[1] E. Guttman (cited p. 148, n. 3 above) at pp. 407, 410, 411. It appears that now the rule laid down in 1920 that English law should guide but not govern the courts in the Sudan has been modified in favour of the doctrine that any system of law may be consulted, English law having no preference.
[2] N. 3 at p. 148.   [3] But see *Namdeo* v *Narmadabai* [1953] S.C.R. 1009.

or other foreign laws is unlikely, if not impossible, as long as the residual sources remain unaffected by legislation. Yet we have seen that there are fields and chapters where English law by no means claims prominence or predominance. The influence exerted by India's long connexion with England, nowhere more subtle or pervasive than in her legal system, seems, none the less, to ensure frequent consultation of English decisions wherever India lacks an authority. The same should apply to relevant parts of Africa.

But in both parts of the globe a proviso exists, which goes back to the origins of the formula. If English law had been meant to be indicated it would indeed have been indicated in so many words. The formula was a device to escape from English law, not to call it in. Because precedent does not govern what the judge may in his discretion regard as consistent with justice, equity and good conscience to anything like the same degree as in other fields it is open to any judge to review other systems of law offered by counsel for his information. It is clear that this source does not mean uncontrolled speculation or personal preference. Reference to another system of law there must be, and provided it is a developed system of law it cannot be said to be against justice, etc., unless it is plainly inconsistent with the needs of the case or markedly incongruent with the rest of the system. So long as the system of customary law applied is one which can provide a valid analogy, the scope for introducing foreign laws does not exist. It is only where positive law, custom, and equitable analogies based upon proved custom cannot be traced that our formula comes into its own. In such cases if the Bar and the Bench are sufficiently learned they may review the whole field of law: customs of neighbouring and similar tribes; written laws of generally similar peoples; the opinions of textbook writers and anthropologists; considerations of peace and public policy; the laws of developed countries starting, naturally, with English law, and reviewing the position in the other colonies or ex-colonies, the Dominions, the United States, and finally the Civil Law world. There is, it is submitted, a case for the employment of a trained comparative lawyer as a legal adviser, from whose opinions, perhaps as *amicus curiae*, it will be possible to determine what would be the *best* law for the circumstances. A rule cannot be consistent with justice, etc., if it relies upon a rule in a particular foreign law, however familiar, when the reverse is normally used amongst a great part of mankind—so long as that latter rule would not be incompatible with the whole chapter of law under consideration.

Finally it is perhaps necessary to point out that some *other* formulae may or may not amount to the same thing as our formula. We have seen that the 'justice and right' of the Original Sides of the Presidency High Courts and their successors has been held to amount to the same thing as 'justice, equity and good conscience', though there are still doubts whether after all the English common law is not the residual source of law there. The repugnancy provisions of various African statutes admitting native law and custom are beyond our concern, for we have seen that 'natural justice, equity and good conscience' was really a mistake, and the question whether 'natural justice' is or is not the same as 'morality', 'humanity', and the like is beyond the scope of this essay.

ADDENDUM

The provision in the law of Ghana for reference to our formula in repugnancy and residual contexts (Courts Ordinance, cap. 4, s. 87 (1)) has been repealed with the rest of that Ordinance by the [Ghana] Courts Act, 1960, s. 156. The savings in s. 154 do not include s. 87 of the earlier law. The new code provides by s. 66 (3) (b) that—

the rules of estoppel and such other of the rules generally known as the doctrines of equity as have heretofore been treated as applicable in all proceedings in Ghana shall continue to be so treated.

Since 'justice, equity and good conscience' is not a rule of common law or equity, and, as we have seen, does not even refer of necessity to common law or equity (though to establish what is consistent with equity and good conscience it would be advisable to inform oneself of what the common law, equity and statute law of England have to say on the topic at issue), it seems to follow that reference to it is abolished in Ghana. It may be asked whether a fundamental rule can be abolished by statute; in other words whether Parliament is bound by fundamental laws which the courts will apply in interpreting the intention of Parliament. Technically the answer in this day and age must be yes to the first question, and no to the second. The result would be that where residual law is needed, or a custom is impugned on the ground of being repugnant to 'natural justice, equity and good conscience' (as distinct from the common law rules of 'reason' and 'public policy'), the plaintiff must fail, or the custom must be admitted, because where the formula is missing, the case must proceed as if no alternative were available. But the function of the judge being what it is (see p. 119 above), decisions (perhaps in contexts other than these last) founded on the principles of justice and natural equity, reason, and good conscience will continue to be given, pending a distinct prohibition from the legislature. As a result the way is still open for the consultation of comparative legal material. Customs will, in any case, be admitted if they are not 'repugnant' in the legally trained opinions of the Ghana judges (see pp. 114, 148 above), and, where necessary, material from foreign systems of law will still be imported at those same judges' discretion to fill gaps left by the positive law.

8

THE LEGAL PROFESSION IN AFRICAN TERRITORIES

SIR SYDNEY LITTLEWOOD

President, The Law Society, 1959–60;
Member, Legal Aid Committee

THE IMPORTANCE OF THE LAWYER IN MODERN SOCIETY

The views that I shall express in the course of this paper are purely my own. I am aware that they differ, in details, from those put forward by Lord Denning's Committee,[1] but I should like to pay tribute to the work done by Lord Denning and his colleagues. They have brought to the notice of the public a state of affairs that few realized, and I hope, and indeed believe, that as a result of their work the countries of Africa that are pushing ahead so rapidly and splendidly will benefit greatly.

In America there is a fused legal profession. Instead of solicitors and barristers, they have Attorneys-at-Law who serve both functions. Some time ago I was being entertained by lawyers in San Francisco. In the course of a chat with my hosts I said I thought the lawyer's job was one of the most important of all in a civilized society and my friends, without exception, expressed surprise at that statement. I asked them to think the matter over; to imagine a country with a legislative body turning out laws, and with its Common Law, but with no judges to interpret the law and see that it was properly administered. They agreed that that would be dreadful; so I said, 'Go a stage further and imagine that country, not only without judges, but without lawyers to advise the public on their rights. Then take another country, with judges but with no lawyers to keep the judges in order'. They thought for a moment and agreed with me that in a modern civilized state both judges and lawyers were of primary importance, and then, of course,

---

[1] Report of the Committee on Legal Education for Students from Africa. Cmnd. 1255, January 1961.

they had to acknowledge that the lawyer's job is one of the most necessary functions in a civilized society.

I want to spend a few moments considering one or two matters in which the client consults his lawyer. First, two people each own land, and are involved in a dispute about a boundary. Any practising lawyer knows how keenly the parties to a boundary dispute feel about the matter, and how each runs off in search of legal advice. In all lands outside the Iron Curtain, and even in some lands inside the Iron Curtain (for I have listened to a boundary dispute in a Polish law court), land ownership is very important to the individual, and he looks to the law to enforce his rights in this respect. To many, their land is almost as important as personal liberty. In the boundary dispute that I have taken as an example, the two disputants know that their lawyers between them, if necessary by having recourse to the court, will establish what is the proper boundary and see that that boundary is maintained. But I wonder how many lawyers engaged in a dispute about a foot or two of land stop to think how serious a thing that is in the life of the community.

A solicitor regards the making of a will as a very ordinary matter. But to the client it is a matter of great importance. He wants to be sure that what he desires to happen to his possessions after his death will in fact happen, and he relies upon his solicitor to advise him so that all pitfalls may be avoided; and, although he is not conscious of this, he also relies upon the courts and the whole administration of the law to see that his wishes as expressed in his will are carried into execution after his death.

You may take any instance you like of the client consulting his lawyer. The client wants his rights protected and he relies upon the law and the lawyer to see that it is done. The most important right of all is the liberty of the subject. Let us suppose a man gets arrested and charged with an offence of which he may be innocent. If there were no judges and no lawyers what hope would that man have of establishing his innocence if his arrest had been brought about by a Government Department or by a very powerful individual? Throughout the British Commonwealth and in all civilized countries that I have visited the man who is arrested, even though he is guilty, can get a lawyer's help; and he knows that when he goes before a judge he will get a fair hearing by a man who has been specially trained and is impartial. And if, by some mischance, the judge should depart from the standard of perfection that is expected of him, the accused man looks to his lawyer to stand up to the judge and prevent him from going wrong. So I can say that for a country to be properly run it needs judges who are learned in the law, who understand people, who know the ways of the world and who are completely impartial. (I know that in some countries judges are politically appointed. Here in England, thank God, and, I believe, in all countries in the British Commonwealth, judges are appointed without regard to their politics and when appointed cease to be politicians, even if they were such before.)

A country also needs a sufficient number of lawyers. These lawyers must know the law, know the practice of the law, be scrupulously honest, understand people, and be independent and fearless where their duty to their clients is concerned. 1 have met lawyers who think that experience can make up for a knowledge of the law. I have known, too, many who, when once they have passed their examinations, have not troubled to keep their knowledge of the law up to date. That is wrong. A lawyer cannot possibly give the best service to his client unless he knows and is up to date in the branch of the law with which he is dealing for that client. And in addition to the many other qualities I have listed the lawyer must be strong. It is not a good service to a client to advise the client in the way he wants to be advised if that advice is unsound in law, but it is fatally easy for the weak man to fall into that trap. Then the lawyer must also have a love of justice and that love must be strong enough to overcome any prejudices he may have. It has been my good fortune to meet lawyers in many different lands and I have found that a love of justice is common to most lawyers after they have had a few years' experience. There is something in the practice of the law that breeds this love of justice.

I should like to tell a true story to show how a love of justice and a sense of duty can overcome prejudice. I was articled many years ago to a man who was a considerable advocate, and on one occasion I went to a magistrates' court with him when he was appearing for the defence of a man of five and twenty who was charged with an indecent offence. This offence was triable summarily and my principal had to plead guilty but put up the most heart-rending plea for mercy. In those days the Probation for Offenders Act was rarely used but, on that occasion, the magistrates listened to the plea and put the young man on probation. As I was walking back to the office with my principal I said to him, 'I was very pleased with that result, weren't you?' He stopped, looked at me and said, with just as much feeling as he had shown in court when putting up such a magnificent plea for the young man: 'No, the dirty fellow should have gone to prison'.

LEGAL TRAINING IN ENGLAND

Having said what I think is required of a lawyer, I want to consider the English system of training. Here we have solicitors who instruct barristers, barristers who appear before judges, and judges who have been practising barristers. That system has stood the test of many centuries and, as I go round the world, I find that most lawyers in foreign countries have a great admiration for our English system of justice. My American friends say they cannot understand how a barrister 'tries' an action when he has not interviewed the witnesses, but, nevertheless, they agree that our legal system commands respect. In England, where we have the two branches, a client consults a solicitor and in the appropriate case the solicitor goes, sometimes with the client, to the barrister. The solicitor, in addition to his legal knowledge, must be a practical man, and a substantial part of his training must be on the practical side. The solicitor in general practice (as the majority of them are) never knows what problem will come to him next. The barrister, on the other hand, always has the solicitor between him and the client; and the barrister has no hope of succeeding at the Bar unless, by what he does, he can convince solicitors that he is to be trusted with their work. The barrister, therefore, always becomes a Common Law man, or a Chancery man or a man who practices in the Probate, Divorce and Admiralty Division. There are, of course, other specialized lines and many become specialists in a very narrow sphere, but it is not necessary for them to be practical people and no part of their training is practical. The Council of Legal Education provides courses in law, and when a barrister is called to the Bar he need have no training beyond that which he has had in his law classes. I should mention here that if a barrister intends to practise in England he must spend a year as a pupil in a barrister's chambers, but that rule does not apply to those who go overseas to practise.

The solicitor, then, has to have a wide knowledge of law, of the way the law works, and of people. When I was adumbrating the qualities required in a lawyer I mentioned that he should be learned in law and in understanding of people. Where there is fusion of the profession those qualities must all be found in the one man; while where we have the two branches the solicitor provides the practical side in its entirety. So the person who wants to be a solicitor, after satisfying the Law Society that his basic education is of a standard high enough to enable him to pursue his legal studies, becomes articled to a practising solicitor, and he must spend a substantial part of his articles in that solicitor's office. There he will learn the every-day practice of the law, how to draft documents, how to issue process and deal with the various steps of actions in various courts, how to get probate, how to make a man bankrupt, in fact all the practical side of the lawyer's practice. He will also learn how to deal with clients and will often see and learn something of their businesses. He will learn to understand a balance sheet—in fact he has to pass an examination in Trust Accounts and Book-keeping. He will learn the etiquette of the profession; and in that connexion I particularly want to mention a solicitor's undertaking. A great deal of work is only possible on solicitors giving undertakings, and these are so important that the Law Society will always compel solicitors to honour them. I hope I have said enough to show the importance of the practical side to a solicitor's training. The barrister who practises in England does not need that practical side to enable him to do his work.

As I am dealing with the work of a solicitor, and many may not realize the extent to which a solicitor can practise advocacy, I must emphasize that he has a right of audience before every court and Tribunal except the High Court, the Court of Appeal and the House of Lords, Assizes and most Quarter Sessions; and here and there one may find a Court of Special Jurisdiction where he has no right of audience. Many solicitors spend most of their business life on advocacy in magistrates' courts, county courts and before administrative tribunals or Government inspectors.

My American friends are always interested to hear about the division between the English solicitor and the English barrister, and time and time again I have had them say to me: 'But you fellows, you solicitors, are what we call lawyers.' Of course, I always point out to them that that is not quite the right way to put it, because in England we do regard the barrister as a lawyer; but the fact is that the bulk of the work that the average firm of lawyers in America does is the work that a solicitor does in England. Put another way, to the man in the street the most important part of a lawyer's work is the work done by the solicitor in England. In case that comes as a surprise to you just remember that there are, in round figures, some 20,000 practising solicitors in England and only 2,000 barristers, of whom it is said that not more than 1,500 make a living. Certainly solicitors are overworked, and at the present time we have ample scope for more solicitors. I am glad to say that I understand that work at the Bar is increasing too, but for our present purpose the important thing that I want you to bear in mind is that we have ten times as many solicitors as we have barristers. On those figures it means that ten-elevenths of a lawyer's work is the work that solicitors do. While I am dealing with figures, you may be interested to know that the last figures given to me of lawyers practising in the United States was 273,000. That figure astounds me. The population of America is about three times as great as the population of England, but they have about twelve times as many lawyers.

Before I deal with legal education in Africa I want to say something about the question of division or fusion within the legal profession. I am satisfied that England is far better off with two separate branches of the profession than it would be with fusion; and while we have two separate branches the system of training for the Bar serves its purpose. I expect you know that there has been much talk of late about bringing the training of the two branches more into line with each other, and of making it easier to transfer from one branch to the other. I think that would be all to the good, but this is not the place to discuss it. I should be horrified, however, if it were suggested that today's training for the Bar fitted a man to be a solicitor. Once a young barrister told me that he thought that fusion would be a good thing and I asked him why. He said, 'I have difficulty in making a living now but if I could practise as a solicitor I could make a good living.' To that I said, 'Let me suppose that fusion comes about tonight and tomorrow morning you can practise as a solicitor. The first client to come to you says, "I have been in business for twenty years. During the last five years things have been going from bad to worse. Now they are desperate. I want you to file my petition for me." What would you do?'—and of course he had no answer. But there are many things more difficult than that. The barrister is not required to know anything about accounts. Many firms of solicitors deal with millions of pounds of clients' money each year and the Law Society requires every penny to be accurately accounted for. The Law Society has the right to inspect any practising solicitor's books at any time and the solicitor whose books are not in order will probably be struck off the Rolls. Again, it is the commonest thing for a client to come in with accounts—either his own or those of a concern in which he is interested—and ask for information upon them. The solicitor must be able to deal with that. He cannot always say 'Go and ask your accountant', as often the client will have come to him with the accounts because a question of law has arisen. It is impossible to over-emphasize the importance of the practical side of a solicitor's training.

A law degree does not confer a right to practise, either as a barrister or a solicitor, in England. In the case of a solicitor it merely exempts him from compulsory attendance at Law School and from part of his examinations.

LEGAL TRAINING IN AFRICA

I was in Central and East Africa in the early part of 1961 and I had the good fortune to be able to discuss the problems of legal education with Chief Justices, politicians, Attorneys-General and practising lawyers. I was able to go over offices run by Africans, offices run by Indians and offices run by Europeans, and to meet the lawyers running those offices. I also learned a certain amount about native courts in the countries I have mentioned.

When I was there, there were in Uganda twenty-three practising African lawyers, in Kenya seven, and in Tanganyika one. In Northern Rhodesia there was one African who had passed the English Bar examinations but had not succeeded in passing an examination that the Northern Rhodesia Law Society insists upon people passing before they can practise in Northern Rhodesia. All of the African lawyers that I have mentioned had been called to the English Bar. Not one had had the training of an English solicitor; but there they were in practice, dealing with clients' money, advising clients on day to day affairs. There were also, of course, a good many Indian and European lawyers.

In all of the countries I have mentioned there is a fused profession. Although I am a strong supporter of the two branches system for England, I recognize that there are many countries where it is impossible, and I believe the fused profession is the only system that can work in East Africa and Northern Rhodesia.

With the coming of independence it is natural that each country should look to its own nationals to administer law and justice; but it follows that those who are to do that must be adequately qualified and, as Lord Denning's Committee has pointed out, that, where there is fusion, training in the practical side of the law is vital.

No one will disagree with me when I say that we want to see a great increase in African lawyers practising in Africa and that we want to see them properly qualified. Now, whatever his nationality or race, any man who sets out to be a lawyer wants to qualify as quickly as he can; but it does not follow that what he wants is the right thing for the nation that he is to serve. An under-trained and under-educated lawyer is a menace to his clients, a danger to himself in a country where an action for negligence can have serious consequences, of little use to his society and a disgrace to his profession; so it is a mistake to let a lawyer qualify too easily.

I have already said that the first requirement of the man who is going to be a lawyer is that he should have a sound general education. It should be at least equal to the standard required for university entrance, because without that basic education it simply is not possible for a man to learn and to understand law. Next, he requires a sound theoretical training in law. Such a training can be given by the Council of Legal Education or by a University (though some English Universities omit certain important legal matters from their curricula). He must also be trained in the ethics of the legal profession; and he must know the practical side of his work. So, if Africans are to run the whole of their legal system, those requirements must be kept in mind when we consider the training of African lawyers.

I have said enough about basic education. The theory of the law can be taught well in a university. A new Law Faculty has been started at Dar es Salaam and from that I expect great things; but, like the man who gets called to the English Bar, the graduate from Dar es Salaam will know nothing of the practical side, nothing of accounts and little or nothing of the other matters I have mentioned. Nor do I think that the system of articles can work in the African countries that I have seen. I say that because the majority of those who are practising there have been trained as barristers only—some in India, and some in England.

I have stressed the importance of accounts. Amongst solicitors in England, the Law Society, by its rules and strict discipline, has brought about a universal system of keeping accounts; and, while some offices are much more efficient than others, all offices are run more or less on the same lines. In East Africa, at any rate, the African lawyer is just beginning to find his feet. It is essential, therefore, that newcomers to the profession there should be properly trained in the work that the solicitor does in England.

In my opinion there are only two ways in which this can be done. Either, after a law student has taken his degree, he should do a spell in an English solicitor's office and take the English solicitors' Trust Accounts and Book-keeping Examination, or there should be a post-graduate law school or law schools which he can attend in the African countries. In such schools first and foremost I would have the graduate train for the book-keeping and trust accounts examination. It may well be that six months would be needed for that purpose, because it is not an easy examination and it is imperative that everyone should pass that examination in such a way that the examiners can be sure that he really knows the subject. Then I would have a further twelve months in the practical application of the law, the working of the legal system and the ethics of the profession. I would have such law schools staffed by practical men and not by academic lawyers, and I should like to see a kind of superman who would keep his eye on all the postgraduate law schools, whether in East Africa, West Africa or any other part of Africa. At the end of the second part of the postgraduate law school course I would require another examination to be passed. For preference I would have an oral examination, and I think that in the early days in Africa that may be possible; but if ever you get such numbers of candidates for the legal profession in Africa as we get for the solicitors' examinations in England, an oral examination would become impossible because of the time factor. Many of those interested would, indeed, like to see every articled clerk put through an oral examination as part of his final, but to do that we should have to have practical lawyers conducting the examination. If they had to give each candidate twenty minutes, and we have a thousand candidates a year, you will appreciate what that would mean; and we could not find enough practical men who could give the time to conduct such examinations.

I understand that the course at Dar es Salaam will be a three-year course. If, therefore, this was followed by the one and a half year postgraduate practical course that I have suggested, it would take the men four and a half years to qualify. I know they can get called to the English Bar in much less time than that; but at the present time, in England, if a man has taken a degree he needs six years to qualify as an English solicitor (three years at University and three years in articles), and if he has not taken a degree, but goes straight into a solicitor's office, he has to do five years' articles.

When I was in Africa it was suggested to me that a law school could be run in their spare time by lawyers carrying on practice. I do not believe that such a scheme would work. The postgraduate law school that I envisage would be a whole time law school where candidates would attend five whole days a week. If a law school were staffed by lawyers engaged in their own practice, the law school would, almost certainly, be an evening affair. That would not be satisfactory. It is essential that those who have taken their degrees should go to the postgraduate school and concentrate on their work there. We should never see a satisfactory result if the classes were evening classes.

At the risk of offending a few people I must say that I think it unfortunate that some men who have been called to the English Bar, and have had no practical experience in the practice of the law, have been allowed, without any further qualification, to practise in countries where there is a fused legal profession.

I mentioned earlier that I have learned something of the native courts in some of the countries that I have visited. Many of these courts administer no written law and have no established practice. More often than not legal representation is not permitted to parties before the court or to accused persons. I have discussed this with European lawyers who have had years of experience in Africa. Many of them would like to see native courts brought more or less into line with the courts manned by Europeans, but they say that only when there is a sufficient number of African lawyers practising will this be possible. The task of bringing these courts up to the standard that every lawyer and most other people would desire will be long and heavy, and it is on that account all the more important that those who eventually tackle it should be well trained.

I understand that in all the East African countries there is much to be done to establish ownership to land and get it all properly registered. That, again, is a task which will call for practical knowledge.

Those Africans who look forward to practising as lawyers in Africa will, therefore, have to face up to a great challenge. Those of us who know the countries that have already attained or are about to attain independence all wish to see them successful. One essential to such success is that their laws shall be administered by people who have been properly trained to that end.

9

ISLAMIC LAW IN AFRICA: PROBLEMS OF TODAY AND TOMORROW

PROFESSOR J. N. D. ANDERSON

Professor of Oriental Laws and Director of the
Institute of Advanced Legal Studies in the
University of London

The subject I have chosen for my contribution to this series is 'Islamic Law in Africa: Problems of Today and Tomorrow'. As such it is, I fear, bound to be somewhat discursive and even disjointed, and can certainly make no claim to being comprehensive. I shall, moreover, confine myself almost exclusively to British, or formerly British, territories 'South of the Sahara'; but I shall refer on occasion, chiefly by way of comparison, to North African and the Arab world.

NORTHERN NIGERIA

The obvious place to start, I suppose, is Northern Nigeria. But here the whole situation has completely changed within the last few months.

It was in Northern Nigeria, in the past, that the major clash occurred between Islamic law and English law—chiefly, though by no means exclusively, in the important matter of homicide cases. A number of attempts had been made, ever since *Tsofo Guba's Case*[1] in 1947, to devise legislation which would reconcile the irreconcilable, and eliminate any injustice resultant from the trying of homicide cases, almost indiscriminately, under two totally different legal systems. But these expedients had not proved very satisfactory in practice.

This situation has now been radically altered by the decision of the Northern Nigerian Government totally to exclude the application of Islamic law—whether substantive or procedural—from the administra-

[1] *Tsofo Guba* v *Gwandu Native Authority*, West African Court of Appeal, XII, 141. Cf. my *Islamic Law in Africa*, pp. 181 ff. and 198 ff. The case was not reported until 1956.

tion of criminal justice in the Region, and to substitute a new Penal Code and Criminal Procedure Code, both based on the corresponding codes in the Sudan (which were themselves inspired by the relevant Indian legislation). This bold and unexpected decision was taken on the recommendation of a 'Panel of Jurists' (four out of six of whom were Muslims) on which I had the honour to serve. As a result the clash between Islamic and English law in Northern Nigeria has been virtually eliminated.

It should, perhaps, be remarked at this point that the Panel fully realized that it would be impossible to transform all the native courts in the Region, overnight as it were, from courts accustomed only to Islamic principles of crime and procedure to courts which applied the radically different principles of the new codes. So it suggested that, for an interim period, the native courts should be 'guided' by these codes rather than strictly bound by their provisions; and it explained that this meant that a genuine attempt must always be made to apply them, but that an appellate court should take a lenient view of any minor lapses.[1] To allay the misgivings of the non-Muslim minorities, more-over, the Panel adopted a suggestion of the Minorities Commission and proposed that non-Muslims should be given the right to 'opt out' of trial by Muslim courts, and vice versa, until the Government felt that all courts had adequately mastered the new legislation.[2]

In the event the progress made in the intervening months seems to have been eminently satisfactory, and to reflect the greatest credit on the Commissioner for Native Courts and the team of instructors who have been training the personnel of these courts in the new systems. But it is inevitable, of course, that much still remains to be done. It is regrettable, therefore, that the Northern Nigerian Government should already have felt compelled to bring the opting-out procedure to an end. The reason given for this action was that the procedure had been manifestly abused—both by false declarations of religious affiliation and by the delays and unnecessary expense often deliberately caused by an insistence on the reference of litigation to distant tribunals. This was deplorable; but action designed to remedy these abuses had already

[1] For a discussion of this question, cf. my article 'Conflict of Laws in Northern Nigeria: A New Start', in *International and Comparative Law Quarterly*, Vol. 8, Part 3, 1959; two articles on the recent legislation in Northern Nigeria by Mr Justin Price and myself in *The Modern Law Review*, September 1961; and correspondence in the next two numbers of the same journal.

[2] Cf. *Statement by the Government of the Northern Region of Nigeria on the Reorganization of the Legal and Judicial Systems of the Northern Region.* Kaduna. December 1958.

been taken by the Native Courts (Amendment) Law, 1960, which somewhat restricted the scope of the option as originally interpreted, and empowered a Resident to reject it where, in his opinion, it was not exercised in good faith. It seems clear, however, that this compromise proved ineffective in practice, and that there was no feasible alternative to bringing the opting-out procedure to what might otherwise appear to be an untimely end.

But the Penal Code Law, as promulgated in 1959, was by no means a mere adoption of its Sudanese model. On the contrary, it was adapted to the needs and circumstances of the Northern Region of Nigeria in a number of different respects. Local Muslim opinion, for example, was by no means satisfied with provisions which penalized drunkenness in public or, in certain circumstances, even in private, and insisted on the inclusion of an article penalizing anyone who 'being of the Moslem faith drinks anything containing alcohol other than for medicinal purpose'.[1] Similarly, under 'Offences relating to marriage and incest', Muslim opinion insisted that sexual intercourse with one whom the man or women concerned 'knows or has reason to believe' is not his or her lawful spouse should be punishable in respect of any person who is 'subject to any native law or custom in which extra-marital sexual intercourse is recognized as a criminal offence'.[2] For both these offences, moreover, the 'haddi lashing' of Muslim law might be imposed, in addition to any other punishment, on Muslim offenders.[3]

FUNDAMENTAL RIGHTS

It is obvious that these provisions—and especially section 403—introduce a distinction between citizens on grounds of the religious or customary law to which they are subject. The question, therefore, seems bound to arise, sooner or later, whether they are compatible with the 'fundamental rights' guaranteed in the Federal Constitution. Section 27 of this Constitution, for example, provides that:

'A citizen of Nigeria of a particular community, tribe, place of origin, religion or political opinion shall not, by reason only that he is such a person—

(a) be subjected either expressly by, or in the practical application of, any law in force in Nigeria or any executive or administrative

---

[1] Sect. 403.　　　　[2] Sects. 387 and 388.
[3] As, also, for offences under articles 392–393 (defamation) and 401–402 (drunkenness).

action of the Government of the Federation or the Government of a Region to disabilities or restrictions to which citizens of Nigeria of other communities, tribes, places of origin, religions or political opinions are not made subject; or

(*b*) be accorded either expressly by, or in the practical application of, any law in force in Nigeria or any such executive or administrative action any privilege or advantage that is not conferred on citizens of Nigeria of other communities, tribes, places of origin, religions or political opinions.'

But 'Nothing in this section shall invalidate any law by reason only that the law imposes any disability or restriction or accords any privilege or advantage that, having regard to its nature and to special circumstances pertaining to the persons to whom it applies, is reasonably justifiable in a democratic society'.

As one might expect, this dilemma is not without parallels—or partial parallels—elsewhere. One of the most interesting is provided by an unreported case from Cyrenaica (*Faraj Ali Sherif Dinali* v *The Public Prosecution of Libya*) which I have had the opportunity to read in typescript. In this case the appellant had been convicted, in Benghazi, of selling intoxicating liquor to a Muslim contrary to the Intoxicating Liquors Control Law of Cyrenaica, Article 4 of which provides that 'No person shall sell . . . any intoxicating liquor . . . to any Moslem, knowing him to be a Moslem'. Against this conviction he appealed to the Court of Appeal in Benghazi, principally on the ground that this law was contrary to Articles 11 and 12 of the Constitution of the United Kingdom of Libya, which provide that:

'Libyans shall be equal before the law. They shall enjoy equal civil and political rights, shall have the same opportunities and be subject to the same public duties and obligations, without distinction of religion, belief, race, language, wealth, kinship or political or social opinions.'[1]

'Personal liberty shall be guaranteed and everyone shall be entitled to equal protection of the laws.'[2]

The Court of Appeal referred this constitutional question in 1955 to the Federal Supreme Court, which delivered a lengthy judgment in 1957. This referred, by way of comparison, to Pakistan, India and the United States of America. It observed that in Pakistan the Con-

[1] Art. 11.   [2] Art. 12.

stitution of 1956 had guaranteed equality before the law for all citizens, yet the 'prohibition of the possession or consumption of liquor by a Muslim' had never been called in question. Under the Indian Constitution, again, the fundamental rights of equality before the law, equal protection of the laws, the absence of discrimination on grounds only of religion or race and equality of opportunity in employment are guaranteed, but 'reasonable restrictions' are permitted, and legislation such as the Bombay Prohibition Act, 1949 (which includes special exceptions in favour of military and naval messes and canteens) has been upheld by the Supreme Court.[1] In the United States of America, moreover, all such questions turn on the formula regarding 'due process of law', and the Supreme Court has ruled that 'state law forbidding possession of liquor was within the police power of the state, and that the right to hold intoxicating liquor for personal use was not one of those fundamental privileges of a citizen of the United States of America which no state could abridge'.[2]

The Court then summarized the issue in the following terms:

'Whereas the Constitution of Libya guarantees to all persons in Libya the rights of legal equality, personal liberty, private property, and religious liberty; and a statute of the Province of Cyrenaica prohibits any person from selling intoxicating liquor to a Muslim; and Muslims comprise nearly the total population of Cyrenaica; and whereas Muslims are prohibited by their Islamic religion from drinking intoxicating liquor; and the Islamic religion is the official state religion of Libya; Therefore, are the constitutional rights of a liquor dealer in Cyrenaica unreasonably interfered with by the statute prohibiting him from selling liquor to a Muslim?'

This question was firmly answered in the negative, for in the light of the fact that Cyrenaica was almost solidly Muslim, that it was well known that the law of Islam forbids alcohol, and that Islam was the official religion of the state, the Court concluded that the prohibition of the sale of liquor to Muslims was not unreasonable as an exercise of 'police power'. On the contrary, they regarded the fact that such sales were permitted to non-Muslims as a broad-minded concession to minority opinion.

There are, of course, a number of factors which distinguish this case from the sort of argument to which the clauses in the Penal Code of Northern Nigeria which we are now considering might give rise.

[1] *State of Bombay* v *Balsara* (1951), Sup. Ct. Rep.
[2] (1918), 245 U.S. 304.

The appellant in Cyrenaica was convicted of selling alcohol to a Muslim, under legislation which might conceivably be regarded as primarily a matter of licence control, rather than of himself drinking alcohol, contrary to an article in the Penal Code which makes this an offence for Muslims only. Again, the inhabitants of Cyrenaica are almost solidly Muslim, and Islam has been proclaimed as the official religion of the state; but this is not true of Northern Nigeria, rigidly Muslim though the Hausa-Fulani rulers traditionally are, for the non-Muslim minority there amounts to at least one-third.

If and when, therefore, this question is brought before the courts, the issue will turn on whether it can be regarded as 'reasonably justifiable in a democratic society' to penalize Muslims, alone, for flouting the dictates of their religion by drinking alcohol. That Article 27 of the Constitution of Nigeria does not exclude all differentiation between citizens on grounds of religion is sufficiently obvious from the fact that the law of marriage, divorce and inheritance to which individuals are subject depends entirely on the religion they profess or on the customary law of their community. This principle has been amply recognized in India, where the courts have reiterated that Article 15 of the Indian Constitution (which prohibits the state from discriminating against any citizen on grounds only of religion, caste, sex or place of birth) does not preclude the application of the personal law of the parties in such matters or, indeed, 'classification based on reasonable grounds for specified objects'[1]—and this even extends to the criminal law in so far as bigamy is concerned. But can this principle properly be extended to the enforcement by penal sanction in the courts, in respect of Muslims only, of a prohibition outside the scope of family law, however emphatically this prohibition may be enjoined upon them by the Islamic texts? It might, in any case, have been preferable to limit the penalty to ritual lashing alone, and to allow a Muslim to claim exemption, if he wished, at the cost of what would no doubt be regarded as a partical repudiation of the authority of his religion. But however this may be, it is quite possible that the Judicial Committee of the Privy Council will one day be called upon to advise Her Majesty as to whether these articles in the Penal Code of the Northern Region are contrary to the Federal Constitution of Nigeria.

Perhaps I might here be permitted an aside. I am reliably informed that there is now a new drink—or at least a new name for a drink—

[1] Cf. *Srinivasa* v *Saraswathi*, I.L.R. 1953 Mad. 78. This case arose out of the Madras Hindu Bigamy (Prevention and Divorce) Act, 1949, which made bigamy an offence for Hindus, but not for Muslims.

in places of refreshment in Northern Nigeria. The customer merely demands a 'Krola Penal Code', and he is given a Krola (a local product rather like coca-cola) suitably 'laced' with brandy or gin, the colour of the latter being adequately disguised by the former!

Incidentally, it is interesting to observe that the penalties for illicit sex-relations, defamation or drinking alcohol, including the 'haddi lashing', can now be imposed after much less stringent rules of evidence have been observed than was previously incumbent in any case involving the 'prescribed offences' of the Sharī'a law. In cases of illicit sex-relations the Sharī'a insists either on a confession or the testimony of four legally competent witnesses to the very act, and in default of this almost impossible standard of evidence imposes the prescribed penalty for slander on the accuser, while defamation or wine-drinking must be proved by a similar confession or by the testimony of two competent witnesses.[1] Under the new statute law, on the other hand, these offences may be proved in all the ordinary ways. This represents an amalgamation of the traditional with the modern in a manner which seems to be of questionable propriety,[2] while the combination of a prescribed and discretionary punishment, for one and the same offence, is totally contrary to principle.

ISLAMIC AND CUSTOMARY LAW

But while the new legislation in Northern Nigeria has largely eliminated conflicts between the Islamic law and the English law, this is by no means true of conflicts between Islamic and customary law. Such conflicts arise to some extent, of course, in every Muslim land; but prior to 1956 the statute law of Nigeria gave ample scope for *ad hoc* solutions. This was because Islamic law was invariably subsumed in Nigeria, up to that date, under the capacious umbrella of 'native law and custom'—an expedient which allowed for an almost unlimited series of gradations from a comparatively rigid application of the Islamic texts, in staunchly Muslim areas, to an exclusively pagan customary law, in the areas into which Islam had never penetrated. But in 1956 the mistake (as I see it) was made of setting up a 'Moslem Court of Appeal' as yet another appellate court for cases 'governed

---

[1] Except that the Mālikī law, alone, regards the pregnancy of an unmarried woman, or the smell of alchohol in a Muslim's breath, as constituting a *prima facie* case against them.

[2] New recommendations regarding these sections of the Penal Code have recently been made by the 'Panel of Jurists', on a return visit at the invitation of the Northern Nigeria Government.

by Moslem law', which were broadly defined as those cases 'to the determination of which it is lawful and appropriate that the principles of Moslem Law shall be applied to the exclusion of any other system of law or of native law and custom';[1] and in such cases the Moslem Court of Appeal was required to 'administer, observe, and enforce the observance of, the principles and provisions of Moslem Law of the Maliki School as interpreted at the place where the trial at first instance took place. . . .'[2]

This may sound reasonable enough. It was obvious from the first, however, that the effect of this innovation would be an increasing tendency towards rigidity and uniformity in the enforcement of the principles of the Mālikī texts even in those respects, and those regions, where local customary law had hitherto prevailed. I stressed this in an article I wrote in 1957 entitled 'Law and Custom in Muslim Areas in Africa: Recent Developments in Nigeria'.[3] Part of this article was concerned with the criminal law and procedure, which have, of course, now been replaced by the new legislation. The Panel of Jurists recommended, indeed, in 1958 that Islamic law, as such, should in future be confined to the personal and family law of Muslim litigants, although it might also be applied, on occasions, as the law under which some contract had in fact been concluded or as the law of tort locally recognized as valid; that the Moslem Court of Appeal, as then constituted, should be abolished; and that a Sharī'a Court of Appeal should be instituted as the final court in matters of personal status and family relationships under the Islamic law.[4] Even so, the question still remains at large as to what cases, precisely, should be so classified.

A few examples will illustrate the problems involved. A disputed point, just at present, concerns litigation regarding rights of inheritance in land. In the past questions of land tenure have been regarded as governed throughout Northern Nigeria—except, perhaps, in the province of Zaria, on the shores of Lake Chad, and to some extent in the immediate environs of Kano and Sokoto—by customary law; and litigation on this subject has normally been handled by the Emirs' Councils rather than the alkalai or, at a lower level, by administrative rather than judicial authorities.[5] Today, however, the alkalai and the

---

[1] Moslem Court of Appeal Law, sect. 3(3), and Native Courts Law, sect. 62(2), both of 1956.

[2] Moslem Court of Appeal Law, sect. 15(1).

[3] *Civilizations*, VII (1957), I, pp. 17–31.

[4] Except that an appeal would still lie to the Federal Supreme Court in any case which involves 'fundamental rights' or other constitutional issues.

[5] Cf. *Islamic Law in Africa*, pp. 184 ff.

Sharī'a Court of Appeal are increasingly insistent that they should themselves administer, under the Islamic law of inheritance, land 'owned' by deceased Muslims. This contention is challenged by the Emirs—partly, no doubt, because they regard questions of land tenure as a vested interest, but also on the ground that rights in land in Northern Nigeria do not, generally speaking, amount to full ownership, but rather to a right to the use and enjoyment of land in which the ultimate title vests in the Government. As such, of course, its legal position might be regarded as similar to that of 'Mīrī' land in the Ottoman Empire, rights in which became progressively assimilated to full ownership in so far as contractual dispositions were concerned, but in regard to which the Islamic law of inheritance was never applied. And it is curious, in this context, to observe that the special law of inheritance enacted for such land in the Ottoman Empire[1] has now been adopted in Iraq as the law of intestate succession applicable to all property, real and personal, to the total exclusion of the Islamic law.[2]

In Northern Nigeria, on the contrary, the tendency is to extend the application of Islamic law in regard to land cases; and it will be interesting to observe how the present conflict of interests and opinions is solved. One possible solution would be for a Native Authority which doubted whether the courts were applying the right law in land cases to make a declaration, under the Native Authority Law, 1954, of the customary law which is locally applicable in this matter.

But besides questions of land, there are parts of Northern Nigeria where the local tribe or community follows its customary law of inheritance regardless of the fact that a few individuals may have embraced Islam. This phenomenon raises problems in many parts of Africa. From the point of view of Muslim orthodoxy, of course, the estate of anyone who has embraced Islam, however rudimentary his knowledge may have been of all that this would entail, should be governed exclusively by the Islamic law—including the rule that all his non-Muslim relatives, however close, should be totally excluded in favour of any Muslim kinsman. From the point of view of tribal opinion, on the other hand, this seems a preposterous requirement. It is interesting to observe that in Tanganyika this dilemma has given rise to a legislative requirement that the estate of a member of a native tribe 'shall be administered according to the law of that tribe unless the deceased at any time professed the Mohammedan

[1] Ottoman Land Law, 1858, as finally amended in 1911.
[2] Cf. my article 'A Law of Personal Status for Iraq', in *The International and Comparative Law Quarterly*, October 1960, pp. 559 ff.

religion and the court exercising jurisdiction over his estate is satisfied from the written or oral declarations of the deceased or his acts or manner of life that the deceased intended his estate to be administered, either wholly or in part, according to Mohammedan law . . .'; but that the estate of a 'Swahili', on the other hand, 'shall be administered according to Mohammedan law unless the court . . . is satisfied from the written or oral declarations of the deceased or his acts or manner of life that he intended his estate to be administered, either wholly or in part, according to any tribal law. . . .'[1] The same enactment also explicitly provides that no one shall 'be deprived of a right to succession to property by reason of that person having renounced or having been excluded from the communion of any religion'.[2] In Kenya, again, the position is somewhat similar; but there the criterion as to whether the Islamic law of succession should be applied is the fact that the deceased must not only have professed Islam but either be the child of a Muslim marriage or have himself contracted a marriage according to Islamic law—which presumably means that he must either be a second generation Muslim or have given proof of a desire to follow the law of Islam in practice.[3] But no such criterion has been adopted in Northern Nigeria, and the question seems very much at large. Unless, therefore, the Native Authorities of the more predominantly pagan areas make suitable declarations of their customary laws of inheritance, there will always be the possibility of a Muslim relative trying to displace all non-Muslims and appropriate the entire estate of a deceased Muslim; and it is exceedingly dubious whether the Sharī'a Court of Appeal would regard even a declaration of this sort as ousting their jurisdiction over the estate of anyone who had professed to embrace Islam.

Other cases of actual or potential conflict are provided by questions of marriage and divorce. Of these three examples must suffice.

When a woman is dissatisfied with her marriage, and wants a divorce, customary law in fact prevails over the strict requirements of Mālikī law even in the most rigidly Muslim areas in Northern Nigeria.[4] As a consequence a woman who is able and willing to refund her 'bride-wealth' can always in practice secure a dissolution of marriage, regardless of whether her husband is prepared to agree. This has, no doubt, been facilitated in West Africa by the fact that the Mālikī law,

---

[1] Administration (Small Estates) (Amendment) Ordinance, 1947, sect. 18(1).
[2] Sect. 18(4).
[3] Mohammedan Marriage, Divorce and Succession Ordinance, 1920, sect. 4.
[4] Cf. *Islamic Law in Africa*, pp. 209 ff.

alone, itself allows this solution of marital discord to be forced on a husband if family 'arbitrators' have been appointed, have concluded that the reconciliation of the parties is impracticable, and have decided that the wife is at least partially to blame. It has also been facilitated by the fact that a recalcitrant wife will never, in West Africa, be forcibly taken back to her marriage home by the police. But the real reason for this phenomenon lies in the customary law, to which even the most rigid alkalai in Northern Nigeria have in practice capitulated in this matter.

Recently, however, the Grand Qāḍī—himself at that time a Sudanese —has persuaded the Commissioner for Native Courts to issue, as a Circular addressed to all the courts, a statement[1] which sets out, in contradistinction, first the current practice in this matter and then the strict requirements of the Mālikī texts. Under these a woman should be given a judicial divorce, without repayment of her dower, if she can prove that she has been cruelly treated. If, on the other hand, a dispute has arisen but she cannot prove such cruelty, then arbitrators should be appointed to attempt to reconcile the parties or, if this proves impossible, to bring the marriage to an end—with or without a refund of dower as circumstances may require. But, in default of either proof of cruelty or a decision by such arbitrators, she should never be given a divorce without the husband's consent. It appears, moreover, from this circular that cases have occurred in which a woman has been given a divorce by an alkali under the customary law, and has in due course remarried; then, on appeal by the husband to the Sharī'a Court of Appeal, this judgment has been reversed and the second marriage annulled—even, on occasions, after the woman has become pregnant by her new husband.

This is clearly a complex question. It is obviously undesirable that a woman should remarry after a divorce which is likely to be reversed on appeal; and it is certainly preferable that a woman who can prove cruelty should not be forced to make any repayment of dower (for the desire for such repayment might well be the motive for the cruelty), and also that the stability of marriage should be safeguarded in any practicable way. But it may pertinently be urged that what is sauce for the goose is sauce for the gander, so while a husband can divorce his wife at any moment and for any (or no) reason, it is difficult to speak convincingly about the sanctity, or stability, of marriage; and it seems highly dubious how far it is wise for the Sharī'a Court of Appeal to attempt to override in this matter the customary law which prevails throughout the whole of West Africa.

[1] Dated August 14, 1961, and prepared by the Grand Qāḍī himself.

Cases occur, moreover, particularly in areas which are pre-dominantly pagan, in which persons who are at least nominally Muslims contract a marriage under native law and custom. A case of this sort has recently been the subject of litigation, I understand, in the High Court of the Northern Region. Here the court was satisfied that two Muslims in Benue Province had in fact concluded their marriage under customary rather than Islamic law; so it dealt with the marriage —very rightly, I would observe with the utmost respect—on the basis of the law of the contract. It is obvious, however, that had this case come before the Sharī'a Court of Appeal the result might have been very different—for the Sharī'a Court of Appeal Law not only gives that court competence to decide 'any question of Moslem law regarding a marriage concluded in accordance with that law . . .',[1] but also, where all the parties to a marriage are Muslims or where the deceased was a Muslim, 'any question of Moslem law regarding a marriage . . . will or succession'.[2]

It is clear, however, that this form of words would *not* give the Sharī'a Court of Appeal any competence in those cases—comparatively frequent in provinces such as Ilorin—where a Christian man marries a Muslim girl. Such a union is, of course, absolutely void under Islamic law, for a Muslim girl may never be given in marriage to any non-Muslim. Litigation arising under such unions is, in practice, taken sometimes to this court and sometimes to that, and the judgments probably vary almost as much as the courts which give them. It seems clear, however, that where the parties to such a union intend their marriage to be governed by customary law, as would almost invariably be the case, no other system of law is properly applicable.

It should, too, be noticed in this context that the Sharī'a Court of Appeal Law also gives that court competence to decide any other questions where 'all the parties to the proceedings (whether or not they are Moslems) have by writing under their hand requested the court that hears the case in the first instance to determine that case in accordance with Moslem law'.[3] This presumably means that the liti-gants can, by their unilateral decision, decide that a case should be governed by Islamic law even where a quite different law would

[1] Sect. 12(*a*).

[2] Sect. 12(*b*) and (*c*). Originally, indeed, these sections did not include the words 'of Moslem law', which were added by the Sharia Court of Appeal (Amendment) Law, 1960, with just such circumstances in view. But the Sharī'a Court of Appeal might well take a very broad view of how these words should be construed.

[3] Sect. 12(*e*).

normally be applied. This seems to be wrong in principle; for it should be for the legislature, rather than the individual, to decide the law that shall be applicable to this matter or that.

EAST AFRICA

To turn from West to East Africa, one of the most controversial questions at the present time is provided by *waqf* cases from Kenya, Tanganyika or Zanzibar. One of these is at present pending before the Judicial Committee of the Privy Council; so I had better restrain myself from making the comments I should like to make on the decision of the Court of Appeal for Eastern Africa which is the subject of this further appeal. I shall confine myself at the moment, therefore, to a general consideration of the points of disharmony, in this matter, between the British courts and competent Muslim opinion.

The law of *waqf*, as applied by courts of a British background in India, Aden and East Africa, has been fundamentally vitiated by a series of cases culminating in the decision of the Judicial Committee in *Abul Fata* v *Russomoy*[1] as long ago as 1894. In this case their Lordships invalidated a family *waqf* on the grounds that the ultimate gift to the poor had 'been put into this settlement merely to give it a colour of piety, and so to legalize arrangements meant to serve for the aggrandizement of a family'; for they could not see how successions of 'inalienable life-interests' could be forbidden under the 'general law of Islam' but could become legal 'if only the settlor says that they are made as a wakf, in the name of God, or for the sake of the poor'. This was, of course, a very natural decision for judges trained in English law, who did not understand, first, that it is exceedingly common in Islamic law for some disposition to be illegal if effected in one way, yet perfectly legal and valid if effected in another way; secondly, that the Islamic law of all the orthodox schools has regarded *waqfs* which provide for the income to be distributed among a series of beneficiaries, generation after generation—whether these represent the descendants of the founder or of any other person—as perfectly valid, provided they are created in the proper form; thirdly, that Abū Yūsuf the Ḥanafī also regarded *waqfs* in which the founder reserved even the whole income for himself for life as equally valid; and, fourthly, that it was only some jurists (such as Muhammad ibn al-Ḥasan al-Shaybānī, the Ḥanafī) who insisted that the *waqf* deed must include an ultimate reservation for the poor or some other charitable purpose which

[1] 22 I.A. 76.

cannot fail, and that the reason for such insistence, where it occurs, is *not* to introduce a charitable element which would otherwise be lacking,[1] but to provide an ultimate disposition which could never come to an end.

This decision caused so much dissatisfaction in India that it had to be remedied by the Mussulman Wakf Validating Act, 1913. The preamble to this recites that 'Whereas doubts have arisen regarding the validity of wakfs created by persons professing the Mussulman faith in favour of themselves, their families, children and descendants ... and whereas it is expedient to remove such doubts;' section 3 explicitly provides for the validity of a *waqf* for, 'among other purposes', the 'maintenance and support wholly or partially' of the founder's 'family, children or descendants' and also, if the founder were a Ḥanafī, for 'his own maintenance and support during his lifetime or for the payment of his debts'—provided only that the 'ultimate benefit' is in such cases 'expressly or impliedly reserved for the poor or for any other purpose recognized by the Mussulman law as a religious, pious or charitable purpose of a permanent character'; while section 4 explicitly declares that no such *waqf* shall be deemed to be invalid 'merely because the benefit reserved therein for the poor or other religious, pious or charitable purpose of a permanent nature is postponed until after the extinction of the family, children or descendants of the person making the wakf'.

There can be little doubt that the intention behind this Act was to restore the principles of the classical texts as they had always been understood by Muslim jurists. It must, of course, be admitted that the drafting, in some respects at least, left a good deal to be desired; but the impression is almost inescapable that the courts have at times given this enactment an unnecessarily restricted interpretation. And it is regrettable—if understandable—that British courts in Aden, Zanzibar and Kenya have all felt bound by the Privy Council decision in *Abul Fata's Case*, in spite of the fact that this has been recognized by all competent persons as a wholly mistaken interpretation of the Islamic law; so the legislature has in each case been compelled to pass a 'Wakf Validating Act', on the Indian model, in order to restore the Islamic law as it was before the courts had misinterpreted it. One Judge in Kenya did, indeed, distinguish the Anglo-Muhammadan law which had grown up in India from the doctrine of the Islamic texts when he remarked that 'A study of the question shows that while the

---

[1] On the contrary, a gift to relatives, even though rich, was regarded as a perfectly valid 'approach to God' if made in this form.

Mahomedan law, uninfluenced from outside sources, permitted perpetuities and the erection of wakfs for family aggrandizement solely, the influence of English Judges and of the Privy Council has gradually encroached on this position'.[1] Unhappily, however, when an appeal from East Africa on this subject reached the Judicial Committee in 1952,[2] their Lordships not only felt unable to reverse their previous decision but even to distinguish it—as they could very easily have done—on the grounds that the Shāfi'ī law certainly does not require a waqf deed to include an ultimate dedication to some purpose which cannot fail. They also made deprecating reference to the words of Hamilton, J., quoted above. Their Lordships were very inadequately assisted by counsel in this appeal; but there can be no doubt (with great respect) that they gave expression to a number of dicta which leave anyone who has studied the matter almost in a state of nervous prostration!

Nor does the tale of woe stop at this point. For the courts in East Africa have also given the most restricted interpretation to the various Wakf Validating Acts which have been passed. I have previously discussed this matter at some length,[3] so must confine myself here to a brief reference to two points only: first, the question whether there must be an explicit dedication to some charity which cannot fail; and, secondly, the nature of the life interest which may be granted to successive generations of beneficiaries. Unhappily, waqfs have repeatedly been invalidated in East Africa simply because their deeds 'contained no specific gift over to the poor or to any other purpose upon the extinction of the descendants of the Settlor', in spite of the fact that the dominant doctrine of the Shāfi'ī law (and these were Shāfi'ī waqfs) makes no such requirement, and that the Kenya Wakf Commissioners Ordinance allows such gift to be implicit 'in any case in which the personal law of the person making the wakf so permits'[4] (and the very use of the word waqf in Shāfi'ī law represents such implicit dedication), while the Ordinance also includes the explicit statement that the 'absence of any reservation of the ultimate benefit in property the subject of the wakf for the poor . . . shall not invalidate the wakf if the personal law of the maker of the wakf does not require

[1] Hamilton, J., in *Talibu bin Mwijaka* v *Executors of Siwa Haji*, (1907) 2 E.A.L.R. 33.

[2] *Fatuma binti Mohamed* v *Mohamed bin Salim Bakhshuwen* [1952] A.C.I. Cf. *Islamic Law in Africa*, pp. 96 ff. and 340 ff.

[3] Cf. 'Waqfs in East Africa', in *Journal of African Law*, III, 3, 1959.

[4] Sect. 4(1) (b) (iii).

any such reservation.' It seems inescapable that this clause was, in fact, inserted in the Ordinance particularly to cover the Shāfiʿī law, but that the courts have frustrated the intention of the legislature.

As for the second point, the provision in the Wakf Validating Acts that establishes the validity of a *waqf* 'for the maintenance and support, either wholly or partly, of any person including the family, children, descendants or kindred of the maker',[1] has been given an excessively restricted meaning—as, indeed, in some Indian cases, but against the general trend of judicial decisions in that sub-continent as this has now become established. Even on a dictionary meaning of these terms, to 'maintain' means, *inter alia*, to 'support one's state of life by expenditure', and to 'support' means 'to strengthen the position of a person by one's assistance'. On this basis, therefore, it would seem to be exclusively within the discretion of the founder of a *waqf* to allow the beneficiaries any sum he may desire, without any question whatever of a *waqf* being invalidated by the mere fact that he provided that the 'income should be paid' to such beneficiary without any intention whatever that this income must only be used to meet the cost of accommodation, food, and clothing. Any such distinction would, indeed, be utterly alien to the Islamic texts, which use the phrase 'eat of the *waqf*' in the sense of 'enjoy its income'. The Indian Wakf Validating Act, moreover, explicitly allows a reservation by a Ḥanafī founder for the 'payment of his debts', without specification of their nature or extent; and it would be exceedingly strange if a founder could do this for himself but not for his family, when the Islamic law is in fact much more reserved regarding what he can do for himself than what he can do for others. It would seem, moreover, that an application of the principles enshrined in *Heydon's Case*[2] would have pointed strongly against giving these words a meaning which frustrates the very purpose for which the legislation was enacted.

I should, perhaps, observe in passing that I am by no means an advocate of family perpetuities, and recent legislation in various countries in the Middle East[3] shows that modern Muslim opinion is also against them. But it is surely preferable to remedy this situation by direct legislation, rather than by what I can only describe—with great respect—as judicial misinterpretation.

[1] Cf. sect. 4(1) (a) in the Kenya Wakf Commissioners Ordinance, 1951.
[2] (1584) 3 Rep. 76—*per* Lord Coke.
[3] Cf. my articles 'The Religious Element in Waqf-Endowments', in *Journal of Royal Central Asian Society*, July 1951; 'Reforms in Islamic Law IX', in *The Muslim World*, XLII, 4, 1952; and references in 'The Reform of Islamic Law in the Sudan', in *Sudan Law Journal and Reports*, 1960, p. 309 f.; etc.

REFORMS IN FAMILY LAW

Space precludes any discussion of another relevant question in Kenya —namely, the law of evidence and procedure applicable in the 'Moslem Courts' of the Protectorate.[1] Instead, I want to turn my attention, finally, to a matter that has not yet arisen in any acute form in any of these countries, but which seems bound to arise before very long— namely, certain reforms which may be required in the family law as this is applied by the courts.

This is, of course, a matter of very considerable delicacy with respect to a law which is regarded as based on divine revelation and considered to be virtually immutable. But it has been effected in recent years in almost all the Arab countries, one after another, by means of a variety of ingenious expedients. In the Sudan, for instance, it is expressly provided that the Sharī'a courts shall follow the authoritative doctrines of the Ḥanafī school except in matters in which the Grand Qāḍī otherwise directs in a Judicial Circular or Memorandum, in which case the decisions shall be in accordance with such other doctrines of the Ḥanafīs or other Muslim jurists as are set forth in such Circular or Memorandum.[2] On occasions, moreover, the reformers—both in the Sudan and elsewhere—have gone well beyond an eclectic choice between the doctrines of the recognized schools and jurists and have adopted a view which is attributed to some extinct or even heterodox school; or which represents a combination in a single whole of parts of two different doctrines that may, in fact, rest on contradictory premises; or which reflects some contemporary deduction from the sacred texts.

It is by means of these expedients that the father's right—under Mālikī and Shāfi'ī law—to give even an adult daughter in forced marriage, provided only that she had not been married before, has been brought to an end in Tunisia, Morocco and the Sudan. To this there is as yet no parallel in East or West Africa—except that in the Somaliland Protectorate the Natives' Betrothal and Marriage Ordinance, 1928, provides that 'Any unmarried woman betrothed by her father or guardian shall have the right to register personally . . . her refusal of the betrothal, and in that event her betrothal shall forthwith be terminated'.[3] There can be little doubt, however, that some change

---

[1] Cf. *Islamic Law in Africa*, pp. 99 ff.
[2] Sudan Mohammedan Law Courts Organisation and Procedure Regulations, 1915, sect. 53.
[3] Sect. 3(1).

in the Shāfi'ī and Mālikī law in this matter, as applied in East and West Africa respectively, will be demanded before very long. It was only in 1960 that the Grand Qāḍī of the Sudan felt compelled to issue a Judicial Circular[1] on this subject which established the following principles:

(1) That a girl who has reached puberty and has already been married can be given in marriage only with her explicit consent to both husband and dower.[2] This is normal Mālikī doctrine.

(2) That a virgin who has reached puberty must give her consent to both husband and dower, although her silence will be taken for consent. Should she, nevertheless, be given in marriage after signifying that she does *not* consent, no subsequent acceptance will validate the contract.[3] This represents what is substantially Ḥanafī doctrine, except that the Ḥanafī girl who has reached puberty, may, alternatively, give herself in marriage without the intervention of her guardian.

(3) That should an adult virgin be informed of a contract of marriage which has been concluded on her behalf without her consent being sought at all, the contract will be void unless she makes an explicit statement of acceptance.[4] This, again, is substantially Ḥanafī doctrine.

Another subject which may well require attention is the matter of child marriage. All the recognized schools of Islamic law allow certain guardians to contract their infant wards in marriage at an age at which consent, even if given, is of no legal effect. Most modern Muslims, however, realize that child marriage is eminently undesirable; and legislation has been introduced in almost all the Arab countries to discourage or prevent it.[5] In East and West Africa the solitary parallel is that the Penal Codes, in some countries only, penalize any attempt by a husband to consummate his marriage with a wife who has not reached a prescribed age.[6] So it is interesting to observe in this context that the Judicial Circular issued in the Sudan last year, to which reference has already been made, dealt with this subject in a single article which provides that where there is anxiety about the morals of a girl who has not reached puberty, but who is not less than ten years old, she may be given in marriage, with consent of court, on condition

---

[1] No. 54 of 1960.   [2] Art. 6, para. 2.   [3] Art. 6, para. 1.   [4] Art. 7.
[5] Cf. my articles on 'Modernisation of Islamic Law in the Sudan', pp. 300–2; on 'Reforms in Family Law in Morocco' (*Journal of African Law*, II, 3, 1958), and on 'A Law of Personal Status for Iraq' (*International and Comparative Law Quarterly*, October 1960).
[6] Cf. *Islamic Law in Africa*, pp. 44, 62, 129 and 255.

that she herself is willing, that her husband is her 'equal', that the dower is appropriate, and that her trousseau is suitable.[1] This presumably means that a minor child cannot be given in marriage in any other circumstances whatever; but it is curious that such a major reform should have been introduced in such implicit, and almost backhanded, fashion.

Yet another subject which is bound to come under discussion, one of these days, is the restriction of polygamy. It is significant that the contraction of polygamous marriages has been submitted to restrictions in recent years in Syria, Morocco and Iraq, and has been forbidden altogether in Tunisia.[2] The juristic basis for so radical a change in the law was provided by the great Egyptian reformer, Muḥammad 'Abduh, who insisted that the Qur'anic 'Verse of Polygamy' should be made the basis for a judicial prohibition of polygamy where the prospective husband cannot be trusted to treat a plurality of wives with equal justice.[3]

Curiously enough, the tendency in Ghana seemed, recently, to be set in the reverse direction. Thus the White Paper on Marriage, Divorce and Inheritance (W.P. No. 3/61) published in May, 1961, suggests that a man should be allowed to register one wife only, but that if he 'marries or has issue with another woman, this will not constitute an offence'[4]—regardless of whether he has previously contracted a marriage under Christian, Muslim or customary law. It is strange that Ghana should be contemplating an extension of the scope of polygamy just when most of the Arab countries are restricting it.

In regard to divorce, the need to give ill-treated wives a right to a judicial dissolution of marriage for cruelty, desertion, etc., may well arise under the Shāfiʿī law applicable in East Africa. But this is already adequately covered by the Mālikī law in force in West Africa; so it

[1] Sect. 8. See my article, to which reference has made been above, p. 302.

[2] For a summary, see *ibid.*, pp. 306-8, or my articles on 'The Syrian Law of Personal Status', on 'The Tunisian Law of Personal Status', and on 'A Law of Personal Status for Iraq', in *The International and Comparative Law Quarterly* for 1955, 1958 and 1960, respectively.

[3] A further condition—that he should be financially able to support his existing dependants as well as the new wife—has also been suggested.

[4] It seems, however, that these proposals met with considerable opposition. As a result, the draft 'Marriage, Divorce and Inheritance Bill' published in May 1962, provides for the registration of only one 'marriage', rather than only one 'wife'; speaks about 'any other woman with whom a man has children', rather than other 'wives'; and makes no explicit mention of the fact that relations with other women would no longer constitute an offence, although this would in fact be the case.

would be simple to enact suitable legislation in East Africa based on Mālikī authority, as has already been done in almost all the Arab countries.[1] Much more difficulty would be experienced in any attempt to discourage unilateral repudiation of a wife by her husband; but this is so common an occurrence in parts of East Africa that something may well have to be done about it. In the Arab countries a certain amount of progress has been made in this matter also; for the 'triple' divorce in a comprehensive formula, or on one and the same occasion, has been reduced to a single, and therefore revocable, divorce, and the scope of suspended or conditional repudiations has been severely limited.[2] In Syria and Morocco, indeed, a husband can be forced to pay financial compensation, in suitable circumstances, to a divorced wife,[3] while in Tunisia and Iraq no divorce is effective unless pronounced—or at least registered—in court.[4]

Much more could be added, but space forbids. Suffice it to say, then, that legislation proposed in Ghana aims at unifying the law of marriage, divorce and inheritance on a national basis, rather than leaving such matters to the religious, customary or 'personal' laws of individual citizens. Such a development would certainly prove attractive in any country in which nationalism provides an urge towards unification and secularization; but it seems most unlikely that public opinion would welcome such a radical change in most of these countries for many years to come. Certainly the suggestions made to this end in the Ghana White Paper were retrogressive rather than progressive; and the unfavourable public reaction to some of these proposals seems to have led to their modification in terminology and ethos, if not in substance and law.[5]

[1] Cf. my book *Islamic Law in the Modern World*, pp. 53 ff., and articles referred to therein.

[2] *Ibid.*, pp. 55 ff.

[3] Cf. *The Syrian Law of Personal Status*, p. 41 f., and *Reforms in Family Law in Morocco*, p. 157.

[4] Cf. *The Tunisian Law of Personal Status*, p. 271, and *A Law of Personal Status for Iraq*, p. 554.

[5] Cf. p.182, and footnote (4).

10

LIABILITY UNDER THE NIGERIA CRIMINAL CODE: A HISTORICAL AND COMPARATIVE STUDY

DR R. Y. HEDGES

Formerly Chief Justice, Western Region of Nigeria

The subject of my paper is 'Liability under the Nigeria Criminal Code'. The words which follow—'A Historical and Comparative Study'— are almost otiose, for it seems to me that the subject could hardly be dealt with in any other way.

Perhaps I should say at the outset that I am only concerned with the Criminal Code which applies in Lagos and in the Western and Eastern Regions of Nigeria. The Northern Region has recently introduced its own Penal Code, of an entirely different nature, and one more suited, in my belief at all events, to a community which is predominantly Muslim.

ORIGIN OF THE CODE

The Nigeria Criminal Code, as we know it, came into force in 1916, and applied to the Colony and to the whole of the Protectorate. It was based on the code then in force in Northern Nigeria. The latter, which was submitted in draft in 1903, was practically the Queensland Code, modified and curtailed—considerably so in parts—to suit local needs. Many of the Queensland provisions were replaced by provisions taken from the Gold Coast Code where they seemed more suitable to the locality, and occasionally sections provided in the Indian Penal Code and in H. L. Stephen's draft of an English Criminal Code were substituted for more or less corresponding provisions of the Queensland Code. In addition, various offences under existing Northern Nigeria Proclamations were introduced.

It seems that the Southern Provinces were not anxious to follow the Northern Nigeria model but wished to introduce a code based on the Straits Settlements model, which in turn is a modification of the Indian Code. There is a minute in the Colonial Office files as follows:

'Southern Nigeria should wait and adopt the Northern Nigeria Code, supplementing it if and when necessary, so that there may be only one main stream of criminal jurisprudence in Nigeria'. One cannot help but reflect, more than half a century later, that Northern Nigeria made a mistake in not adopting the Indian Code at the outset, whilst Southern Nigeria made a mistake in wanting to do so.

Nigerian lawyers may be surprised to hear that their Criminal Code is largely a product of Australia. Perhaps they would be surprised even more to learn that it embodies much that was good in the Italian Penal Code of 1888, one of the finest Codes in existence at that time, whilst a few of its provisions are derived from the Penal Code of New York State.

Before pursuing this matter further I think I ought to say a little on the subject of codification of criminal law generally. In 1880 a Criminal Code Bill was introduced into the English Parliament, but owing to organized opposition in the House of Commons it was not even read a second time. It has been said that the history of codification of criminal law in England stopped at that point. Much has been done in the way of consolidation, but that of course is a different matter. The work done on the Bill was not, however, in any way wasted. The draft English Code of 1880, with suitable adaptations, was adopted by various Colonial legislatures. The English model was followed in New Zealand (Act No. 56 of 1893) and in Canada (55 & 56 Vict., c. 29), and oddly enough in certain native territories in South Africa. It had some influence on the Queensland Code, but I shall have something more to say about that later.

Colonial legislatures in the Far East have been more inclined to adopt the Indian model. Work on the Indian Penal Code was begun by a draft by Lord Macaulay, framed during his tenure of office on the Viceroy's Council between the years 1834 and 1838. During twenty years it remained a draft, as the English Code remains to this day, but after an elaborate revision by the Legislative Council it became law in 1860. Since that date it has been introduced in one form or another into several parts of Her Majesty's dominions in the Far East. Perhaps the best known version is the Straits Settlements model. This was introduced, with local variations, in Sarawak and elsewhere. British North Borneo, during the period of rule by the Chartered Company, used the Indian Penal Code, and it was left to the Courts to make suitable adaptations. The territory became a Colony in 1946, and not very long afterwards North Borneo found it more convenient to adopt the Sarawak Code. Brunei followed suit for the same reason.

It is clear that both the English model (although the original draft never found its way onto the Statute Book) and the Indian model have had a profound effect on the criminal law in the component parts of the British Commonwealth. A bold legislative experiment in Australia has produced a third model, which may be called the Queensland model. The Queensland Criminal Code was passed in 1899 and came into force on January 1, 1901. It had a great influence on the Code of Western Australia, and to a lesser extent on the Tasmanian Code. It was also introduced into the territory of Papua and what was formerly the Mandated Territory of New Guinea.

The Queensland Criminal Code was largely the work of Sir Samuel Griffith, who later became the first Chief Justice of the High Court of Australia. The final draft was settled after considering the report of a Royal Commission. Sir Samuel Griffith embodied in the Code a good many provisions which were not to be found in the draft English Code of 1880, but which he considered to be correct statements of the common law or propositions which he thought would commend themselves as rules which ought to be recognized as the law. He was also at pains to acknowledge his indebtedness to the framers of the Italian Penal Code of 1888, of which he was a great admirer. To quote his own words:

'I have derived very great assistance from this Code which is I believe in many respects the most complete and perfect Penal Code in existence. I have also derived much help from the masterly Ministerial explanation (*Relazione*) of Signor Zanardelli, who had charge of this Code during its passage through Parliament.'

As I mentioned earlier, he also had frequent recourse to the Penal Code of New York State.

To return to the subject of my paper, the Nigeria Criminal Code is based on the Queensland model. I have dealt with the history of the matter at some length, because I believe it to be very important. It opens the way for a comparative study, which so far has never been undertaken. A substantial portion of the two Codes is in identical language. It seems to me that with the aid of the technique of comparative law the jurisprudence of Nigeria could be greatly enriched. The subject is so vast, and the implications so far-reaching, that I shall try to illustrate my point by dealing here with only one small, but important, chapter in the Nigeria Criminal Code.

GENERAL PRINCIPLES OF LIABILITY

Chapter V of the Nigeria Code is headed 'Criminal Responsibility'. Chapter V of the Queensland Code has the same heading. The contents of the two chapters are the same; the wording is almost identical; even the marginal notes are the same. Many questions will of course at once occur to my readers, as they have occurred to me. Has interpretation in the Courts of the two territories proceeded on parallel lines? If not, why not? How much case law is to be found? What degree of persuasive authority is accorded to decisions of the Queensland Supreme Court? Are decisions of the High Court of Australia on the interpretation of the Queensland Criminal Code usually followed in Nigeria?

The answer to these questions I will leave to the end. Meanwhile, I invite your attention to some of the detailed provisions of Chapter V of the Nigeria Criminal Code. Almost all of them are statements of general principle. I will omit the sections which deal with (a) the liability of judicial officers, (b) offences by partners and members of companies with respect to partnership or corporate property, and (c) the liability of husband and wife for offences committed by either with respect to the other's property.

22. Ignorance of the law does not afford any excuse for any act or omission which would otherwise constitute an offence, unless knowledge of the law by the offender is expressly declared to be an element of the offence.

23. A person is not criminally responsible, as for an offence relating to property, for an act done or omitted to be done by him with respect to any property in the exercise of an honest claim of right and without intention to defraud.

24. Subject to the express provisions of this Code relating to negligent acts and omissions, a person is not criminally responsible for an act or omission, which occurs independently of the exercise of his will, or for an event which occurs by accident.

Unless the intention to cause a particular result is expressly declared to be an element of the offence constituted, in whole or in part, by an act or omission, the result intended to be caused by an act or omission is immaterial.

Unless otherwise expressly declared, the motive by which a person is induced to do or omit to do an act, or to form an intention, is immaterial so far as regards criminal responsibility.

25. A person who does or omits to do an act under an honest and reasonable, but mistaken, belief in the existence of any state of things is not criminally responsible for the act or omission to any greater extent than if the real state of things had been such as he believed to exist.

The operation of this rule may be excluded by the express or implied provisions of the law relating to the subject.

In a letter to the Attorney-General which accompanied the submission of the draft Queensland Code, Sir Samuel Griffith said: 'No part of the draft Code has occasioned me more anxiety, but I may add that I regard no part of the work with greater satisfaction.' He was referring to the whole of Chapter V. The particular sections I have quoted he seemed to regard as embodying the common law, except part of section 24 which was taken from the Italian Code. Certainly at first sight these provisions appear on the face of them to correspond generally with English law. The rules as to ignorance of law and mistake of fact bring to mind the famous cases of *Wheat*[1] and *Tolson*.[2] I must confess that as a law student I could not understand them at all. Later as a teacher of law I tried to explain them but had little confidence in what I was saying. Today, I am able to say, with no sense of shame, that I think it is a waste of time to attempt to reconcile the irreconcilable, and if text-writers would cease to quote these cases the Judges would cease to discuss them and they might safely pass into oblivion. I am comforted by the words of Latham, C.J., of the High Court of Australia, who said that any suggested reconciliation between *Wheat* and *Tolson* was based on wrong premises. That was in *Thomas* v *The King*.[3]

Let us see how these identical provisions have been interpreted in Australia and in Nigeria. Griffith made it quite clear when he submitted his draft that he intended to introduce the doctrine of *mens rea* into Queensland law. Some years later he had the delightful task of interpreting his own work judicially. This is what he said as Chief Justice: 'Under the law of Queensland, as defined in the Criminal Code, it is never necessary to have recourse to the old doctrine of *mens rea*. . . The test now to be applied is whether the prohibited act was or was not done accidentally or independently of the exercise of the will of the accused person.'[4] The doctrines of the common law were in essence flexible, and in the process of codification it is inevitable that the written

---

[1] (1921) 2 K.B. 119.   [2] (1889) 23 Q.B.D. 168.   [3] 59 C.L.R. 279.
Widgee Shire Council v *Bonney*, (1907) 4 C.L.R. 977.

form should produce a certain rigidiy and so lead to some change. In more recent cases, McCawley, J., in the Queensland Supreme Court, seemed to think that if the question arose whether the *mens rea* doctrine should be read into a particular statutory provision, the answer should be the same as that which would be given by the common law.[1] A similar approach was made by Webb, C.J.[2] On the other hand, in the same cases Real, J., and Philp, J., both took the view that the problem could only be solved by an examination of the specific provision of the code in each case according to the ordinary rules of construction and without recourse to common law doctrine. The present tendency seems to be to get right away from the *mens rea* doctrine.

What is the attitude of the Courts in Nigeria on identical provisions of the Code? Look at the Index to the decisions of the West African Court of Appeal and you will not find the phrase *mens rea*. You would also look in vain for it in the Index to the Federal Supreme Court Reports. Perhaps half a dozen cases could be found in the decisions of Courts of first instance, especially customs cases, where the phrase is used, but there would be little more than a passing reference to the English doctrine with an unquestioned acceptance that it was applicable. Whether it is applicable in interpreting the Code or not seems to be undecided, if indeed it has been considered at all. Perhaps some enterprising Nigerian lawyer will study the Queensland cases and argue the point. At all events it should open up a fruitful line of inquiry.

MENTAL DISEASE OR INFIRMITY

The Nigeria Criminal Code goes on to deal with the question of criminal liability in so far as it may be affected by mental disease or infirmity. There are two sections on this matter.

27. Every person is presumed to be of sound mind, and to have been of sound mind at any time which comes in question, until the contrary is proved.

28. A person is not criminally responsible for an act or omission if at the time of doing the act or making the omission he is in such a state of mental disease or natural mental infirmity as to deprive him of capacity to understand what he is doing, or of capacity to control his actions, or of capacity to know that he ought not to do the act or make the omission.

A person whose mind, at the time of doing or omitting to do an

---

[1] *Thomas* v *McEather*, [1920] St. R. Qd. 166.
[2] *Anderson* v *Nystrom*, [1941] St. R. Qd. 56.

act, is affected by delusions on some specific matter or matters, but who is not otherwise entitled to the benefit of the foregoing provisions of this section, is criminally responsible for the act or omission to the same extent as if the real state of things had been such as he was induced by the delusions to believe to exist.

There is a familiar ring about these words, and naturally one thinks of the McNaughten Rules. And here I must give a word of warning. Many an advocate in Nigeria, having received his legal education in this country, has observed the similarity between provisions of the Nigeria Code and the English criminal law in which he has been trained. He then makes the mistake of rushing to Archbold in search of suitable authorities, only to find that the Judges are not impressed. This is a case in point. In Nigeria the McNaughten Rules have been both modified and extended. Not only has the code departed from the phraseology of the Rules but it has introduced two entirely new factors.

In the first place, the Code introduces the concept of 'natural mental infirmity'. One of the McNaughten Rules enunciates the proposition that, to establish a defence on the ground of insanity, it must be clearly proved that at the time of committing the act the party accused was labouring under such a defect of reason from disease of the mind as not to know the nature and quality of the act he was doing, or, if he did know it, that he did not know that what he was doing was wrong. It may well be that the words 'such a state of mental disease' in section 28 of the code are equivalent to the words 'such a defect of reason from disease of the mind' used in the Rules, but the introduction of the words 'or natural infirmity' certainly goes beyond the latter words. As the West African Court of Appeal observed in *Sunday Omoni's Case*,[1] to which I will refer shortly, the code has shown a clear intention to distinguish between mental disease and natural mental infirmity, and the latter phrase should be interpreted to mean 'a defect in mental power neither produced by his own default nor the result of disease of the mind.'

Secondly, an even more marked extension of the law of England is to be found in the Nigeria Code by the inclusion in section 28 of the words 'to deprive him of capacity to control his actions'. On this aspect of the matter, Sir John Verity, C.J., delivering the judgment of the Court in Omoni's Case, said this:

'Not only do these words depart from the rules in McNaughten's Case, but they are in direct conflict with the line of English decisions

[1] 12 W.A.C.A. 511.

subsequent thereto in which the Judges in England have declined to accept the defence of 'irresistible impulse' which these words appear to have introduced into the law of Nigeria. As to the wisdom of introducing or maintaining this departure from English law, it is for the legislature to judge; this Court can only apply the law as we find it. Nothing could emphasize more pointedly the contrast between the English and the Nigerian law in this respect than the words of Hewart, L.C.J., in the well-known case of *R.* v *Kopsch*, 10 Cr. App. R. 50, where the learned Lord Chief Justice said, "The complaint against the Judge is that he did not tell the jury that something was the law which was not the law... It is the fantastic theory of uncontrollable impulse which, if it were to become part of our criminal law, would be mostly subversive. It is not yet part of our law, and it is to be hoped that the time is far distant when it will be made so." '

If there were time, it would be interesting to look at some of the cases from three of the Australian States, other than Queensland, where a tendency showed itself to find judicial support for the proposition that there was room for the defence of uncontrollable impulse even within the framework of the McNaughten Rules, though this line of reasoning received a set-back from the decision of the Judicial Committee of the Privy Council in *A.-G. for South Australia* v *Brown*.[1]

The Australian cases are certainly interesting; but for an authoritative statement of the Nigerian law on the subject of insanity and criminal responsibility *Omoni's Case* must still be regarded as the principal source. Unless the conditions laid down in that case are satisfied, a defence of insanity will fail. There have been attempts recently to raise the defence of 'mental black-out', whatever that phrase may mean, but the defence is quite unknown to the law. As Jibowu, A.G. S.P.J., pointed out in *R.* v *Dim*,[2] such a defence would be exploited and become prevalent if allowed without adequate proof. The defence must prove affirmatively that the circumstances are such as to bring the case within section 28 of the code, as interpreted in *Omoni's Case*, and evidence of a 'black-out' which falls short of such proof will be of no avail.

The presumption of sanity continues until the contrary is proved, as provided by section 27, and the burden of proving insanity is on the accused person. The Code does not say so, but this is provided in section 140(3) (c) of the Evidence Ordinance. The burden is a lighter one than that imposed on the prosecution. I need not mention this

[1] 44 Cr. App. R. 100.   [2] 14 W.A.C.A. 154.

further because the law is the same as in England. This was decided recently by the Federal Supreme Court in *Onakpoya* v *The Queen*.[1] It had already been so decided by the West African Court of Appeal some years before, but curiously enough the earlier cases were not cited, and the Court was content merely to follow the English decision of *R.* v *Carr-Bryant*.[2]

Before leaving this question the point I should like to emphasize is this. The statute law of Nigeria is identical with that of Queensland. The case law of Nigeria has developed on parallel lines with that of Queensland—in other words the same result has been reached quite independently—but I am unable to trace a single instance in which an Australian decision on the subject of insanity has been brought to the attention of a Nigerian Court.

INTOXICATION

The only other matter I shall have time to deal with, and only very briefly, is that of intoxication. The general rule is that intoxication does not consitute a defence to any criminal charge. This is stated in section 29 of the Code, but the same section goes on to qualify the general principle in two ways.

29(2). Intoxication shall be a defence to any criminal charge if by reason thereof the person charged at the time of the act or omission complained of did not know that such act or omission was wrong or did not know what he was doing and—

(*a*) the state of intoxication was caused without his consent by the malicious or negligent act of another person; or
(*b*) the person charged was by reason of intoxication insane, temporarily or otherwise, at the time of such act or omission.

29(4). Intoxication shall be taken into account for the purpose of determining whether the person charged had formed any intention, specific or otherwise, in the absence of which he would not be guilty of the offence.

29(5). For the purposes of this section 'intoxication' shall be deemed to include a state produced by narcotics or drugs.

The Nigerian law on this matter appears to be the same as that of England. It is for this reason no doubt that there are very few reported

[1] 4 F.S.C. 150.   [2] 29 Cr. App. R. 76.

decisions on the subject, although the matter has been fully discussed in two or three judgments of the West African Court of Appeal.

In the case of *R.* v *Owarey*,[1] the Court did no more than approve the statement of the law contained in the judgment of the Court of first instance in which the Judge, after referring to the principles of English law laid down in *Beard's Case*,[2] said: 'That is the law also in this country.' Perhaps I ought to add that although those principles are followed, on the same *facts* as *Beard's Case* in Nigeria the decision would be different and the offence committed would be manslaughter only and not murder. But that is due to a difference in the definition of murder, and not to any difference in the law as to the effect of drunkenness on criminal liability.

CONCLUSIONS

In this paper I have been able to cover only a very small field, and not in the detail which the subject deserves. But I hope I have said enough to warrant one or two conclusions. We have seen that the Nigeria Criminal Code follows the Queensland model. I asked some questions earlier as to how far the Nigerian Courts are influenced by Queensland decisions. The answer I can give in one sentence. I have been unable to find a single instance in which Queensland decisions have been brought to the attention of the Courts and discussed. The West African Court of Appeal heard appeals from other territories as well as Nigeria—for instance, from the Gold Coast and Sierra Leone—where the Queensland model had not been introduced; whereas the new Federal Supreme Court hears appeals only from Nigeria. I can only repeat the hope that there will be some enterprising Nigerian lawyer who appreciates the value of comparative law, and will see in this link between Nigeria and Australia not merely something of academic interest, but a challenge, and an opportunity to develop the jurisprudence of his own country.

[1] 5 W.A.C.A. 66. [2] [1920] A.C. 479.

11

LEGAL DEVELOPMENT AND ECONOMIC GROWTH IN AFRICA

DR A. N. ALLOTT

Reader in African Law in the University of London

The study of the means to economic growth doubtless has an attraction all its own for the professional economist; but to the average lawyer it might seem a dry and dusty subject, and in any event no concern of his. Even if this reaction on the part of the lawyer were correct for this country (and I believe it is not), it is certainly far from the truth in contemporary Africa. The lawyer has, in the developing countries of Africa, a highly creative role to perform; and in the term 'lawyer' I shall include both those who devise the laws—the law reformers, the legislators, the draftsmen; those who administer them—the judges, the practitioners; and those who study and criticize the law—the academic lawyers such as myself.

What are the economic problems with which African countries are now faced? What are the legal implications of those problems? To what extent can the law act as a brake on economic progress, or alternatively stimulate or harness such progress? What is to be the role of the lawyer in all this? In my attempt to answer these questions, I shall be taking a closer look at one or two fields of the law which have particular economic significance: pre-eminent among these is the law of property; almost equally important is the structure of credit and the laws which govern or guarantee its supply; and lastly, for readers outside Africa, it will perhaps be useful to examine the ways in which improvements in the law can encourage foreign investment in African countries.

THE ECONOMIC PROBLEM

Let us look, first of all, at the economic problem of African countries today. All these countries, independent or still dependent, are 'developing' countries, by which is meant that their economies are growing and must be rapidly expanded if the new-found wants of their peoples are to be satisfied. (Incidentally, may I be allowed to enter a mild protest at the description so often given to such countries of 'under-developed territories'? I would suggest that *all* countries are economically underdeveloped in the sense that they have not yet realized their full economic potential; Great Britain, and even the United States, are thus 'underdeveloped'. The alternative consequence must be that we recognize some countries as being overdeveloped!) It is, however, in the newly independent countries that the passion for economic and social progress is most deeply felt. The good life means in part a rapid rise in standards of living; this in its turn implies a rapid growth in the economy. Even where the road to speedy economic growth is not seen to lie through industrialization (as with Ghana), a government must take every step to ensure that production from existing assets is maximized; this is one reason for the long and critical look which many governments are now taking at their existing agricultural practices and land laws (as with Tanganyika, Kenya, Basutoland). Economic growth depends on the accumulation of capital and the stimulation of trade and investment: hence the paramount importance of the laws governing investment, commercial enterprise, and the grant of credit.

The development of a new economy inevitably means a break with the past: a break both with the traditional peasant economies of subsistence agriculture and local markets, and with the colonial-style extractive or monoculture economies which relations between colony and mother-country too often implied. Diversification and strengthening of the economy are called for today. But let us not over-emphasize the magnitude of the break that must be made: after all, there had been some development of local industry even in colonial times; and in many parts of Africa African farmers had already taken wholeheartedly to commercial agriculture (cocoa in Ghana and Western Nigeria; oil-products and groundnuts in West Africa; coffee, tea, and cotton in East Africa—and so on). The position is thus not as simple as it is sometimes presented; and often it is a question of reinforcing tendencies which are already there rather than of sweeping away all that exists today.

THE LEGAL IMPLICATIONS OF ECONOMIC DEVELOPMENT

What are the legal implications of this quest for economic growth? They arise in several different ways: first of all, any major change in economic or social arrangements which a government wishes to introduce has to be procured by revision of the law; change of the law is thus an *instrument* or *consequence* of economic change. For example, the movement towards consolidation and registration of individual African titles to land in Kenya was inspired by economic considerations; it was intended to increase the economic potential of land in African occupation. To carry this policy out, radical changes were required in the whole structure of the law governing land tenure in the African-occupied areas; a new substantive law of land had to be created and machinery had to be devised for passing from the old system of tenure to the new.[1] Here legal development *follows* economic change.

But there is another and more subtle way in which law reform may be tied up with economic growth; and that is where change in the law is seen, not as a mechanical consequence of economic development, but as a stimulant to economic development. The existing law, it may be felt, restricts economic growth in one way or another: for example, the traditional systems of land tenure may be thought to inhibit efficient use of the land; or the absence of legislation on bankruptcy inhibits the supply of credit; or the out-of-date character of the commercial law deters foreign concerns from investing in the country. Change in the existing law can then facilitate or liberate economic expansion.

The indirect promotion of economic development by legal change can proceed even more generally than that, as where it is felt that the whole legal climate or structure of the law is a deterrent to economic growth. One or two instances which occur to me are: (*i*) in East Africa, the Royal Commission's[2] desire to create an individualistic and competitive society inspired by the profit motive (but not too much, like the famous advertisement for shaving soap!), which led them to attack the existing features of the customary law which they thought were anti-individualistic and 'communal' in tendency; (*ii*) in West Africa, a book I was reading the other day on the economic development of French-speaking West Africa, which placed among the obstacles to economic growth the customary institutions of polygamous marriage, the giving of bride-price, and the family system; and (*iii*) in Northern Nigeria, the advice of the Panel of Jurists convened

---

[1] For which see F. D. Homan, 'Consolidation, enclosure and registration of title in Kenya' (1962), 1J. Local Admin. Overseas 4.

[2] *East Africa Royal Commission* 1953–1955 *Report* (London, 1955, H.M.S.O., Cmd. 9475).

to examine the penal law of the Region, which felt that foreign investors might well shrink from commercial contact with countries with an out-of-date criminal law.[1]

How do particular economic changes affect the law, or particular legal changes affect economic growth? What are the legal obstacles to economic growth? I propose to answer these questions through three case-studies, which reveal how African countries view the existing state of their legal systems when examined through economic spectacles. After this, I hope we shall be in a position to define more clearly the sort of law and the sort of lawyer that are capable of meeting the novel challenges posed by these problems.

THREE CASE-STUDIES: (A) LAND LAW

The first problem that I turn to is that of the land law, which is surely the most pressing of all the economico-legal problems in every African country. I find it difficult to think of a single intertropical African country which could say at the present moment that it was entirely satisfied with its land law. And yet for a long time to come it will be from the land that most of the wealth of all the African countries will come, whether they succeed in progressive industrialization or not. Land is the major resource of such countries; the way it is used today and the obstacles to its more efficient use are thus of paramount importance.

What is wrong with the existing land laws? Many things. I shall overlook the purely political defects, such as under the Land Apportionment Act in Southern Rhodesia, and concentrate on the legal and economic deficiencies. First of all, there is the fact that in practically every territory there is not a single system of land law: most territories have at least two kinds of land law—a territorial law of European origin or inspiration, and African customary land laws applying to the African section of the population. But even this simple picture is obscured, since in some territories there is a multiplicity of different statutory régimes governing the tenure and transfer of land in different parts of the country or for different kinds of property (e.g. in Ghana[2] and in Kenya); and in Tanganyika one finds it necessary to have a knowledge of the German and English law relating to title and

---

[1] See J. N. D. Anderson, 'Conflict of laws in Northern Nigeria: a new start' (1959), 8 I.C.L.Q. 442, at p. 452.

[2] The position in Ghana has very recently been changed with the enactment of the Administration of Lands Act, 1962.

conveyancing, as well as of the locally enacted Land Ordinance, before one can appreciate what is the general law relating to land. Yet another complicating factor is the multiplicity of customary land laws, and in West Africa at any rate one has all the uncertainties caused by the possibility of combining English and customary land laws in a single transaction, or of converting an interest held under the one system into an analogous one under the other system and back again. Multiplicity of laws is thus the first handicap.

The next thing that is wrong with the territorial laws is that they are often out of date. The conveyancing law imported into most of the common law West African countries (excluding the Western Region of Nigeria) and into Tanganyika was the pre-1926 law of England.

The conflicts which can arise between one sort of law and another, and the difficulties in finding out the details of the correct law, whether statutory or customary, are productive very often of *uncertainty* as to the law or as to the validity of a particular title. Such uncertainty is undoubtedly increased by the restricted use made of registration of title as guaranteeing the interest which a holder of land may possess and which he may wish to market, or at least to use as security.

The defects which I have so far mentioned are technical defects, which one might well expect a competent property lawyer, given the necessary time and information, to be able to put right without too much difficulty. But the next problem is of quite a different character. It has been suggested, especially in East and Central Africa, that the whole system under which peasant farming has hitherto been carried on is basically unacceptable in a modern economy, and that this system must be radically modified, or even abolished altogether, in favour of a new approach to land-holding and exploitation. The most articulate expression of this view is to be found in the Report of the Royal Commission on Land and Population in East Africa,[1] which reported in 1955 (though its sentiments have been echoed by other commissions and government spokesmen from time to time). What is the burden of the East African Royal Commission's criticisms?

In the cattle-keeping societies, the major criticism of customary law is that it permits so-called 'communal' grazing, i.e., that grazing land is open to all members of a particular local community or kinship group, whilst ownership of cattle is 'individual'. This leads to an absence of pasture management and deterioration of the pastures.

In the agricultural societies, the main alleged faults are: shifting

[1] *Supra*, Chaps. 21, 22.

cultivation; the vesting of land-rights in the so-called clan or tribe, with, as stated consequences,

'the unrestricted right of the individual to run stock on what is held to be the common asset of land; the right of all in the clan to claim to be supported from the clan's land; and the understanding that ownership, if such an idea exists at all, is vested in the community, so that sale, mortgage, capital value, lease and rental were terms unknown.'

And next there is a wide variety of authorities controlling the administration of the land of various groups, including religious and chiefly authorities. In modern times, new deficiencies have appeared, it is suggested: the divisory system of succession, coupled with expansion of population, leading to fragmentation and sub-division of holdings; insecurity of tenure; a vicious struggle for survival due to the growing of cash-crops and the realization that land has a cash-value; tribal parochialism and exclusiveness; and all the ills traceable to the uncontrolled evolution of customary land laws in the direction of greater individualization of land-rights.

What does the Royal Commission recommend? 'The smallness of the monetary needs of the pastoral tribes' is seen as a major difficulty (fortunate people, we might well say!); therefore a commercial instinct must be encouraged among them. Restriction of cattle numbers is one of the solutions, together with improved marketing of stock.

It is in regard to the agricultural societies that the major recommendations are made. The technical agricultural faults are isolated as: erosion; lack of integration between stock and the carrying capacity of the land they occupy; insufficiency of the resting period in the cultivation cycle; and fragmentation. The answers to these problems, the Commission says, mainly lie in integrated, consolidated, planned holdings run on a more scientific basis. There must be an encouragement of individual tenure, as this gives the proprietor a sense of responsibility, an interest in improvement of his land, and a feeling of security. At the same time the Commission wisely recognizes that:

'From a land usage angle there is nothing necessarily associated as more beneficial either with a communal or an individual approach. Neither individual tenure nor co-operatives, nor collective farming necessarily make crops grow better.'

What counts, said the Commission, is that there should be some form of control and planning of land use. But equally there ought to be encouragement of the 'progressive individual', who may pioneer new ways of land use.

Views such as these have been influential in East and Central Africa. In Kenya the process of consolidation and registration of holding under African occupation is in close conformity with the Commission's proposals; in Southern Rhodesia something similar has been introduced by the Native Land Husbandry Act; in Uganda there has been a cautious acceptance of some of the major planks in the 'individualizing' platform; while for Basutoland the Morse Commission[1] said that

'traditional law and custom concerning the tenure of land throughout Africa appear clearly to be out of step with the requirements for a modern cash crop agriculture, where the individual must take certain risks and therefore be assured that the reward of so doing will fall to him. In many African countries changes have already been made (e.g. Southern Rhodesia and parts of Kenya), apparently with considerable success. It may not be too optimistic to hope that by the end of the present century these traditional tenure systems will be only a memory in every progressive African country.'

The Morse Commission went on to suggest that there might be introduced 'a system of tenure based on conditional individual tenure'. At the same time their advice was *festina lente*, at least till there had been an expert study of the whole problem.

I am afraid that it is not possible to document my criticisms of these attitudes and recommendations in detail here; but let me summarize my general position by saying that I feel that many of these criticisms of existing customary land tenure systems are exaggerated or ill-informed, and rest on insufficient knowledge of how the systems function in practice today (for example, there may be a very wide variation in the structure and details of the land law from one part of a single territory to another, let alone as between different territories; and the assumption that there is some common factor labelled 'communal customary land tenure' betrays a gross misunderstanding of the customary laws). Whilst one would concede that *in some areas* the faults mentioned by these critics exist—e.g. insecurity of tenure is undoubtedly a difficulty in some places, overcrowding conspicuous in others—it is doubtful how far these faults are due to deficiencies in the land *law*, as opposed to backwardness in land *use*, or whether it is justifiable to criticize the whole of a customary land tenure system

[1] *Basutoland, Bechuanaland Protectorate and Swaziland—Report of an economic survey mission* (London, 1960, H.M.S.O.), pp. 242–5.

because one of its features is unsatisfactory (e.g. where the system of intestate succession is divisory, and where there is no fresh land available for occupation, the continual sub-division of holdings cannot be avoided if the population continually expands; but this is just as much the fault of the British, for introducing peace and medicine, as it is of the customary law; and the remedy lies in a voluntary or compulsory change in the succession law rather than in an alteration of customary land law as a whole).

Again, much of the criticism of customary land law for its alleged failure to adapt to new economic demands, and its resistance to individual interests, strikes me as wide of the mark; customary land law has changed radically in many areas in response to the arrival of commercial crops, and individual interests of a strong and durable kind have appeared spontaneously and without benefit of Royal Commissions in various regions of Africa (a short look at the land law of West Africa might have been a help here). Indeed, one of the criticisms of customary land law, as we have seen, has been of its over-successful adaptation to the business of making money rather than keeping alive.

And, finally, it seems to me that these critics often fail to consider, because they are not technically equipped to do so, how to build on the good features of existing customary land laws, while eliminating those which are definitely inimical to the increase of yields and the protection of natural resources. This lack of specialist knowledge is compounded, perhaps, by a certain psychological reluctance to look beyond the rather narrow prescriptions of the western-orientated expert in economics or agriculture.

(B) CREDIT

The second field which I wish to use as an illustration of the ways in which law and economic development are intermingled is in some respects connected with that which I have just been discussing: it is the law governing the supply of credit, prescribing what security can be given in return for credit, and what is to happen to the debtor who does not pay.

The function of credit in a modern economy cannot be over-estimated. Allow me to quote a few words from the admirable report of the Commission appointed to investigate insolvency law in Ghana:

'Credit is the lifeblood of the Ghanaian economy. It flows through every sector of the economy. Without credit the economy would come to a standstill... For the economy to expand at the rate envisaged in the Second Development Plan will need considerable and increasing infusions of credit both from abroad and at home. . . . It is often said of the Ghanaian economy that the whole economy runs on credit. Taken literally this is an exaggeration... Nevertheless, in relative terms, credit transactions, though a minority of all transactions, probably bulk larger in the Ghanaian economy than they do in many other countries.'[1]

One could in this context speak of the legal machinery governing the formation of capital, of investment and lending for development generally; or of the importance of the structure of the law relating to banking, insurance, friendly societies, stock exchanges, and so on in so far as it favours or impedes the dynamic growth of the economy. But I have chosen to restrict what I have to say about credit to those aspects which most intimately affect the individual African, however humble his circumstances; and I shall speak mainly about two aspects of credit supply: (*i*) the nature of the security that can be given for it, and (*ii*) the legislation for the enforcement of debts and the supervision of the insolvent debtor.

Security. Borrowing requires or implies a willing lender, and hence usually a credit-worthy borrower. A borrower is credit-worthy if he can assure the lender (*a*) that he will get his capital back at the time agreed for repayment, and (*b*) that the loan will be serviced, i.e., that instalments of interest where payable will be met at the due time. Usually a lender does not trust a borrower to pay back the capital, and demands some form of security for his loan against which recourse may be had if the borrower fails in his obligation to repay. The East African Royal Commission assumed, in their interesting study of this topic, that the security must be 'negotiable', as they called it; in so far as lending on land was concerned, they stated that persons can only expect to borrow on the security of land 'if the land is a negotiable asset, and . . . the value of land as a security increases in proportion to the absence of restraints on its disposal'.[2]

---

[1] *Report of the Commissioners appointed to enquire into the insolvency law of Ghana* (Accra, 1961), at pp. 18–19.
[2] *Supra*, Chap. 9, pp. 97, 98.

The Commission further stated:

'In the traditional subsistence economies these conditions do not exist; there is no negotiable security and, by its very nature, subsistence production precludes the possibility that any income above what is required for subsistence will be available for the service of the loan.'

And finally the Commission accused the Africans of misunderstanding the basic principles underlying the securing of loans.

I should like to lay the same charge at the door of the Commission. In its broadest sense security for a loan must mean some assurance independent of the good faith or will of the debtor that the loan will be duly repaid, to which recourse can be had by the creditor in the event of default. So-called 'negotiability' is by no means the only consideration here, and one can imagine forms of security which are not negotiable assets at all (e.g. a guarantee by a third party; judicial or administrative supervision of the debtor).

And, secondly, I do not think their criticism of traditional customary laws is generally merited. One of the commonest features of customary land laws in many parts of Africa is the pledge of land, where the lender goes into possession of the land pledged and works the land for his own benefit, taking the yield as the interest on his loan. As the land once pledged remains redeemable whenever the debtor can tender the capital sum he borrowed, the arrangement is in the interests of both creditor and debtor. It is only on an extremely narrow definition of a 'subsistence economy' that it could be said that such arrangements do not exist in traditional subsistence economies.

Not only are such customary pledges of land common in Africa, but we also find pledges of movables as well. In the developed customary laws (especially in West Africa) new forms of security are continually being devised. In Ghana I found, when I was conducting research into customary land law among the Akan there, that the ancient usufructuary kind of pledge was being largely superseded by new types of charge: for example, pledges with a fixed term with rights of foreclosure and sale as remedies for non-payment; self-liquidating mortgages where the debtor remained in possession as agent of the creditor and the annual yield of the land was divided into three parts, one of which went to the creditor to pay off the capital, one-third went as interest, and one-third to the debtor for his management services. The blanket criticisms made by the Royal Commission, even if they are confined to East Africa, I do not therefore consider to be fair.

The reasons why commercial, especially non-African, lenders are reluctant to lend money to African peasant farmers lie mainly (*i*) in the uncertainties, as they see it, of the existing customary systems of land tenure, and hence doubts as to the validity of the title of the potential borrower; (*ii*) in doubts as to the credit-worthiness of the applicant (which seem to me far more serious than the question of security as such)—doubts which arise mainly from the fact that the African farmer is undercapitalized, and that he is perhaps unfamiliar with the most fruitful ways of putting the money he borrows to work so as permanently to enhance his productive capacity; and (*iii*) in the inter-racial legal difficulties which have in the past restricted both the grant of credit by non-Africans to Africans in East Africa and the enforcement of any real security in such circumstances. Uncertainties as to customary land law can be removed by various means, not all of which require changes in the land law so much as its clarification either generally or in particular cases. Registration of title is one such device; government guarantees another; while official bodies may themselves enter the market as lending agencies. It is noteworthy that a comparatively large number of loans to African farmers in the consolidated areas of Kenya have been made by commercial agencies since consolidation was introduced.

Enforcement of debts and insolvency legislation. One of the more peculiar features of the law of Ghana has been the absence of legislation governing insolvency (or bankruptcy), i.e., the administration of the affairs of insolvents. In the past there has been an almost universal distrust of any proposal to introduce such insolvency legislation into Ghana; recently the picture has startlingly changed, perhaps due to the educative work of the Insolvency Commission[1] itself. The Commission also found that the existing machinery for the enforcement of debts was inadequate and that there was an absence of effective remedies against defaulting debtors. The Commission commented:

'One of the principal aims of Government is to create in Ghana a modern agricultural, commercial and industrial system. It is our considered conclusion ... that adequate legal machinery for the determination and settlement of debts must play an important part in this.'

[1] *Supra.*

It is our further conclusion that the need for this machinery is urgent and that its introduction cannot now be delayed without markedly retarding the healthy expansion of the economy.'[1]

In making their specific proposals, the Insolvency Commission took special care to ensure that they would fit in with the two most relevant aspects of the customary law, that relating to the giving of real security, and that concerned with the liability of families and family and stool property for the debts of their members. The Commission also kept in mind the sociological fact that 'many Ghanaians are dilatory about paying their debts and that a not inconsiderable minority default altogether in whole or in part'. (Let me add that this is a complaint by no means confined to Ghana.) The enactment of legislation with teeth in it was thus necessary to restore confidence in the credit-worthiness of the potential Ghanaian borrower, both at home and abroad.

(C) ENCOURAGEMENT OF FOREIGN INVESTMENT

Finally, I wish to discuss the effect that the desire to encourage foreign investment may have on the demand for and scale of legal reform in the receiving countries. To examine this problem it is necessary to ask: who is the potential foreign investor? what is he looking for before he will agree to invest?

Much of the investment in African countries is coming from public sources of one kind or another—some national, some international. I would suggest that such investors or lenders are not particularly interested in the state of the law in the countries to which they lend; what they will look for is efficient government capable of making proper use of the money lent or invested, and some assurance (though this is sometimes weakened for political reasons to vanishing point) that the loan will be serviced and the money will eventually be repaid.

Private investors are in another category altogether. One might think that as commercial concerns they would be principally interested in the state of the commercial law, especially the company legislation. The terms of reference given to Professor Gower as Commissioner for the reform of company law in Ghana specially instructed the Commissioner when making his recommendations to 'take into account the encouragement of foreign investment' in Ghana. Yet the Commissioner himself in his Final Report[2] rather doubted how far reform

[1] *Op. cit.*, p. 23.
[2] *Final report of the Commission of Enquiry into the working and administration of the present company law of Ghana* (Accra, 1961, Government Printer), p. 9.

of company legislation contributes specifically to the encouragement of foreign investment, or more generally to economic growth; and he suggested that other branches of the law, such as tax law, exchange control and immigration law, have perhaps a greater influence on potential foreign investors. For Basutoland the Morse Commission would add[1] that the system of land law (with its absence of formal security of tenure for non-Basuto) is a deterrent to commercial expansion.

This analysis is undoubtedly correct, though one must not carry the point too far. One could, however, go even farther and say that what principally influences the decision to invest are in fact non-legal considerations such as: (1) the economic and social climate in the country in question; (2) the attitude of the government now and in the foreseeable future to foreign investors as a class; and (3) the profitability of the particular enterprise under consideration. Stability and a friendly reception are thus more important than the details of the laws. This is not to say that a foreign company's legal advisers will not scrutinize the legal framework under which the company will have to operate, and that where that law is manifestly uncertain, onerous, inflexible or out-of-date this may not act as a marginal deterrent. The mere fact that the law is foreign is usually no obstacle at all, provided —and it is an important proviso—competent legal advice is available to explain it. (This may well be a reason in some African countries either for training or evolving more local practitioners who are expert in commercial law, or alternatively for changing the law to one which is more generally familiar to lawyers in the great trading nations.)

The larger commercial concerns are already in many ways international rather than national bodies; this fact, coupled with the ever-increasing interchange of practices and multiplication of contacts, naturally leads commercial concerns generally to welcome any step towards the unification on an international level of the laws under which they operate. Much has already been achieved in the unification of private law. The question of the harmonization of national laws has an additional interest in Africa today, however, since it may at the inter-African level contribute to a closer association, and eventually to a political unity, between African states on a regional or continental basis. From the standpoint of inter-African trade there is little compelling reason, of course, for unification of commercial law in Africa at present; on the other hand, there is equally no major technical obstacle to a harmonization of commercial laws. Such a harmonization

[1] *Op. cit.*, p. 244.

involves in essence a reconciliation between the ideas and forms of two types of legal system: those systems of the common law tradition, and those which belong to the civil or Roman law tradition. Experience in the harmonization of laws in juridically mixed countries such as the United States and Canada (each with its civil law component)—or even as between England and Scotland, for that matter—will be useful here. Nor is this merely an academic exercise. As new bonds are forged between civil law and common law countries in Africa (e.g. as in the Cameroun and Somali Republics, and, though this problem has not yet come up, as between Ghana, Guinea and Mali), harmonization of laws becomes a matter requiring urgent administrative action. The Federation of Rhodesia and Nyasaland has a similar problem on its hands, owing to the fact that Southern Rhodesia has a Roman-Dutch type of legal system, whereas Northern Rhodesia and Nyasaland have systems based on English law.

THE ROLE OF THE LAWYER

I turn now to consider the role of the lawyer. The promotion of economic growth in the countries of Africa necessarily entails, as we have seen, revision of the laws of those countries, not merely as the consequence of economic change, but in some cases as a pre-condition for it. Sometimes the legal changes required will mean radical reform of the law. Obviously the lawyer is going to be involved in all this; but what sort of lawyer, and at what stage in the process will he be brought in for consultation?

The legal and economic changes we have been discussing are likely to have grave social repercussions. This is most obviously so with reform of land tenure, but it is equally the case where a right of testamentary disposition is introduced or the status of women altered, or the procedure for recovery of debts made more effective. Many of these changes involve major alterations in, or supersession of, the customary law.

Thus if we require the co-operation of lawyers for any purpose more ambitious than that of merely writing down in legal language what the economists and administrators have already decided on— and I believe most strongly that we do need more than this—we shall have to look for lawyers of a new type. The practitioner (or even the academic expert) whose legal knowledge is confined to a single system of European-type law is unfortunately not good enough; we need a person with such knowledge, but coupled with an intimate understanding of customary law and an appreciation of what I hope you will allow me to christen 'sociolegal dynamics'.

Nor is it much use consulting legal experts of this type (practitioners in sociolegal dynamics!) only in the closing stages of an enquiry; they must be associated with the examination of the existing law, and the exploration of new legal structures to replace it, right from the very beginning. Every economic mission of the kind now customary in Africa should have its lawyer-member.

What do we find in practice? So far as I can discover, none of the economic missions or commissions has had a legal member, still less one qualified in the way I suggest; from East Africa and Tanganyika to the High Commission Territories and Nigeria, it is the same story: the missions include bankers, economists, agricultural experts, technical experts, administrators, geographers—but the lawyers are strangely absent.[1]

It is to this reason that I attribute some of the deficiencies (which I mentioned earlier) in the reports of these missions and commissions. The basic, correct and relevant legal information has not been presented to the mission; or, if duly presented, the inter-relations between it and the social and economic context have not been correctly appreciated and analysed. From these strictures I would except the two reports I have already referred to, both from Ghana, the one relating to company law and the other to insolvency legislation. Both strike me as being models of the way in which the historical, sociological and legal factors should be handled in any study of law reform in Africa. (I have already noted the careful way in which the Insolvency Commission attempted to dovetail its recommendations in with the customary law; equally Professor Gower in his report was much concerned with the connexion between the life of small private businesses and the customary system of intestate succession by the family.) Both reports embodied relevant research into these factors, some original, some already carried out for other purposes.

It is not only the aid of specially qualified legal experts that is necessary; there must also be made available the necessary research, both into the existing law, statutory and customary, and into the specific inter-relations between that law and social and economic organization. And here I should like to quote some words of Professor Dudley Stamp. He was speaking about the stages in the work of putting

[1] Apart from references already given, see: *The economic development of Tanganyika* (Baltimore, 1961); *The economic development of Nigeria* (Baltimore, 1955).

land to the best possible use, but what he says applies to legal development for economic purposes in Africa as well. There ought really to be three stages, he said:[1]

'There ought first to be the stage of survey, the recording of the present position; secondly, the stage of analysis, seeking to understand the reasons for that position and of seeing what are the existing trends in development; and then, thirdly, the actual planning for the future, which must take the present and the present trends into full consideration. Unfortunately this concept of land-use planning is far from being universally accepted. There is an idea that surely there must be a short cut, that one can ignore the past, one can ignore the present, and go straight on to say what should be done for the future. Speaking personally I regard this as an extremely dangerous point of view. . . .'

President Nkrumah, in a recent speech[2] at the opening of the Ghana Law School, drew special attention to the need for such research, and particularly into 'the basic concepts of African law'. We hope that here at this School we are contributing to this fundamental research into African laws. We are also beginning, in collaboration with experts in economics, sociology and politics, to institute a series of special studies and seminars devoted to the second kind of research that I have just mentioned. In these studies we hope to explore the social, economic, political and historical factors determining or affecting the shape of the legal systems in Africa; and we have already made a start with a pilot study of the evolution and future of land law in Tanganyika. As President Nkrumah put it in the same speech:

'The law should be the legal expression of the political, economic, and social conditions of the people and of their aims for progress.'

It is to contribute to this incarnation in legal form of the economic and social aspirations of African peoples that we are developing our own interdisciplinary studies in this new, exciting, and growing intellectual field, which we consider to be of the highest significance for the economic development of Africa today.

[1] L. Dudley Stamp, *Applied geography* (London, 1961), pp. 37–8.
[2] January 4th, 1962; reported in *Journal of African Law* at [1962] J.A.L. 103.

12

WOMEN'S STATUS AND LAW REFORM

J. S. READ

*Lecturer in African Law, School of Oriental
and African Studies, University of London*

Women's status is a topic of considerable importance. Its significance is indicated by the fact that it would seem odd indeed in most societies to discuss the status of men. Instead, the rights and duties enjoyed, or owed, by men are generally the norm by differentiation from which women acquire their distinctive status. Thus the *Encyclopaedia of the Social Sciences* contains articles on 'Woman, Position in Society',[1] but the only entry under 'Man'[2] deals with the evolution of *homo sapiens* and gives as its first reference *Man's Place Among the Mammals*. It seems inevitable to start at this point, although the risk is run thereby of forfeiting the attention of those who enjoy—or suffer—the status here discussed and who may question this writer's sincerity because he does not. Women no doubt accept the voluminous attention accorded them in modern times as a compliment to their sex. The spate of literature specifically concerned with women's status is so great that, in the later stages of preparing this discussion, one is tempted to ask the poet's question:

> Why do I prate
> Of women, that are things against my fate?[3]

No defence can be offered for this attempt to add to the flood of documentation, but two pleas may be allowed in mitigation. First, the urgency of some problems calling for reform of the law to keep pace with the fast changing position of women in developing countries of Africa justifies repetition. Secondly, the writer would say, with the

---

[1] Vol. XV, pp. 439 ff.   [2] Vol. X, pp. 71–6.
[3] Thomas Randolph (1605–1635), 'An Ode to Mr Anthony Stafford to Hasten Him into the Country'.

author of a recent book on the *Women of Africa*, 'the more of them I met the more interested I became'.[1]

It is well, however, to commence this consideration by recalling some lines of an eminent transatlantic authority:

> I attribute much of our modern tension
> To a misguided striving for intersexual comprehension.
> It's about time to realize, brethren, as best we can,
> That a woman is not just a female man.[2]

EQUALITY OF THE SEXES

The Universal Declaration of Human Rights reflects the fact that the rights of women are measured by reference to the rights of men:

'Article 16. (1) Men and women of full age, without any limitation due to race, nationality or religion, have the right to marry and to found a family. They are entitled to equal rights as to marriage, during marriage and at its dissolution.

(2) Marriage shall be entered into only with the free and full consent of the intending spouses.'

The principle of equality between the sexes in marriage has been elaborated by the Economic and Social Council of the United Nations, which

'*Believing* that legal equality of husband and wife and the sharing by spouses of the authority, prerogatives and responsibilities involved in marriage are of benefit not only to the status of women but also to the family as an institution,
Noting that the legal systems of many countries result in a subordinate status of the wife in family matters of fundamental importance, and that under numerous legal systems women are, during marriage, deprived of important personal and property rights or are subject to the authority and control of their husbands in the exercise of these rights,
Recommends that governments:
(*a*) Take all possible measures to ensure equality of rights and duties of husband and wife in family matters;
(*b*) Take all possible measures to ensure to the wife full legal capacity, the right to engage in work outside the home and the right, on equal

[1] Alastair Scobie, *Women of Africa*, 1960, p. 1.   [2] Ogden Nash, *The Private Dining-Room and other new verses* (London, 1953, Dent), p. 123.

terms with her husband, to acquire, administer, enjoy and dispose of property."[1]

The work of the United Nations through its specialized agencies, and particularly through the Economic and Social Council and its Commission on the Status of Women, has been an important force behind the recent world wide movement of opinion regarding the position of women. This tide of opinion, changing the heart as well as the face of societies of diverse patterns throughout the world, is one of the outstanding social revolutions of this century. It has removed inequalities in the rights enjoyed by men and women respectively; but more, by its spreading of a common philosophy based on equality of status, and by the instruments it has used, such as the international feminist organizations, it has broken down barriers between nations themselves, increasing the understanding by women of each country of the problems of their sisters elsewhere, and removing many of the more extreme divergences of social patterns between different nations.

Ideas have changed, and are changing still. But in practice much remains to be accomplished. The lawyer's task is clearly only part of the whole. There is still much prejudice, and much in law or custom that imposes on some women not merely an inferior, but sometimes a degrading status. But in many countries too, and certainly at the international level, the broad lines of social and therefore legal change have been charted.

Pressure for law reform may come from several sources: from the educated and vocal women who usually, in developing countries, form a small but powerful minority; but also, not nowadays to be overlooked, from the ordinary women of the country, awakened as they so often are to the possibilities of tomorrow, and wielding the power of the vote; from progressive politicians responding to that power and planning the creation of modern states; from economic forces; and from international sources.

So swift has been modern political and economic development that existing legal systems are often sorely strained to deal even with the present social patterns. Many African territories have legal systems embracing several types of law. Often these systems are creaking under the strain of social changes, already accomplished, to which they have not been adapted. In two spheres in particular this strain is most evident—land law and family law. The laws relating to marriage

---

[1] Resolution 503 D (XVI) of the Economic and Social Council, at its 736th plenary meeting, July 23, 1953.

in parts of East Africa will shortly be discussed; but it may be remarked here that they result in situations which would certainly have seemed too fanciful for comic opera plots by W. S. Gilbert. Unfortunately that analogy, accurate as a matter of fact, fails utterly to indicate the tragedies of personal and social confusion which result from the confusion of the law. Reform of the law relating to women would often be an urgent necessity even if it were not for the widespread change in commonly held notions about woman's proper place.

The principle of equality of the sexes may sometimes be accepted only with reluctance, especially when it is construed as an alien notion reflecting adversely upon a traditional social system. The point has been stated for India by Derrett:

'The notion "equality of the sexes" is a foreign importation in India, and is viewed with suspicion to this day. The educated Hindu who is in a position to discuss this matter with a foreigner will not hesitate to say that there is something indecent or improper in positing 'equality' between brother and sister, or between husband and wife. They are unequal because they are dissimilar, and girls' inequality may in fact be a sign of their superiority: in other words females may be given special treatment not because they are despised, but because they are peculiarly honoured and protected.'[1]

A man's feelings of respect and tenderness towards certain women is a characteristic of the Hindu family: in particular, 'the apotheosis of the mother has reached a greater height in India than anywhere else'.[2]

Nevertheless, in modern India the need has been felt for sweeping measures of law reform designed to improve women's status. In surveying *The Position of Women in Hindu Civilization*, Altekar refers to this contrast between popular male attitudes and actual legal disabilities:

'Even during the last two thousand years the average woman continued to lead a happy and contented life, fondled by her parents, loved by her husband and revered by her children. It must be, however, admitted that her cup of happiness was more frequently spilt in this period than ever before by the prohibition of widow remarriage, the revival of the Sati custom, the spread of the Purda and the greater

---

[1] J. Duncan M. Derrett, 'The Legal Status of Women in India from the most ancient times to the present day', *Recueils de la Société Jean Bodin*, 1959, Vol. XI, pp. 239-40.
[2] A. S. Altekar, *The Position of Women in Hindu Civilization*, Banaras, 2nd edition, 1956, p. 101.

prevalence of polygamy and supersession. Society's attitude towards her was also one of patronizing condescension.'[1]

Such conflicting attitudes in a society often make it difficult to assess succinctly the general position of women. In Elizabethan England women, distinctly subordinate to men in legal rights to property or in political influence, nevertheless received considerable respect from their menfolk, especially among the upper classes:

'The passionate but formal romance of the days of chivalry, the long ages of adoration of the Virgin Mother in the medieval church, had given the lady a place in the sun. It was artificial enough. Much of the formal courtesy disappeared when the ownership of an estate or estates was in question; but in ordinary times the lady received a homage that was emphasized by the fantastic theatricality Elizabeth demanded from her courtiers. This could not but have influenced the behaviour of all men to all women.'[2]

The principal concern of this discussion is with the relevance of the law and its reform to the position of women; but women's status is clearly not a matter of law alone. Concentration on the law may give misleading impressions. It is said to be difficult

'to generalize about the position of the English country-women in the Middle Ages. The law is clear enough and the Church's view is clear enough. But men and women are never ruled in their personal relationships by law alone or by the Church alone. No farmer could get along without a wife. It is probably not far from the truth to say that the nearer the household was to the land the stronger the tie between man and wife, the more nearly were they on equal terms.'[3]

And a similar contrast between law and everyday life may be found in Africa. Thus among the Bamenda of the Cameroons it was recorded that although legal rights to land are vested in the men, 'in the domestic context women, as wives of these men, exercise real control over land use by virtue of their rights as producers over the crops they grow'.[4]

Two matters are of particular relevance. First, in considering the position of women in any society it is seldom possible to collect and

[1] *Op. cit.*, pp. 360–1.
[2] G. E. & K. R. Fussell, *The English Countrywoman*, 1953, p. 19.
[3] Doris Mary Stenton, *The English Woman in History*, 1957, p. 98.
[4] Daryll Forde, *Preface* to Phyllis M. Kaberry, *Women of the Grassfields*, 1952, p. vi.

assess the relevant evidence from law, social and economic life, religion and ethics, and on that basis to award the women of that society a definite rung on the fictitious ladder of women's status. This is essentially a subjective assessment of numerous and complex factors. Kaberry concluded that any attempt 'by a species of anthropological or moral arithmetic, to decide whether the position of women in general is high or low, or good or bad is . . . likely to prove profitless'.[1] She illustrates this by quoting two contradictory views of the position of Bamenda women from experienced missionaries. One thought they had 'achieved a remarkable degree of freedom and independence', while the other described their status as 'alarmingly low'.[2]

Secondly, just as law is only one factor in the total position of women, although of course a highly significant one, so too reform of the law is only one of the instruments by which that position may be altered. And law reform is not necessarily always the first weapon in a feminist campaign. In his study of *Law and Public Opinion in England during the Nineteenth Century*, Dicey records that the law reform of today is often based upon the opinion of yesterday.[3] This may have been especially true of Victorian England, but it is less applicable to modern African states. The dynamic urge for progress felt by many in the new Africa, plus the international encouragement and aid for modernizing social and economic life, the swift expansion of educational facilities, the solidarity aroused by popular nationalist philosophies and the disproportionate influence of the small élites of these countries (élites by no means entirely male in their composition) ——these factors combine to speed considerably the process of reform of the law. Instead of being, as so often in English history, a means of bringing the law into slow and often grudging accord with changes already accomplished in public opinion and social and economic patterns, reform of the law will be seen in Africa as a means of promoting such changes in these spheres of life. But law reform as an instrument of, or catalyst in, social change must be finely calculated if it is not to confuse still further an already complicated system; it would be no improvement to replace laws at present out of touch with actual social behaviour, and perhaps unenforceable, with new laws equally out of accord with the way people subject to them do in fact behave. In this field the law reformer must lean heavily upon the sociologist.

Apart from law reform, other factors of vital significance to the improvement of women's status lie within governmental control to

---

[1] *Op. cit.*, p. vii.   [2] *Op. cit.*, p. vii.   [3] 2nd. edition, 1926, p. 33.

some extent. Changes in public opinion are of course of prime importance. Such changes are very closely linked with the expansion of education. It is unfortunately true that in Africa women have benefitted in markedly smaller numbers than men from the limited educational facilities which have been available. The proportion of girls who ever commence school attendance is much lower for most countries than the proportion of boys; and the falling off in numbers proceeding from each school grade to the next, considerable as it is for boys, is even higher for girls. This is partly why the proportion of women students at universities in tropical Africa is so low (rarely as high as ten per cent of the student body). Needless to say neither law nor Government policy is necessarily to blame for the deficiencies of female education. Economic demands upon the family, social patterns such as early marriage for girls, and the general climate of opinion giving priority to boys, are all involved. In reporting on African education in Uganda in 1953, de Bunsen gave other reasons including the moral dangers involved in travelling long distances to attend senior classes which are perhaps coeducational. Few modern African governments need to be convinced of the importance of education at all levels to the development of their countries. Probably no other factor will be of more significance in the improvement of women's position in society. Special provision may well be necessary, such as the 'Fundamental Educational Programme for Women' proposed by the Democratic Party of Uganda in its policy statement, *Uganda Women March to Freedom*, or special projects of community development.

A second factor, the increased participation of women in the economic life of a developing nation, depends to a great extent of course upon national economic policies: perhaps in encouraging the establishment or development of those industries in which women's labour can most effectively be used or where, as in many parts of Africa, women's work is traditionally in agriculture, in seeking to improve the level of efficiency in production or marketing of crops. (In so far as much of the wealth looked for by developing African countries can come only from their soil, women in such societies will play a key part in economic development—a point which does not appear to have been fully discussed at the meeting of the International Institute of Differing Civilizations in 1958, when 'Women's Role in the Development of Tropical and Sub-Tropical Countries' was under consideration.) Economists have stressed that industrialization does not necessarily involve the absorption of women into industry, unless there is a shortage of male labour or unless women's present occupations are relatively unproductive. Thus, in Uganda,

'Whether a transfer of women from their traditional occupation as farmers into industry will increase the national income must depend upon their relative marginal productivity in the two spheres.'[1]

While it may not always be in the national interest to encourage women to enter industrial employment, clearly there should be no legal restriction on the freedom of a woman to choose her occupation that does not apply to a man. The Economic and Social Council of the United Nations has resolved in this sense:

'*Noting* that in the legal systems of many countries the husband has the power to prevent his wife from engaging in independent work and that in some he has control over her earnings,
Believing that this limitation of the legal capacity and of the property rights of married women is incompatible with the principle of equality of spouses during marriage as proclaimed in the Universal Declaration of Human Rights,
Recommends that governments take all necessary measures to ensure the right of a married woman to undertake independent work, to carry it on and to administer and dispose of her earnings without the necessity of securing her husband's authorization.'[2]

Further, some special protection for women in industry may be desirable even though it gives them unequal (favourable) treatment in comparison with men. Many common law African countries have such provisions, often at present in an embryo form only, prohibiting, for example, the employment of women at night or on underground work in mines. Other countries, such as Egypt, have more complex systems of protection. There is a danger in excessive legislation on this topic: if the employer of female labour has too many special rules to observe he may decide to employ men instead. It is possible to legislate women out of employment in this way. This may also happen if equal pay for men and women becomes obligatory, as recommended, though not unanimously, by the meeting on 'Women's Role 'organized by the I.N.C.I.D.I.

In parts of Africa, it may be a serious breach of traditional custom for women to engage in employment in towns—often due to an

---

[1] W. Elkan, *The Employment of Women in Uganda*, p. 6 (a roneoed Conference Paper of the East African Institute of Social Research).
[2] Resolution 547 J (XVIII), 805th plenary meeting, July 12, 1954.

association in the minds of their menfolk between urban employment and prostitution. But there is in this respect a striking difference between, for example, East and West Africa: and women from the former would be astonished to see the extent to which their sisters in the towns of West Africa engage in trade at all levels, but particularly petty trade, on their own account. A recent study shows that of 171 women interviewed in central Lagos, 87 per cent were trading and only 8 per cent were not working; and of the many hundred stall holders in the markets of Lagos Island, five-sixths were women.[1] Another report from Nigeria shows that among the Afikpo Ibo, 'almost all the women both farm and buy and sell in the market'.[2] In the professions there is seldom any legal discrimination against women, but the lack of educational opportunities has limited the numbers of them who could acquire professional qualifications. In West Africa there are not a few African women doctors and lawyers, including some magistrates; but in East Africa these are rare indeed.

WOMEN IN PUBLIC LIFE

So great has been the change in women's participation in public life in the modern world that it is all too easy to infer, mistakenly, that women have now for the first time been released from some age-old subjection to men. This is far from true in many civilizations. Thus the small part played by women in medieval English public life represented a decline in this respect from the days of bustling Anglo-Saxon ladies who, for example, exercised authority over the newly developed 'double monasteries' with communities of men as well as women under their rule.[3] In Anglo-Saxon royal circles such women as Offa's wife Cynethryth and her more tyrannical daughter Eadburg left their mark.[4] Derrett refers to examples of women in ancient India exercising public office even to the the highest level, before the decline of the last two thousand years which resulted partly from a decline in female education.[5]

There is not wanting evidence that parts of Africa have seen a similar decline from an earlier time when women exercised greater public influence. It is possible to accept this without accepting in full

---

[1] P. Marris, *Family and Social Change in an African City*, 1961, pp. 68, 75.

[2] Phoebe N. Ottenberg, 'The Changing Economic Position of Women among the Afikpo Ibo', in *Continuity and Change in African Cultures*, edited by Bascom and Herskovits, 1959, p. 208.

[3] Stenton, *op. cit.*, p. 13.   [4] Stenton, *op. cit.*, pp. 2–3.

[5] Derrett, *op. cit.*, pp. 246–7.

Talbot's report that the men's societies among the Ibibio of south-eastern Nigeria were originally women's societies penetrated and subverted in the past by male spies. 'In the old, old days Ibibio women were more powerful than the men. . .'[1] Talbot records the modern importance of the *Ebere* societies which 'form the only safeguard of Ibibio women against the tyranny of their menfolk'.[2] Among the Kamba of Kenya there were semi-formalized means by which women of a community enforced their views, even interfering with judicial proceedings with success:

'When the women come thus in a body, beating their drums and carrying boughs in their hands, the men try to keep out of the way as much as possible.'[3]

A conflicting picture of the decline of women's influence is given by the Culwicks, who wrote of the Babena of Tanganyika:

'Now and again a royal lady of outstanding ability might have her own village. . . But it was not customary for a woman to have more than a village settlement under her, and old Wabena can hardly have envisaged the possibility of one holding office as an Mtwa Mwenyelutenana [i.e. provincial ruler] as Semudodera's daughter has done successfully for many years. Towegale bemoans the way the women of the royal family have slipped out of public life now, fallen back in education and intelligence, while the men have on the whole gone forward. . . The Semukomi of today is quite incapable of doing as did the Mtema's senior wife in former times, holding her own court of law while travelling from one part of the country to another, weighing up the claims of rival litigants in the light of tribal law, making valid decisions in disputes: indeed, the idea is laughable to anyone who knows the simple-minded, shy, and unambitious chief wife of these days. The senior wife of the past admittedly dealt only with minor cases, passing on the more serious ones to a higher court, but she of the present would be overcome with confusion if called upon to decide the pettiest of disputes in public. Not one of the royal ladies now troubles to attend at the Mtema's court-house when he is transacting public business as their predecessors used to do.'[4]

[1] Talbot, *Women's Mysteries of a Primitive People*, 1915, p. 196 ff.
[2] *Op. cit.*, p. 190.
[3] Lindblom, *The Akamba in British East Africa*, 2nd edition, 1920, p. 181.
[4] A. T. and G. M. Culwick, *Ubena of the Rivers*, 1935, pp. 138-9.

Of course it does not follow that women in general had a higher status because certain individual women were prominent in public life, even holding positions of the highest prestige and power. England under Queen Victoria is a sufficient illustration of the fallacy of any such argument. In centralized societies in different parts of Africa, the queen-mother or queen-sister exercising real power is a recurrent phenomenon—found for example in Buganda, Ankole, Bunyoro, Ruanda and Toro. Thus, in the kingdom of Ankole 'the king's mother had judicial and administrative functions. No man could be executed without her consent. She sat beside the Mugabe at all important judicial cases and helped in deciding questions of war and peace.'[1] Even among the Muslim Kanuri of Bornu near Lake Chad a similar system appears to exist:

'The position of women in Bornu can be judged by the fact that certain ladies of the old Court of the Shehu (the *Magira* or official mother, and the *Magiram* or official sister, who acted as the King's advisers, though they were not necessarily actually related to him) attained such importance that the British at one time thought of ranking them as second class chiefs and giving them staves of office.'[2] African women have also been notable military leaders, such as for example Queen Zhinga of Matamba; she has her parallels in Aethelflaed of tenth century England and in Akkadevi and Umadevi a century or two later in India. The most amusing and vivid account of a nineteenth century woman chief in Africa is perhaps found in the description by Livingstone of his rebuff at the hands of Manenko.[3]

In more modern times, the political significance of women's views has sometimes been dramatically expressed, e.g. in the Aba Riots of 1929 in Eastern Nigeria:

'In the history of the British administration of Nigeria, Ibo women have constituted a unique and unforgettable human force. When they changed almost overnight from apparently peaceable, home-loving villagers into a frenzied mob of thousands who in December, 1929, attacked administration authorities while their men stood passively by, they brought about a sudden interest in the previously little-known

---

[1] K. Oberg, 'The Kingdom of Ankole in Uganda' in *African Political Systems*, edited by M. Fortes and E. E. Evans-Pritchard, 1940, pp. 160–1. See further, J. Roscoe, *The Banyankole*, 1923, chapter VI, pp. 59 ff.

[2] Douglas Botting, *The Knights of Bornu*, 1961, p. 55.

[3] See Livingstone's *Missionary Travels and Researches in South Africa*, 1857, pp. 275 ff. The relevant parts are included in *Livingstone's Travels*, edited by the Rev. James I. Macnair, 1954, pp. 75 ff.

Ibo-speaking peoples. This uprising, precipitated by an unfounded rumour that Ibo women were to be taxed by the Government, arose from uneasiness on the part of the women concerning their economic position. . .'[1]

Another example of women's resistance to unpopular administrative measures, in this case real ones, is found in the reaction of the Bafurutse women of South Africa to the extension to them and their sisters throughout the Union of the Reference Book system by an Act of 1952.[2] Today women's participation in public life may appear to be considerably less than that of men—except at elections.

'It would shock the Ibibio peasant woman to hear that, in Switzerland, women do not have the vote. In many of the polling stations at the last election, more women voted than men.'[3]

Yet this is not a field in which reform of the law would seem to be generally necessary. In the political slogan, 'One man—one vote', which has swept Africa in the past decade, the masculine has been taken to include the feminine. Women as well as men have been granted the right to vote, to stand for election and to have access to public offices. Where the progressive extension of the franchise, with property or financial qualifications at different stages, occurred, it was generally provided that married women could qualify to vote in right of their husband's qualifications (although educational qualifications, where relevant, were of course personal). Some anomalous situations arose: in Buganda before 1962 women were eligible to stand as candidates in elections to the Lukiko but were not eligible to vote! Under the qualified franchise provisions in both the old and the new constitutions of Southern Rhodesia, which include *inter alia* qualifications to vote based on income, it is provided that a married woman without a means qualification in her own right is deemed to have the same qualification as her husband: but 'in the case of a man married under a polygamous system, only the wife to whom he has been married for the longest period may be deemed to have the same qualification as her husband'.[4] In the Northern Region of Nigeria Islamic influence led to the franchise being withheld from women. In the Sudan, there is considerable feminist activity directed to

---

[1] Ottenberg, *op. cit.*, p. 205.
[2] Native (Abolition of Passes and Co-ordination of Documents) Act, No. 67 of 1952. See Charles Hooper, *Brief Authority*.
[3] Naomi Mitchison, *Other People's Worlds*, 1958, p. 93.
[4] *Southern Rhodesia Constitution*, Cmnd. 1399, 1961, p. 14.

ensuring that women receive political rights in the new Constitution now under preparation (formerly only men were enfranchised, except that some women graduates voted in the Graduates' Consituency, which has now disappeared).

Despite the general equality of legal rights, women do not in fact appear to take an equal part in government. Thus the proportion of women members of parliaments is consistently low. In 1955 it was estimated that for most countries except the Soviet Union, where women made up 17 per cent of the Supreme Soviet, 'the maximum percentage of women elected to the various parliaments seems to be about 5'.[1] Nevertheless, owing to the survival of local prejudices most strongly at village level, it may well be possible for women to play more significant roles in national than in local politics. Can the law assist in this situation? It can be provided that certain seats are reserved in the assembly for women members, or specially created for them, as was done in Ghana as a temporary expedient.[2] The value of such a measure on a permanent basis is open to serious doubt; but apparently unequal measures are sometimes necessary to promote genuine 'equality'.

The Convention on the Nationality of Married Women opened by the United Nations in 1957 provides in essence for separate nationality for wives, independent of that of their husbands. The British Nationality Act, 1948, of course, reverting to the earlier common law, is in accordance with this. It applies in dependent territories in Africa and independent Commonwealth states generally legislate in similar terms. The Economic and Social Council of the U.N. Organization has stated its belief that legal systems which allow the wife only a dependent domicile following that of her husband are incompatible with the principle of equality of the spouses set forward in the Declaration of Human Rights; it recommended that governments make provision to give wives the right to independent domicile.[3] To effect this would

[1] Duverger, *The Political Role of Women*, 1955, p. 145.

[2] By the Representation of the People (Women Members) Acts, 1959 and 1960, later repealed. The 1959 Act provided for the election of ten women Members by electoral colleges themselves elected by registered female voters. This conflicted with the principle of 'one woman, one vote' and was replaced by Act No. 8 of 1960 which provided that the Members of the Assembly themselves should elect ten women Members as a temporary measure. The women so elected will remain members until dissolution of the Assembly, when these special seats will disappear. See, further, *African Women*, Vol. IV, No. 1, 1960, and L. Rubin and P. Murray, *The Constitution and Government of Ghana*, 1961, p. 67.

[3] Resolution 587 D (XX), 890th plenary meeting, August 3, 1955.

involve legislation in most common law African countries where the English rule which does not give such a right is normally followed. But in most of these countries there is found a provision analogous to that in the English Matrimonial Causes Act, 1950, section 18, which gives to the courts jurisdiction in divorce where the wife, although not domiciled in the country, has resided there for three years.

The wish of the participants in the United Nations Seminar on the Participation of Women in Public Life, 1960, that wives should have complete freedom to retain their own names or take those of their husbands, does not involve reform of the law in common law jurisdictions, which already afford this right (although the position in customary law is not clear).

With regard to women and the criminal law, the little evidence documented for African territories indicates that, as in other parts of the world, women commit far less crime than men. But for some crimes statistics may, for reasons peculiar to Africa, number more women than men among the offenders: such is the offence of illegally brewing beer, at least in Northern Rhodesia.[1]

WOMEN IN PRIVATE LAW

It is proposed first to consider women's rights in general in systems of customary law in Africa, with reference to the need for law reform; secondly, a more detailed examination will be given to the remarkable situations which result from the conflicts between different systems of law coexisting territorially—taking one territory, Uganda, as a somewhat extreme example of the need for law reform in this respect.

It would be futile to generalize about the status of African women in customary law. Even where there is a common religion with its own legal system, such as Islam, striking differences occur. Thus, of the Kanuri Botting writes as follows:

'The position of women in Bornu society is much freer than in most Muslim countries, for the veil is unknown and seclusion in the house of parent or husband is much rarer. Women may dance in public with men, walk freely around the streets and talk openly with anyone they choose, and they play an active and significant part in ordinary day-to-day business, especially on market day. Women in Bornu are not usually regarded as either chattels, slaves or beasts of burden, and the

[1] See W. Clifford, *Crime in Northern Rhodesia*, 1960, Rhodes-Livingstone Communication No. 18, pp. 72-3.

Kanuri's prime occupation of agriculture is shared by both men and women.'[1]

But in Muslim societies where the rule of the seclusion of women is strictly followed, men are responsible for all agricultural labour. And in Zaria and Nupe, in Nigeria, men in practice do the major part of the work of cultivating, the degree of seclusion in the former depending upon the agreement made at the time of the marriage.[2]

Other differences occur between different societies as a result of different ethnic backgrounds and history, and different political and economic systems (thus the herding of cattle in pastoral societies tends to be exclusively a male prerogative, except for the domestic beasts such as sheep and goats). Some differences in women's status are explicable as resulting from the differences between matrilineal and patrilineal systems of relationship and inheritance. In the former, where women transmit—but do not necessarily enjoy—rights to property, it may be expected that they will receive greater protection from the law than in societies where the line of descent for inheritance or relationship purposes (such as clan membership) is traced through males. Where property is held by right of membership in a patrilineal clan, a wife, being of course of a different clan from her husband, may find herself destitute on his death; unless she has been able to acquire property for her own enjoyment (which the customary law may not permit) she will, as a widow, be dependent upon either her own children, or her own family or her deceased husband's clan relatives.

On the other hand, in many matrilineal societies the husband commonly goes to live with his wife and her family, at least during the early years of the marriage. His position there[3] is inevitably different from that of the husband in a patrilineal society whose wife must normally join him at his home and may often visit her own relatives only with his permission (which should not, however, be unreasonably withheld).

To discuss the position of women in customary law is to discuss the position of women in marriage, for spinsterhood was a rare thing in traditional societies. But in the changed economic circumstances of today the unmarried woman may attain a status in independence superior to her married sister:

[1] Botting, op. cit., p. 54.
[2] L. P. Mair, 'African Marriage and Social Change', in Survey of African Marriage and Family Life, edited by Arthur Phillips, 1953, p. 137.
[3] See Mair, op. cit., p. 74.

'... the free-lance woman may forfeit respectability and general esteem, yet can undoubtedly win an economic and jural status as an independent business woman and property owner which is not open to her respectable sister.'[1]

A commonly expressed view in the past has stressed the inferior position of wives of customary law marriages.

'The inferior status of women is believed to be evident in the institution of polygyny (and still more of polyandry where it is found), child betrothal, the inheritance of widows and all procedures whereby women can be disposed of in marriage without their consent;. . . .'[2]

The general nature of African marriage is sometimes seen as subordinating the individuals to the wider families and their interests. Much authority suggests that customary marriage is 'an alliance between two kinship groups and only in a secondary aspect . . . a union between two individual persons'.[3] Phillips emphasises that it must be viewed as an integral part of the kinship system as a whole, but the first trend he discusses in the changing pattern of marriage is the shifting of emphasis 'to the individual aspect of marriage as a relationship between two persons'.[4]

Were both husband and wife subordinated in this way it would not necessarily involve a diminution of the wife's rights compared with those of her husband; but in South Africa it is alleged that the subordination in fact affects the wife more particularly. Indeed, a modern authority maintains that the bride is not even recognized in law as a party to the contract of marriage.[5]

'Forced marriage', often connected with child betrothal, has been alleged to be typical of customary law. Free consent to marriage is one of several matters incorporated in a Draft Convention relating to the formation of marriage and adopted by the Third Committee of the United Nations General Assembly in December 1961. After recalling Article 16 of the Universal Declaration of Human Rights, and an earlier resolution of the General Assembly declaring certain customs, ancient laws and practices to be inconsistent therewith,

---

[1] A. Southall, 'Introductory Summary', in *Social Change in Modern Africa*, edited by Southall, 1961, p. 22.

[2] Mair, *op. cit.*, p. 7.

[3] A. Phillips, 'An Introductory Essay', in Phillips (ed.), *Survey of African Marriage and Family Life*, 1953, p. xv.

[4] Phillips, *op. cit.*, p. xvii.

[5] S. M. Seymour, *Native Law in South Africa*, 2nd edition, 1960, p. 77.

the preamble reaffirms that all states should take appropriate measures to abolish such customs. The substantive articles follow:

'Article 1. No marriage shall be legally entered into without the full and free consent of both parties, such consent to be expressed by them in person after due publicity and in the presence of the authority competent to solemnize the marriage and of witnesses, as prescribed by law.

Article 2. States parties to this convention shall take legislative action to specify a minimum age for marriage. No marriage shall be legally entered into by any person under this age, except where a competent authority has granted a dispensation as to age, for serious reasons, in the interest of the intending spouses.

Article 3. All marriages shall be registered in an appropriate official register by the competent authority.'[1]

Each of these articles calls for measures of reform of the law in different parts of Africa. Allegations of forced marriages have in the past given rise to considerable concern and public discussion, leading on one occasion to a notable general investigation by the Secretary of State for the Colonies.[2] The nature of the subject, however, complicates investigation and conclusion. It is obviously difficult (in any society) to analyse the degree of 'freedom' with which a person consents to marry—pressure of various kinds may operate in different degrees, much of it not realized even by the person concerned. Investigation may be misled by the recurrence in many African societies of the custom of ritual, formalized resistance to the marriage by the bride who may, or may not, at heart be content with the match. There are well-documented individual cases of girls fleeing from husbands whom their parents have chosen for them, often no doubt because of an affectionate attachment for another. One aspect of law reform in this matter might well be to improve the legal mechanisms for overriding the unreasonable refusal of parents or guardian to consent to a match desired by the daughter herself. But in the villages of Africa the day has not yet come when young daughters will readily invoke the aid of local judicial authorities to defy their parents' wishes. A good precedent for legislation exists in that part of the Somali Republic which was formerly British Somaliland.[3] Phillips concludes that 'general legisla-

---

[1] Adopted by the Third Committee on December 14, 1961.
[2] The White Paper documenting this investigation is *Correspondence relating to the Welfare of Women in Tropical Africa 1935–37, 1938*, Cmd. 5784.
[3] Natives' Betrothal and Marriage Ordinance, Cap. 67, section 3 (2), which gave a woman the right to register her refusal of a betrothal.

tion on this subject is perhaps in itself of slight value' but he cites some other examples of enactments.[1] The Natal Code of Native Law requires a public declaration by the bride of her free consent,[2] and in other parts of the Republic of South Africa where there is no express legislation the courts on grounds of public policy require her consent for the validity of a customary union;[3] agreements by parents for the subsequent marriage of young children are void, but subsequent ratification by the partners will validate the union from the date of such ratification.[4]

If there is any doubt as to the need to deal with this problem, reference may be made to some of the tragic cases recorded in *African Homicide and Suicide*.[5] Two cases among the Luo of Kenya emphasize that conflicts of wills in this matter may lead to bitter consequences.

'A very young girl, little more than a child, objected in the traditional way to the union which her parents had arranged. The parents insisted that she be sent or "dragged" to her husband. On the night of the ceremonial defloration she committed suicide by hanging... Her mother was so struck by grief that she committed suicide later.'[6]

In another case, a girl, when she was three years old, had been promised by her father to his friend. The girl was well educated (her father being a headmaster) and fell in love with a teacher at another school. He begged her father to allow him to marry the girl, asking to be permitted to return the bride-wealth animals the father had already received. The father refused. On the night before her wedding to her betrothed, the girl ran away to join the young teacher; he was arrested, but his brothers took the girl to Nairobi. She was eventually found there by her father, forcibly returned to her home and married to her betrothed, who took her by force to the place of his employment 700 miles away. The teacher and his brother were heavily fined for taking the girl from her father. Meanwhile the girl reached her husband's home to find that he already had a Christian wife who refused to have the girl in the home. As a result of their quarrels the husband was

---

[1] *Op. cit.*, pp. 203–5.
[2] Section 59 (1). Section 29 of Cape Proclamation 140 of 1885 makes it unlawful 'for any person to compel any woman to marry against her wish'.
[3] *Sila* v *Masuku*, 1937 N.A.C. (T. & N.) 121, cited by Seymour, *op. cit.*, p. 73; see also the cases cited by Phillips, *op. cit.*, p. 205.
[4] Seymour, *op. cit.*, p. 74.
[5] Edited by Paul Bohannan, 1960.
[6] G. M. Wilson, 'Homicide and Suicide among the Joluo of Kenya' in *African Homicide and Suicide*, ed. Bohannan, pp. 205–6.

obliged to return the girl to her father and ask for a divorce. Instead of returning home, the girl joined her sweetheart in Nairobi; it was her father who hanged himself in a classroom in his school, in shame and humiliation. But his last act was to write letters to those involved blaming his daughter for the tragedy.[1]

This case is of particular interest because the girl's action in running away was the last traditional way for her to assert her refusal of an unwanted match. By Luo customary law, the elopement would have been justified and legal. But the modern increase in illegal unions forces African courts to deal severely with young couples who run off possibly to evade bride-price obligations.

The question of forced marriage is of course intimately connected with the point dealt with in article 2 of the Draft Convention. In general, 'governments have . . . shown caution and even reluctance'[2] to legislate for a minimum age for customary marriage. For many reasons it is often thought that such a reform would be unenforceable. In particular, child betrothal rather than child marriage may be the problem. A general provision in the French territories stipulated minimum ages of 14 for women and 16 for men.[3] The Penal Code of Tanganyika makes it an offence for a husband to have sexual inter-course with a wife under twelve years of age, but it expressly does not affect the validity of marriage under that age where consummation is postponed.[4] This may merely reflect customary law. In Buganda, 'it was an abomination (kivve) to have sexual intercourse with a girl before her puberty'.[5] In other societies, girls could marry only after completing the initiation ceremonies which took place at or after puberty. But it is clear that in some societies child betrothal was common.[6]

The third article in the Draft Convention refers to a matter which has been the subject of considerable discussion for many years. Should registration of customary marriages be introduced? If so, what should be the effect of registration? If registration does not affect the validity of the marriage, provision for it may be relatively ineffective; if registration is made essential for validity, this amounts to the introduc-tion of a compulsory non-customary solemnization.[7] But it is difficult

[1] Wilson, op. cit., 201–4. [2] Phillips, op. cit., p. 200.
[3] Décret Mandel, 1939. [4] Section 138.
[5] E. S. Haydon, Law and Justice in Buganda, 1960, p. 84.
[6] See, for example, J. C. D. Lawrance, The Iteso, 1957, p. 93.
[7] The dilemma is stated in these terms by Phillips, op. cit., p. 217, following his discussion of the problem and its history.

to see how any other reform in the customary laws of marriage, or in resolving conflicts between different systems of marriage, can be effective without this initial regulatory step. The article quoted above was passed by the Third Committee with no opposing votes (though there were seven abstentions). The Report of the Committee's discussion includes the following:

'The importance of registration of marriages as a protective measure, particularly in the developing countries, was recognized. One representative, while pointing out that the trend in her country was towards registration, emphasised that customary law had applied there for over one thousand years, and that education to the idea of registration must necessarily take time.'[1]

The present writer was present in the Lukiko of Buganda in 1960 when that all-male assembly overwhelmingly (and not for the first time) rejected a motion for registration.

Two features common to marriage under most systems of African customary law are of vital significance; and yet their ultimate effect on the position of women is open to endless inconclusive debate. These are the polygamous nature of marriage by customary law and the economic exchange, whether by cash, livestock, goods or services, which generally characterizes the inception of such marriages—the 'bride-price'.

'Africa remains a continent of polygamy. Polygyny is the undoubted goal of men in rural society, though comparatively few reach it until their later years.'[2]

Southall points out that where economic change has undermined the traditional basis of the compound polygynous family, the old norms and values have found new expression in successive monogamy or a combination of monogamy with concubinage. Moreover, he sees the movement towards equality of status for women as having this result: that of those few women who do not remain subject to the traditional sanctions of rural life, many demand the right, which men enjoy, to have a number of sexual partners.[3]

By way of deferring this problem, it is often stated that economic and other changes will abolish polygamy in due course. This view may be based on a mistaken assessment of the extent of polygamy in ancient

---

[1] Report of the Third Committee, December 14, 1961, para 12.
[2] Southall, *op. cit.*, p. 52.   [3] *Op. cit.*, p. 53.

times. In the course of his detailed study,[1] Dorjahn concludes that 'lacking the necessary quantitative data, one can only say that no certain overall tendency toward increase or decrease is discernible for sub-Saharan Africa during the last forty years'.[2] His tables show that the incidence of polygamy is lower in southern and eastern Africa than in the Congo and western Sudan; it is highest in the Guinea Coast.

'In general, the data show that about 35 per cent of all married African males are polygynous, that this 35 per cent averages about 245 wives per 100 polygynously married men (or households), while the number of wives to 100 husbands, monogamously and polygamously married, is about 150'.[3]

Whatever the effect of polygyny upon the position of women, even when practised merely to this limited extent, it has often an unfortunate effect upon the status of young men who may, by reason of competition for brides from older, more prosperous polygamists, be obliged to postpone their own marriages. Dorjahn suggests that it is the difference in the mean ages of first marriages of men and women which provides the surplus of women who serve as second or subsequent wives.[4] This is the sort of factor with which the law cannot deal—no one would suggest a maximum as well as a minimum age for marriage.

Phillips cites legislation prohibiting polygamy:[5] a Belgian Decree withheld recognition from polygamous marriages contracted after 1950. In Angola permanent residents in towns were forbidden to marry polygamously: apart from penal sanctions, polygamous Africans were disqualified from employment in government service. Schapera records legislation by Tswana chiefs prohibiting polygamy without the chief's permission to men of the two junior age regiments. This is enforced by annulment of the second marriage and punishment, but Phillips points out that it falls far short of a general ban, merely restricting polygamy to old and middle-aged men.[6]

Other legal measures may discourage polygamy: e.g. differential taxing provisions. Phillips emphasises the importance of providing an alternative form of legally binding monogamous marriage for those who wish for it[7]—an alternative not yet available to Africans in

---

[1] Vernon R. Dorjahn, 'Polygyny in African Demography', in *Continuity and Change in African Cultures*, edited by Bascom and Herskovits, 1959, pp. 87–112; see also Dorjahn, *African Polygyny*, 1954.

[2] *Op. cit.*, p. 101.   [3] *Op. cit.*, p. 104.   [4] *Op. cit.*, p. 108.
[5] *Op. cit.*, p. 192.   [6] Cited by Phillips, *op. cit.*, pp. 192–3.
[7] *Op. cit.*, p. 194.

Northern Rhodesia where the need for reform on this point seems urgent.[1] Here the option of statutory marriage is not available to Africans, and even if they have a religious ceremony an African couple can enter into a customary law marriage only. It might well be argued that, if a couple avoid fulfilling the requirements of customary law (which otherwise would be the law of their marriage) and marry in Christian form in church, they will have contracted a valid common law marriage, no local form of monogamous marriage being available to them. The obstacle to be surmounted by such argument would be the reply that local legislation expressly withheld monogamous forms of marriage from persons of this class. Phillips also refers to the possibility of African courts giving effect to express promises of monogamy in marriage contracts, a precedent for which is found in Islamic law.[2] In the English Court of Appeal, Harman, L.J., has suggested this possibility to the Ghanaian wife of a customary marriage according to Ghanaian law, whose application to an English magistrates' court for a maintenance order against her husband was held to be outside the jurisdiction of English courts, which cannot give matrimonial remedies in cases of even potentially polygamous marriages.[3]

Except for the minority expressing definite Christian or moral convictions, there does not appear to be a clear-cut demand from educated African women for the general prohibition of polygamy at present. Under existing economic conditions, where wives are so often responsible for cultivation of both food and cash crops, the wife without co-wives may find herself at a serious disadvantage. Views of participants in the U.N. Seminar in 1960 were clearly divided, but it is recorded that 'the great majority of participants agreed that polygamy was undesirable and outmoded'.[4]

Clearly, when it is felt that public opinion will support such a measure, it is possible to legislate simply for the prohibition of polygamy, as was done in India by the Hindu Marriage Act, 1955. (Similar provisions have been introduced for Hindu marriages in Uganda, for which no previous provision had been made despite the presence of a large immigrant Indian community.)[5]

---

[1] By section 47, the Marriage Ordinance, Cap. 109, does not apply to 'natives'.
[2] *Op. cit.*, p. 194.   [3] *Sowa* v *Sowa*, [1961] 2 W.L.R. 313, 318.
[4] U.N. Seminar on the Participation of Women in Public Life, Addis Ababa. 1960.
[5] See now the Hindu Marriage and Divorce Ordinance, 1961. For other examples, see Anderson, *Islamic Laws in the Modern World*, 1959.

Views about bride-price are similarly conflicting and uncertain, partly reflecting the different nature of this factor in different areas today as a result of local developments. At this time it is unnecessary to commence a discussion of the real nature of marriage payments in traditional customary law; that they performed a valuable function, and did not amount merely to a purchase of the bride, is scarcely open to doubt. Modern changes seem to have had effects differing considerably, but producing *inter alia* two opposite extremes: in societies such as Buganda the bride-price has become a formal token or ritual transfer, not inflated in amount and often not recovered on dissolution of the marriage; in other (often pastoral) societies the amount of bride-price has been proportionately inflated—some would say commercialized—leading to real abuse. It is ironical that in such societies the bride-price may have tended to become in modern times the thing it was originally thought to be by early observers, a means of purchasing a wife. Few would doubt that in many areas reform of the law is called for; but views would be divided on the nature of that reform.

Where a maximum limit for marriage payments has been fixed by law it has in practice often been evaded—perhaps wholesale as among the Iteso of Uganda, who find it profitable to pay the legal penalty of a 150 shilling fine in the unlikely event of detection.[1] But among the Ngwato of Bechuanaland, a chief's edict prohibiting bride-price appears to have been effective.[2]

The Committee set up by the Government of the Eastern Region of Nigeria in 1954 'to investigate the social effects of bride-price and to make . . . recommendations' reported that inflation of the payment forced men and women to postpone marriage, and increased prostitution and the number of children born outside wedlock. £50 for an illiterate girl and three or four times that sum for one well educated were quoted as examples of payments made. But the Committee did not include abolition among its recommendations—the mere suggestion having been generally received with consternation; it did recommend limitations on the amount of the 'dowry' and marriage expenses, with registration to include the recording of the details of the payments agreed and made. Participants in the 1960 U.N. Seminar were divided on this matter. So too were the women who took part in the Uganda Council of Women Conference in 1960, and who did not

---

[1] See Lawrance, *op. cit.*, pp. 202–3.
[2] I. Schapera, *A Handbook of Tswana Law and Custom*, 2nd edition, 1955, pp. 145–6.

recommend abolition of the payment of bride-price but did recommend abolition of the refund of the payment on divorce. Unfortunately, such refund is still often the equivalent of the 'decree' of dissolution and it is not clear what would be substituted for the refund as a mark of divorce. Perhaps the best proposal comes from the meeting of the I.N.C.I.D.I. on 'Women's Role':

'In regions where customs provide for the payment of dowry, legislation should have as a principal aim ensuring that the new family itself shall be the beneficiary.'[1]

As a basis for law reform, the transfer of the benefit of the bride-price rather than its total abolition would certainly be more likely to command general acceptance.

With several other topics of law affecting the position of women there is not room to deal here. Property rights are obviously of fundamental importance; here again it is impossible to draw general statements valid for the different systems of customary law. Matrimonial property regimes, for example, vary from the typical South African 'native law' system under which the wife has no individual right to own property, everything acquired by her belonging to her 'House' within the wider polygamous family, which is controlled by her husband, to (at the other extreme) the separation in law of the property of the spouses among the matrilineal Akan of the Guinea Coast. Central African peoples seem to occupy appropriately a mean between these extremes, the wife's property being kept distinct and the husband's strict rights being modified by everyday practice: thus among the Nkundo the husband can claim the proceeds of the sales of objects made by his wife, but in disposing of property during marriage the spouses consult together 'and the husband is censured if he presses his claims on the fruit of his wife's labours too far'.[2] There are other societies where wives complain that their husbands seize the proceeds of their labours; but any proposals for the introduction of legislative modifications of the customary law on the lines of the Married Women's Property Act, 1882, must be based on careful local examination of the requirements of different societies. Yet the principle of equality certainly demands that wives be able to claim for themselves their own earnings at the very least; and this is already the position in many parts of West Africa and in North-Eastern Rhodesia and Nyasaland.

[1] Final Recommendations, II, 5, p. 530.
[2] Mair, *op. cit.*, p. 96.

The position of widows in African customary law is one which may cause concern to those who would improve women's status. Apart from the levirate custom which raises special questions, a widow may be left with the unhappy alternative of returning destitute to her own family and depending on them for support, or of remaining with her deceased husband's family usually as the wife of one of his kinsmen. This is often the result of the exclusion of women from inheritance; but even the admission of women to equal rights of participation in, for example, family property in Yorubaland may not benefit widows as such—for they will not come of the right line of descent to inherit; women participate in Yoruba family property as children, not as wives.[1] A widow may of course be supported by her children but the lot of a childless widow may be hard indeed. It should be possible to devise legislation which would afford the widow genuine freedom of choice—perhaps through a special application to the local African court which could be given discretion to make appropriate orders in different cases. But in some cases, such as when the deceased leaves insufficient property to satisfy the reasonable requirements of his widow or widows *and* his children and kinsmen, the conflict of interests between wives claiming equal rights which result essentially from a new concept of marriage, and clansmen claiming traditional rights based on an older social pattern, will be crystallized and will demand solution.

Similar considerations apply to the question of affording wives equal rights with their husbands over their children. Rights to children, perhaps deriving in the past at least from the payment of marriage cattle for the mother (irrespective often of the actual progenitor of the child) repose, through the father, in a patrilineal clan in many societies. The child's mother is not a member of this clan. It is easy to see that in this situation the struggle by women for equal rights will bring them into conflict not only with their husbands' claims but with those of their clans; and it is difficult to see how ultimately the claims of the clan can be reconciled with the rights of the wife based on the notion of the smaller, nuclear family.

The final complication with regard to customary marriage to which reference can now be made results from the problem of conflicting laws which is typical of the multiple legal systems of modern Africa. How far is a customary law marriage recognized by the 'general' (i.e. statute and common) law? Is the wife of such a marriage entitled to the status of wife to the same extent as the wife of a monogamous marriage in

[1] G. B. A. Coker, *Family Property among the Yorubas*, 1958, pp. 159 ff.

statutory form? Once again diversity is found in the law. Most of the consequences of a customary law marriage will, of course, be governed by that system of law under which it is contracted and under which the spouses live. On this basis, in most territories the wife will be recognized as a wife, though as subject to different legal consequences in respect of the marriage itself from the wife of a marriage in statutory form. In South Africa, however, even the term 'marriage' is denied to the 'customary union' and the existence of the latter is no bar (as it is in many other parts of Africa) to a subsequent statutory marriage by either spouse, which automatically dissolves the customary union. As a result of recent decisions of the Judicial Committee, the recognition of customary law marriage has been extended much further in other parts of Africa, in allowing children and wives of customary law marriages to share in the distribution of a deceased husband's estate as children and wives within the meaning of those terms in English statutes concerning succession, as applied in Africa.[1] Similar developments have been authoritatively proposed for South Africa, i.e. that the law should be reformed to allow all legitimate children to share equally in their father's (or mother's) estate, whether the issue of a marriage or a customary union.[2] The widow should also receive at least a child's share (under 'native' law a woman has no right of inheritance at all).[3]

LAW REFORM IN UGANDA

Women of Uganda are considerably dissatisfied with the laws of marriage in that country. A women teacher has written:

'The laws and customs which govern marriage, inheritance and the custody of children are in a hopeless state of the utmost confusion and complication. It will need long, patient and careful study of the Protectorate Laws and African customary laws to bring about the much needed reform in integrating the two systems.'[4]

[1] *Bamgbose* v *Daniel* [1955] A.C. 107 (P.C.); *Mawji* v *The Queen* [1957] A.C. 126 (P.C.); *Coleman* v *Shang* [1961] A.C. 481 (P.C.).
[2] Julius Lewin *et al.*, 'The Legal Status of African Women', *Race Relations Journal* (South African Institute of Race Relations, Johannesburg), Vol. XXVI, No. 4, pp. 152–9, at p. 153.
[3] Lewin, *op. cit.*, p. 153; Seymour, *op. cit.*, p. 175: in some tribes of the Sotho-Tswana group a woman may inherit property.
[4] E. S. Nyendwoha, 'Uganda', in *Women's Role in the Development of Tropical and Sub-Tropical Countries*, 1959 (International Institute of Differing Civilizations, Report of the XXXIst Meeting), pp. 174–85 at p. 176.

For his Presidential Address to the Uganda Society in 1959, Dr. H. F. Morris, then Native Courts Adviser, chose as his subject 'marriage in Uganda, and in particular the anomalies and difficulties to which the present legal position gives rise'.[1] The present writer was privileged in 1960 to attend in Uganda two sets of discussions upon this urgent theme—a national conference called by the Uganda Council of Women and a special committee appointed by the Upper Nile Diocese of the Native Anglican Church to recommend possible lines of reform.

A major source of discontent arises from uncertainty in the present law; and this in turn is due to the inextricable confusion of different systems of law. In common with most African territories, Uganda has a complex legal system based upon the coexistence of the 'general' or 'Protectorate' law (composed mainly of the law of England of 1902 with statutes subsequently enacted in Uganda) with various local systems of customary law, of which Uganda has a wide variety. (Some rules of Islamic and Hindu law are also applied in the field of marriage under special local Ordinances.) The divisions of the judicial system —the High Court and magistrates' courts on the one side and the Buganda or African or native courts on the other—do not correspond precisely with the divisions of law but do so very nearly: the High Court administers principally the general law; the African courts apply mainly the unwritten customary law prevailing in the areas of their jurisdiction, with some sections of the enacted laws and local bye-laws, and they must now be guided by certain general enactments, especially in criminal law or procedure.

Various types of marriage are available in Uganda. Customary law marriages may be entered into by Africans. The Marriage Ordinance[2] and the Marriage of Africans Ordinance[3] both came into force in 1904. The former governs the formation of monogamous type marriage, in civil or religious form, by any persons. The Registrar must be satisfied that neither party is already married by customary law to another spouse. The Ordinance also provides for the conversion of customary law marriages into legally binding monogamous marriages by a civil ceremony. During the continuance of an 'Ordinance marriage' neither spouse can contract a valid customary law marriage: to do so (that is, to purport to do so, the second marriage being void), or to enter into an Ordinance 'marriage' while married by customary law, is an offence akin to bigamy punishable with up to

---

[1] H. F. Morris, 'Marriage and Divorce in Uganda', *Uganda Journal*, Vol. 24, 1960, pp. 197–206.

[2] Chapter 109 of the Revised Laws, 1951.   [3] Chapter 111.

five years' imprisonment. The Marriage of Africans Ordinance provide for marriages between African Christians or Muslims respectively, and the Marriage and Divorce of Mohammedans Ordinance of 1906[1] dispensing with certain preliminaries required by the main Ordinance.

The Divorce Ordinance, 1904,[2] which governs the dissolution (in the case of Africans by the High Court or a First Class Magistrate's court) of a marriage under the Marriage Ordinance, is based on the English law of that date, which was then found in the original Matrimonial Causes Act, 1857. This law discriminated in favour of men, who could petition for divorce on the ground of their wives' adultery only, whereas a wife's petition had to be based—and still does, in Uganda —on the husband's adultery plus one of the aggravating circumstances: desertion, cruelty, bigamy, incest, etc. Dr. Morris describes this Ordinance as having 'almost a medieval ring about it'; it is an archaism which should no longer be tolerated on the statute book of Uganda.

Confusion arises because some Africans in Uganda, while attaining the social ideal of a church wedding under the Ordinance, also perform all the requirements of customary marriage; they therefore contract a curious kind of double marriage, the two aspects of which have inconsistent consequences.[3] It would require specialized legal advice clearly to apprise the spouses in this situation of their legal rights and duties, especially as clear judicial authority is lacking. One case of note in fact serves only to confuse the position still further. In *Bishan Singh* v *R.*,[4] the High Court held that the Marriage Ordinances were imperative as to native Christians, so that a marriage between such persons celebrated according to customary law was a nullity and the accused Sikh therefore committed no offence in taking away the 'wife' of such 'marriage'. This decision would not seem to have been required by the terms of the Ordinances, which appear essentially permissive, not mandatory.

African courts have no jurisdiction over marriages contracted under the Ordinances—except that they can hear claims for refund of brideprice or for adultery, founded on native law or custom.[5] When this

---

[1] Chapter 110.   [2] Chapter 112.

[3] J. V. Taylor, *The Growth of the Church in Buganda*, 1958, p. 176.

[4] Criminal Appeal No. 13 of 1923, reported in the *Uganda Herald* on January 26, 1924. The decision gave rise to considerable anxiety, not least among officers of the government.

[5] Native Courts Ordinance, Chapter 76, section 10 (*b*); African Courts Ordinance, 1957, section 8 (*b*). However, the Buganda Courts Ordinance,

exception was provided for (in the face of considerable opposition from missionaries) its implications were perhaps not fully recognised. For the refund of the bride-price is normally the means of dissolution of the customary marriage. Thus the situation arises in which, following a 'double marriage' between two partners, the customary marriage may be dissolved by the refund of the bride-price in the native courts and the spouses may not appreciate that they are still bound by the Ordinance marriage, which is dissoluble only in a higher court. If either spouse marries another person, he or she will become liable to the penalty for an offence akin to bigamy described above. Dr. Morris gives 'the tortuous but not impossible example of the man—let us call him James—who was married in church accompanied by a native marriage contract, to Anne. The pair separate and the customary contract is dissolved by a Native Court, the bride wealth being returned. Anne is then married by native custom to William. James, however, later visits and sleeps with her and is discovered by William, who takes a case against him in the Native Court for adultery which of course has been committed with a woman who is still in Protectorate Law the adulterer's wife. What is the Native Court to which this case is brought to do?'[1]

This is one of the possible situations which, it has already been suggested, is too fantastic for the plot of a comic opera. And yet Uganda presents only a slightly more extreme example of the problem of conflicting laws than that which is found in many parts of common law Africa, where a similar framework of marriage law is provided. It was this sort of situation that the Ghana Government made proposals to reform in their White Paper on Marriage, Divorce and Inheritance in 1961.[2] The suggestion that all sanctions maintaining monogamy be removed could hardly be expected to be acceptable to Christian opinion, which would insist that some form of monogamous marriage should be available in the state.[3] The proposals for divorce were more interesting, apparently representing a genuine attempt to reconcile modern needs (judicial procedure and sanction) with traditional customary law (attempts made privately to reconcile the

Chapter 77, section 9 (b), excludes jurisdiction over 'Ordinance marriage' with no exceptions.

[1] Op. cit. For problems arising from the application of Islamic law, see Anderson, *Islamic Law in Africa*, 1954, pp. 148 ff.

[2] No. 3 of 1961.

[3] It is interesting to note that the President of another West African state, Guinea, with which indeed Ghana has a union, is reported as stressing that polygamy must disappear in order that his country may develop.

spouses, with divorce as the solution only if it becomes clear that the marriage has irretrievably broken down—thus departing from the English law notion of the matrimonial offence as a basis for divorce).

CONCLUSION

In this discussion it has been possible only to consider a few of the fields within which reform of the law might be expected to be of relevance in improving the status of women in the developing countries of Africa. It has been seen that many of the problems turn on the position of women in marriage, and in particular on the incidents of customary law marriage and on the complex situations which result from the internal conflicts of laws on this subject.

Even in England law reform to give women equality with men in private law is still needed in certain matters.[1] But the difficulties of the task in Africa are intensified by the speed and extent of the social changes now taking place. African women are impatient to assert and enjoy in all respects their equality with men and such is the tempo of the times that they may well accomplish in a decade advances which took their sisters in other continents a generation. Is it too much to hope that the laws of their countries will advance with them?

[1] These matters were considered by the Law Reform Committee in its Ninth Report, *Liability in Tort between Husband and Wife*, 1961, Cmd. 1268.

13

ISLAMIC FAMILY LAW: PROGRESS IN PAKISTAN

N. J. COULSON

Lecturer in Islamic Law, School of Oriental and
African Studies, University of London

'Certain depraved elements have again raised their head and are con-
spiring to rob the weaker sex of their cherished treasure of chastity
by holding out false prospects of their rights in an attempt to push
them again into the abyss of disgrace in which they had been rotting
in the dark ages.' Maulana Ihtisham-ul-Haq thus forcefully expressed
his dissent from the proposals of his colleagues on a Commission set
up in 1955 in Pakistan[1] to consider possible reform of the traditional
Islamic law of the family and particularly of the position of women.
The Commission had proposed, *inter alia*, that a husband should not
be allowed to exercise either his right of polygamy or his right of
unilateral repudiation without the consent of the court. This consent
to a second marriage should only be given, it was suggested, where
the first wife was insane, or was suffering from some incurable disease
or there were other exceptional circumstances, but not where the
husband merely wished to marry a prettier or a younger woman than
his existing wife. Permission to repudiate should only be given when
the position of the wife could be adequately safeguarded by requiring
payment of the dower and suitable maintenance until her remarriage,
or for life if necessary. It is perhaps a little difficult to see in such
proposals a depraved conspiracy against the chastity of Muslim wives;
but the intensely hostile reaction of the traditionalist member may be
better appreciated when it is remembered how revolutionary these

---

[1] The report of the Commission was published in the *Gazette of Pakistan,*
Extraordinary, dated June 20, 1956, and the note of dissent in the issue of the
same journal dated August 30, 1956. I have discussed the work of the Commission
in my article: *Reform of Family Law in Pakistan* in *Studia Islamica, Fasc. VII,*
1957.

proposals in fact were at the time. A brief account of the contemporary state of Islamic law will serve to explain this.

GENERAL ISLAMIC BACKGROUND

The twin pillars of patriarchy—polygamy and unilateral repudiation by the husband—had been the unshakeable supports of the structure of Islamic family law for more than thirteen centuries. Nor, in the Islamic context, was it simply a matter of attachment to long-standing tradition: a fundamental problem of legal principle was involved. For Islamic law is theoretically the command of Allāh which no human authority has the power to modify or abrogate and, in orthodox belief, Allāh has vouchsafed to no one since the death of the prophet Muḥammad in AD 632 the communication of his will to man. It is true that the last few decades had witnessed intense legal activity in the Muslim world, particularly in the Middle East.[1] Under the impact of modern conditions and the pressing need to align a family law which was mediaeval in outlook to the demands of society many changes had been effected in the law as traditionally applied. But prior to 1955 these reforms had almost everywhere been achieved upon a juristic basis which was, formally at any rate, legitimate according to traditional principles.

The juristic basis concerned lay in the doctrine of *siyāsa*, which in general terms defines the position of the political authority vis-à-vis the Sharī'a law and in particular affords him the power to make administrative regulations defining the jurisdiction of his courts.Such administrative regulations, for the purpose of modern reform, fall into two distinct categories.

The first defines the jurisdiction of the courts in the sense that it orders them to apply one particular among several variant legal rules on the same question. Divergence of doctrine is an outstanding characteristic of Sharī'a law and one inherent in its very nature. For the law represents the attempt of scholars to define the will of Allāh for Muslim society by interpreting and expanding the basic material

---

[1] The phenomenon of Islamic legal modernism in the Middle East was first analysed by J. Schacht in 1932, and his most recent article on this subject is *Problems of Modern Islamic Legislation* in *Studia Islamica, Fasc. XII*, 1960. The detailed documentation of the various modern codes of Sharī'a law is the work of J. N. D. Anderson. See his *Islamic Law in the Modern World* for a bibliography of articles on the subject. From my former tutor and present colleague respectively I have borrowed liberally, and to save innumerable references here acknowledge my general indebtedness.

of divine revelation. This basic material—the text of the Qur'ān and the recorded precedents of the prophet—is extremely limited in its amount and scope, and accordingly the vast bulk of Sharī'a law is the product of the reasoning of jurists. This potential for divergent views was greatly accentuated by the fragmentary growth of the law during the early formative period, where geographical division, local allegiances and conflicts of principle produced numerous competing systems. By AD 900 the divergence had crystallized in the formation of four distinct schools of Sharī'a law—not to mention the systems of the minority sects—and within each school the doctrine was further ramified by the various opinions of its own splinter groups and individual jurists. At this stage the process of disintegration was arrested. A belief that all the necessary work of interpretation and expansion had been completed came gradually to be expressed as an infallible consensus of opinion that no jurist henceforth had the right to interpet the original texts independently. The right of individual reasoning or *ijtihād* was denied. It was replaced by the duty of *taqlīd* or adherence to the established law. This doctrine, though not un-challenged in theory, in practice had been consistently observed, with one minor exception to which we shall later refer, when the Pakistani Commission was set up in 1955. Whatever the aims and aspirations of a Muslim State it was in theory bound to follow the doctrine emanating from jurists of the tenth century and now sys-tematically enshrined in the mediaeval handbooks of Sharī'a law, which possessed a final and unquestionable authority.

Accordingly it is only, in strict principle, by a choice from among the authoritative opinions recorded in these texts that the Muslim political authority may define the jurisdiction of his courts. On this basis indeed the face of Sharī'a law in the Middle East has been greatly altered in recent times. For example, in place of the Ḥanafī law tradi-tionally dominant in this area, which confines a wife's petition for divorce to the one ground of the sexual impotence of her husband, the Mālikī law, under which a wife's petition may be grounded on the husband's incurable and contagious disease, desertion, failure to maintain or cruelty, has been widely adopted. But the limits of this process are readily apparent. The reformers were soon forced to forage beyond the limits established by the general consensus. Doctrines of isolated jurists outside the four Sunnī schools, mentioned in the texts as historical curiosities, were selected and embodied in the modern codifications. To suit the preconceived purposes of the reformers legal rules were 'patched up', by a procedure aptly termed *talfīq*, from a combination of the views, or particular elements from the views, of different schools and jurists. And yet, though strained beyond any legitimate bounds of orthodoxy, formally the doctrine of *taqlīd* still held sway.

The second category of administrative regulations admissible under the doctrine of *siyāsa* is that by which the sovereign defines the jurisdiction of his courts in the sense that he restricts their competence to certain types of case. A limited number of important reforms have been achieved by this method in the Middle East. Under traditional Ḥanafī law, for instance, a child born to a widow or divorcee within two years of the dissolution of her marriage was presumed legitimate, for such was the maximum period of gestation laid down in the Ḥanafī texts. The Egyptian Law No. 25 of 1920 declared that the courts would not entertain any disputed claim of legitimacy on behalf of a child born more than one year after the dissolution of the marriage of the child's mother and alleged father, and thus restricted jurisdiction in such matters to claims in which the factual situation involved was in accord with modern medical opinion concerning the gestation period.

But while this is a procedural method which formally leaves the substantive law untouched, its limits in practice are even more obvious than those of the method of selection. The denial of judicial relief to parties whose acts or relationships are admittedly valid is a harsh method of reform and obviously, if carried to its ultimate conclusion, would wrest all semblance of authority from the Sharī'a courts. For this reason it has been used very sparingly and only in regard to matters which are essentially matters of evidence. Thus, in addition to the matter of the gestation period already mentioned, the Sharī'a courts have been forbidden to entertain suits involving disputed claims of a marriage or a repudiation which had not been registered. These are, of course, essentially matters of legal proof and therefore a proper subject for administrative regulations. Admittedly, when in Egypt in 1923 officials competent to register marriages were forbidden to register marriages between parties below certain minimum prescribed ages, and the courts were precluded from entertaining claims dependent upon the existence of such a marriage when it was disputed, this directly affected the substantive right of marriage guardians under the Sharī'a to contract their minor wards in marriage; but this seems to be the only occasion on which the principle has been thus extended. In any event, even when so used, it is a principle which has been manifestly wrenched out of all historical perspective; for its traditional formulation merely visualized the apportionment of different types of case between several different courts.

This, in broad outline, was the scope for reform of the Sharī'a law offered by the exploitation of traditional principles. As such it had proved the generally acceptable middle way between the two extremes of total abandonment of the Sharī'a or rigid adherence to its traditional form. The former solution was adopted by Turkey in the 1920's, while the traditionalist attitude of Saudi Arabia was strong enough to reject King Ibn Saud's proposal in 1927 to compile a code of Islamic law embodying doctrines from schools other than the Ḥanbalī school. The same conservatism, it may be remarked, was also strong enough to defeat a proposal to introduce a form of income tax in 1951.[1]

But, far reaching though some of the reforms introduced by the methods discussed may have been, these methods were of no avail against the two institutions of the Sharī'a which were obviously bound to be the ultimate concern of the modern reformer—the husband's rights of polygamy and repudiation or ṭalāq. Both rights rested squarely upon divine revelation, in the form of the text of the Qur'ān or the practice of the prophet. No variant opinion at all could be adduced to challenge them; nor could the method of denial of judicial relief be contemplated in regard to such firmly entrenched substantive rights for the reasons already mentioned. It is true that by the process of selection certain harsh details of the Ḥanafī law of ṭalāq had been whittled away. For example the rule that a repudiation pronounced in drunkenness was valid and effective was discarded in favour of the contrary opinion of the other schools. Similarly, as a step towards the limitation of polygamy, the Ottoman Law of Family Rights, 1917, followed by the later Middle Eastern codifications, adopted the Ḥanbalī view that a husband who agreed in his marriage contract not to take a second wife during the continuance of the marriage would be bound by such a stipulation, in the sense that the first wife would be entitled to a dissolution of the marriage in the event of its breach. The Ḥanafī law holds such a stipulation to be wholly void. But in order seriously to challenge the essence of these traditional rights of the husband some more extreme and incisive approach was required.

Such an approach had indeed been suggested by the great Egyptian reformer Muḥammad 'Abduh as early as 1898. His argument, as developed, may be presented in the following terms. The Qur'ān may be so interpreted as to deny both the right of polygamy and the

[1] Schacht, *Islamic Law in Contemporary States*, in the *American Journal of Comparative Law*, 1959, p. 146 f.

right of extra-judicial divorce by repudiation. In the first place the Qur'ān qualifies its permission of polygamy by requiring that the husband should be financially capable of supporting a plurality of wives and that he should be able to treat them impartially. If these qualifications should be interpreted not as mere moral injunctions, but as positive legal conditions precedent to the exercise of the right itself, then it would be open to a modern court, in the light of present social circumstances, to hold that these conditions, particularly the second, were incapable of fulfilment, and thus refuse to sanction a second marriage. In the second place the Qur'ān orders the appointment of arbitrators in the event of 'discord' between husband and wife. What more obvious instance of 'discord' than the pronouncement of a repudiation by the husband? Who then more fitted to assume the necessary function of arbitration than the established courts? In short, a repudiation should not be *per se* effective, but should require at least the consent of the court. Implicit in this approach is the power of the court to consider the husband's motive and to give its consent only upon such terms, particularly as to financial provision for the divorced wife, as it sees fit.

Attractive though such proposals might appear, and powerful though the personality and advocacy of their initiator may have been, they had no immediate success. For such an open assertion of the right of *ijtihād* represented an outright and radical break with the tradition of more than ten centuries standing and proved unacceptable to contemporary Muslim opinion.

It was not until 1953 that the first hesitant steps were taken in the actual implementation of this novel approach. The Syrian Law of Personal Status, 1953, required the consent of the court for a second marriage, and such consent was only to be given where the husband could establish his financial ability to support his co-wives adequately. Polygamy became the privilege of the wealthy. In regard to *ṭalāq* the approach was less extreme and in fact the terms of the law itself come as something of an anti-climax after a resounding preamble on the need for a fresh interpretation of the original sources. For the only provision of consequence is that which enables the court to award a repudiated wife compensation, within the maximum of one year's maintenance, where the repudiation was pronounced without just or proper motive and was injurious to the wife.

PARTICULAR BACKGROUND IN THE INDIAN SUB-CONTINENT

Such had been the progress achieved in the reform of Islamic family law in the Middle East when the Pakistani Commission was appointed in 1955. At this time the state of Islamic family law in the Indian sub-continent was, in substance, broadly similar to that in the Middle East, though such changes as had taken place in the traditional Ḥanafī law were the result of a process quite different from, and indeed wholly alien to, the Middle Eastern legal tradition.

In India the interaction of English and Islamic law had moulded the latter into a unique form, aptly termed Anglo-Muhammadan law, where the application of the law of the authoritative Ḥanafī texts was subject to the twin influences of the doctrine of precedent and over-riding legislation, both of which are utterly foreign to pure Sharī'a doctrine. Thus, to confine ourselves to the concrete examples already noted, while the Middle Eastern reformers had chosen to apply the Mālikī law concerning the possible grounds of a wife's petition for dissolution, substantially the same reforms were effected in India by the direct and overriding legislation of the Dissolution of Muslim Marriages Act, 1939. But though the terms of the Act are generally parallel with the Mālikī law there are some notable differences; and indeed, as its preamble points out, the Act was only necessary because the courts were hesitant to apply Mālikī law in these cases. Similarly, where the Middle Eastern reformers had used the indirect procedural device of denying judicial relief, the Indian Evidence Act, 1872,[1] super-ceded the traditional Ḥanafī law concerning the maximum period of gestation by adopting, broadly speaking, the English law relating to presumptions of legitimacy; while the Child Marriage Restraint Act, 1929, imposed penalties,[2] in cases of child[3] marriage, upon the male party if adult, the celebrant of the marriage and the guardian of the child concerned. Finally, the practice of the courts in enforcing stipu-lations in marriage contracts, including a stipulation against a second marriage, if they are 'reasonable and not contrary to the provisions or policy of the law',[4] would appear to be a case of judge-made law stemming from English influence. It is certainly not a conscious or deliberate application of the Ḥanbalī doctrine.

[1] Section 112.
[2] Imprisonment of up to one month or a fine of up to 1,000 rupees, or both.
[3] Boys under eighteen and girls under fourteen years of age.
[4] Fyzee, *Outlines of Muhammadan Law*, O.U.P., 1953, p. 104 *et seq.* The report of the Pakistani Commission claims 'a consensus of opinion' that such conditions are valid and enforceable.

But, notwithstanding such changes, no serious attempt had been made to challenge the husband's right of polygamy and *ṭalāq*. Like the Middle East India had also known its advocates of a dynamic reinterpretation of the Qur'ān, but the thesis of scholars like S. Khuda Buksh had remained a matter of theoretical speculation.

At a time, therefore, when a workable equilibrium between traditional Islamic law and modern Muslim society had been gradually established in the sub-continent, and when in the rest of the Muslim world reforms had not seriously disrupted the continuity of the Islamic legal tradition, the advocation by the Pakistani Commission of a sudden and total break with past tradition by the reopening of the door of *ijtihād* as the foundation for comprehensive reform naturally shocked the conservative element into violent reaction. The particular circumstances prevailing in Pakistan, of course, heightened the controversy. For the State was to be founded on Islamic principles and it was precisely the nature of those principles which was in issue. Furthermore, the majority of the members of the Commission hardly justified their claim to be exercising any genuine form of *ijtihād*. On the contrary, their often arbitrary and specious reasoning demonstrated only the most superficial familiarity with Islamic legal history. It is not surprising, therefore, that their proposals were condemned by their traditionalist colleague as an unwarranted interference by laymen in the realm of the sacred law and an attempt 'to undermine the accepted tenets of Islam and the fundamentals of the Islamic Shariat.'

It was the strength of the traditionalist reaction which brought into stark relief the magnitude of the issues involved in the conflict and which, no less than the unsettled political situation, caused considerable delay in Governmental decision on the proposals. In the interim, however, significant events had taken place elsewhere in the Muslim world. New codes of family law were promulgated in Tunisia, Morocco and Iraq in 1957, 1958 and 1959 respectively. The Tunisian code, carrying the thesis of Muḥammad 'Abduh to its logical conclusion, had outrightly prohibited polygamy and made *ṭalāq* dependent upon the consent of the court. When, therefore, President Ayub Khan promulgated the Muslim Family Laws Ordinance in March, 1961,[1] the recommendations of the Commission no longer bore the same

---

[1] The Ordinance came into force on July 15, 1961. It was published in the *Gazette of Pakistan, Extraordinary*, March 2, 1961, and now appears as *Supplement I—to The Muslim Law of Marriage* in *All Pakistan Legal Decisions*, 1961.

revolutionary aspect. And, as will be observed, the terms of the Ordinance are not only far less extreme than the Tunisian Law: they by no means wholly implement the recommendations of the Commission.

THE MUSLIM FAMILY LAWS ORDINANCE, 1961

To consider, then, the substance of the Ordinance.[1] If there were those who hoped that the Islamic State of Pakistan would set an example for the rest of the Muslim world by a sweeping revision of the existing legal structure and the translation of modernistic Islamic thought into a comprehensive code of family law, those hopes have been disappointed. The codes of family law which have recently appeared in the Islamic world have been notoriously brief. But for brevity this enactment can claim pride of place: it consists in all of thirteen short sections.

Following the recommendations of the Commission, the registration of marriages, on a standard form of marriage contract or *nikahnama*, is made compulsory under pain of penalties—three months imprisonment or a fine of 1,000 rupees, or both—much heavier than those suggested by the Commission,[2] though marriages not so registered are still valid. This is perhaps the one occasion where reform appears as genuine *ijtihād*. For whereas the same reform in Middle Eastern countries was invariably regarded as a species of administrative regulation, the proposal was based by the Commission on a verse of the Qur'ān,[3] ignored by thirteen centuries of Muslim jurisprudence, which enjoins that contracts should be made in writing.

However, the outstanding reform which does follow closely the spirit and letter of the Qur'ān is contained in Section 2 of the Ordinance. This provides for the setting up of Arbitration Councils, consisting of the Chairman of the Union Council constituted under the Basic Democracies Order, 1959, provided such a person is a Muslim, and a representative of each of the parties to any one of the three principal matters dealt with in the Ordinance, i.e. a second marriage, a repudiation or a wife's claim for maintenance. A verse of the Qur'ān does, in fact, as we have noted, order the appointment of arbitrators

---

[1] J. Roussier, of Algiers, has analysed the Ordinance, with customary clarity, in the French periodical *Actualités et Informations*, 1962, pp. 799–808.

[2] For infraction of registration provisions the Commission had suggested only a fine of 500 rupees.

[3] Sura II, Verse 282.

in case of 'discord' between spouses. And though the system of arbitration has previously operated only in cases where a wife sought dissolution of her marriage on the grounds of her husband's cruelty which she was unable to prove,[1] obviously 'discord' equally exists between the spouses in the three cases mentioned. But, eminently Qur'ānic though the system may be, this would appear to be coincidental rather than the result of any conscious or deliberate attempt by the drafters of the law to implement the Qur'ānic provision, for there was certainly no specific reference to this text in the report of the Commission. They had indeed recommended the establishment of 'special Matrimonial and Family Laws courts' to deal expeditiously with suits relating to family law, but obviously visualized courts properly so-called with a far greater competence than that which the Ordinance affords to the Arbitration Councils. However this may be, the reform is a most important and salutary one and one which, to the knowledge of the writer, is unique in the Muslim world.

We turn now to the three principle matters which will occupy the attention of the Arbitration Councils. The Ordinance gives effect to the recommendations of the Commission on the subject of polygamy *in toto*. A second marriage during the subsistence of an existing marriage is prohibited without the written permission of the Arbitration Council, and such permission may only be given where the Council is 'satisfied that the proposed marriage is necessary and just', and may be given 'subject to such conditions, if any, as may be deemed fit'. There are limited provisions for appeal from the Council's decision.[2] As to when a second marriage will be considered 'necessary and just' it is obvious from the Ordinance that the consent or otherwise of the existing wife or wives will be a highly relevant factor. Apart from this the rules made under the authority of the Ordinance[3] by the Provincial Governments afford the necessary guidance and criteria. 'The Arbitration Council may, without prejudice to its general powers to consider what is just and necessary, have regard to such circumstances as the following, amongst others: Sterility, physical infirmity, physical unfitness for the conjugal relation, wilful avoidance of a decree for restitution of conjugal rights, or insanity on the part of an existing wife.' The rules made by the Provincial

---

[1] This is the system of traditional Mālikī law, and it has now been adopted in certain Ḥanafī countries, e.g. by the Ottoman Law of Family Rights, 1917 and by the Egyptian Law, No. 25 of 1920.

[2] In West Pakistan the appeal lies to the Collector and in East Pakistan to the Sub-Divisional Officer, whose decisions are final.

[3] Section 11.

Governments of West and East Pakistan respectively in this regard are couched in identical terms. Indeed, the only point upon which the two sets of rules as a whole differ is on the question of the fee which must accompany the application for the Council's permission for a second marriage. It is 25 rupees in East Pakistan and four times that amount in West Pakistan.

Failure to obtain the Council's permission before contracting a second marriage does not render such marriage invalid, but entails a threefold sanction. The husband becomes liable to imprisonment for up to one year or a fine of up to 5,000 rupees, or both; he is obliged to pay forthwith the entire dower of his existing wife or wives, even where the payment of a portion of the dower was specifically deferred;[1] and finally the existing wife has a right to the dissolution of her marriage, an express clause to this effect being added by the Ordinance to the Dissolution of Muslim Marriages Act, 1939.

By contrast with the provisions concerning polygamy those relating to *ṭalāq* by no means follow the Commission's recommendations. It may be recalled that the Commission had suggested that a *ṭalāq* should require the permission of the court, and that such permission should only be granted after any outstanding dower had been paid to the wife and, in cases where the husband had no legitimate motive for repudiation, when suitable provision had been made for the maintenance of the divorced wife. Section 7 of the Ordinance, however, merely requires that the husband, after pronouncing a *ṭalāq*, shall give notice in writing of his having done so to the Chairman of the Arbitration Council, and to his wife. Failure to comply with this provision makes the husband liable to imprisonment for a term of up to one year or a fine of up to 5,000 rupees, or both.[2]

[1] A minor reform introduced by the Ordinance, on the recommendation of the Commission, is that, where the dower is not specifically divided into prompt and deferred portions, the whole amount will be presumed to be payable promptly. Ḥanafī law decides the apportionment in these cases on the basis of local custom, and failing proof of such custom presumes half the dower to be prompt and half deferred.

[2] According to section 8 these provisions are also to apply where a wife exercises a duly delegated power of *ṭalāq* or 'where any of the parties to a marriage wishes to dissolve the marriage otherwise than by *ṭalāq*'. This last phrase certainly includes divorce by mutual consent (known as *khul'* in Sharī'a law) but I find it difficult to suppose, as Roussier does (*op. cit.*, p. 803), that it was also intended to cover proceedings under the Dissolution of Muslim Marriages Act, 1939. In these cases the requirement of additional notice would seem to serve little useful purpose. It was the extra-judicial forms of divorce which were the concern of the framers of the Ordinance.

The *ṭalāq* is not to be effective until ninety days after the delivery of notice to the Chairman or, where the repudiated wife is pregnant, until delivery of the child, whichever period be longer. This is, of course, substantially the traditional *'idda* period of Sharī'a law, and since it is to apply after the pronouncement of a *ṭalāq* 'in any form whatsoever' the immediate effect of the various forms of irrevocable *ṭalāq* known to traditional Sharī'a law is thereby nullified.[1] During the said period the function of the Arbitration Council, which must be constituted within thirty days of the receipt of notice of the repudiation, is confined to attempting a reconciliation between the parties. And though the Council is empowered to 'take all steps necessary to bring about such reconciliation' this cannot conceivably include effecting such safeguards for the position of the repudiated wife as were suggested in the Commission's report. In sum, therefore, the husband's traditional power of unilateral repudiation at his discretion is left substantially unimpaired.

It may finally be remarked, on the general subject of divorce, that the Ordinance does not attempt to implement the suggestion of the Commission that incompatability of temperament should give a wife the right to demand a divorce in the *khul'* form. The Commission, indeed, had stated that 'there is a consensus of opinion that Islam has granted this right (of *khul'* divorce) to the woman if she forgoes the *mahr* (dower) or part of it, if it is so demanded by the husband'. It remains to be seen whether the courts of Pakistan will endorse this statement or whether they will adhere to the true Sharī'a law under which *khul'* divorce is entirely dependent upon the consent of the husband.

Equally disappointing to the Commission and their supporters must be the terms of the Ordinance in regard to the matter of a wife's maintenance. When Section 9 enacts that in cases of dispute under this head the Arbitration Council may determine what maintenance is adequate for the wife or wives concerned and may issue a certificate to this effect, and that any arrears of maintenance specified in—and, presumably, accruing after the issue of—such a certificate may be

---

[1] This applies, in particular, to the so-called 'triple' form of *ṭalāq*, i.e. where the husband repeats the words 'I repudiate you' three times or where he says 'I repudiate you three times'. It is also noteworthy that the principal effect of such a repudiation, namely the prohibition of remarriage between the divorced couple until the wife has contracted and consummated an intervening marriage, is also abolished by the terms of Section 7, sub-section 6, though the rule still applies in the case of a wife who is effectively repudiated for the third time under the provisions of this Section.

recovered as arrears of land revenue, it simply provides additional alternative machinery for the application of traditional Ḥanafī law. Under this law arrears of unpaid maintenance cannot be claimed by the wife unless a mutual agreement between the spouses or a judicial decree has fixed the amount of such maintenance; and it was this rule, admittedly the cause of considerable hardship to abandoned wives,[1] which was the primary concern, in this context, of the Commission. But the Ordinance contains no reference at all to their proposal that a wife should in all cases be able to claim past maintenance for a period of three years prior to the institution of the suit.

In the final aspect of the marriage laws dealt with in the Ordinance —the subject of child marriage—two relatively minor modifications only of the existing law are introduced. The age below which it is prohibited, under the Child Marriage Restraint Act, 1929, to contract a girl in marriage is raised from fourteen to sixteen by amendment of the Act.[2] Marriages of minors concluded by their guardians exercising their traditional powers in defiance of these provisions remain valid, but the child concerned may repudiate the marriage, provided it has not been consummated, on the attainment of puberty and before the age of eighteen under the terms of the Dissolution of Muslim Marriages Act, 1939. Under this Act the option was exercisable by a girl who had been given in marriage before she was fifteen. Accordingly this Act also is amended by the Ordinance and the age of sixteen substituted. The second modification is procedural only and consists of a further amendment to the Child Marriage Restraint Act which provides that no court shall take cognizance of any offence under the Act except on a complaint made by the Union Council.

INTESTATE SUCCESSION

Apart from the matter of polygamy, then, the changes effected by the Ordinance in the current substantive law of marriage and divorce are far from radical, particularly when compared with the corresponding Tunisian reforms. But in one respect the Ordinance goes

---

[1] This Ḥanafī rule has been replaced in most Middle Eastern countries by the more favourable doctrine of the other Sunnī schools.

[2] This adopts the suggestion of the Commission. The vague wording of the Commission's report made it doubtful at the time how they visualized their recommendation being carried into effect. It now appears, as I suggested in my article (p. 144, Note 1), that the intention was to continue the policy of the Child Marriage Restraint Act, 1929.

far beyond the Tunisian law and introduces a reform which is positively shattering in its impact upon the traditional law; for one terse, and perhaps to the Western lawyer seemingly innocuous, section[1] completely disrupts the Sharī'a law of intestate succession. We quote the section *in extenso*. 'In the event of the death of any son or daughter of the *propositus* before the opening of succession, the children of such son or daughter, if any, living at the time the succession opens, shall *per stirpes* receive a share equivalent to the share which such son or daughter, as the case may be, would have received, if alive.'

The traditional Sharī'a law of intestate succession recognizes two principal categories of heirs: the so-called 'Qur'ānic sharers', twelve relatives in all and mainly women, who receive a specific fraction of the estate, and the residuary heirs or '*aṣaba* who are the agnate kindred of the deceased. The simple rule regulating succession by the latter class to the residue left after the deduction of the Qur'anic shares is that the nearest '*aṣaba* only takes. For this purpose these relatives are divided into four classes, each class completely excluding all lower classes and within each class the nearer relative in degree excluding the more remote. It is this last rule, of course, which completely precludes any principle of representation in the traditional law. As might be supposed, modern Muslim reformers have been concerned to remedy the hardship occasioned by this rule where orphaned grandchildren are excluded from inheritance by the survival of a son of the deceased. Yet the fact that inheritance is one of the subjects regulated in detail by the Qur'ān itself and that the 'no representation' rule has been the subject of a consensus of opinion of all Muslim jurists since the days of the prophet necessitated a cautious approach.

In the event Egypt adopted, in 1946, the system known as 'obligatory bequests' under which, notwithstanding the absence of any testamentary disposition to this effect by the deceased, the orphaned grandchildren of the deceased are entitled, in the presence of his surviving son, to the share their own parent would have received had he or she survived, within the maximum of one-third of the nett estate.[2] This system, since adopted by Syria, Morocco and Tunisia,[3] is based, convincingly enough, on principles adduced from the traditional authorities, and since the 'obligatory legatees' are never

---

[1] Section 4.

[2] The limit imposed by Sharī'a law on the power of testamentary disposition.

[3] In Syria and Morocco the rule is confined to children of the deceased's son and children of the deceased's daughter do not benefit. This, of course, is more in line with the traditional criterion of agnate relationship.

legal heirs in their own right it harmonizes well with the general Sharī'a scheme of succession. The Pakistani provision, on the contrary, is clearly not confined in operation to the case where grandchildren are excluded from succession by a son of the deceased, and the havoc it plays with the traditional Sharī'a system may be shortly illustrated. Where there is no immediate child of the deceased surviving, a daughter's son or daughter's daughter, who would previously not have inherited at all, may now take the lion's share of the estate. The son's daughter, in competition with a daughter of the deceased, previously took, as a Qur'ānic share, one-third as much as her aunt. She will now take, as a residuary heir, twice as much as her aunt. Furthermore, the son's daughter will now completely exclude any brothers or sisters of the deceased, though the deceased's daughter will not.

Leaving many other complications aside, this is perhaps sufficient to show how the delicate balance achieved by the Sharī'a between the two distinct categories of heirs is completely upset. In effect this simple reform, apart from destroying the fundamental rule of residuary succession by the nearest 'aṣaba, both adds to and subtracts from the list of Qur'ānic sharers and admits as primary heirs relatives who would previously never have inherited at all. By comparison the Tunisian reform of 1959, under which a daughter or son's daughter of the deceased excludes all collateral relatives,[1] important though it is, is far less disruptive of traditional doctrine. The only Islamic precedent for the Pakistani reform lies in the Iraqi Code of Personal Status, 1959. This, in fact, adopts the representation rule.[2] But the whole system of succession therein enacted departs completely from the traditional Sharī'a system, an approach presumably dictated by the demands of national unity. For the population of Iraq is approximately evenly divided between Sunnīs and Shī'īs, and though a uniform system of marriage and divorce on a traditional basis might be supportable, the divergencies between the Sunnī and the Shī'ī systems of succession are too fundamental to admit of any such compromise. Such factors were in no way relevant to Pakistan. The reform is obviously intended to operate within the framework of the traditional law, but its effect is so far reaching that one may perhaps be excused for wondering whether all its implications were fully appreciated

---

[1] See J. Roussier, *Dispositions Nouvelles dans le Statut Successoral en Droit Tunisien*, in *Studia Islamica*, Fasc. *XII*, 1960, p. 138 *et seq.*

[2] See J. N. D. Anderson, *A Law of Personal Status for Iraq*, in *The International and Comparative Law Quarterly*, October, 1960, p. 559.

or whether the reformers have in fact gone further than they intended.

SUMMARY

We may now, in conclusion, briefly summarize the scope and nature of the Ordinance both as regards its substance and the juristic method on which it rests.

While by far the most radical reform introduced—the rule of representation in succession—affects both sexes equally, it was, of course, the amelioration of the position of women under the family law which was the major objective of the reformers. There has perhaps been in modern times an understandable tendency to exaggerate the picture of Muslim women labouring under the heavy shackles of the traditional law. For, by the elaboration of such devices as the deferred dower and suspended and delegated repudiation, the law had evinced a positive concern to establish some kind of equilibrium between husband and wife, and the miserable lot of Muslim wives in practice has often been the responsibility of society—inasmuch as the failure to make due use of existing legal machinery may be attributed to the denial of educational facilities to women and their resultant ignorance of their legal rights—rather than the direct result of the terms of Sharī'a law itself. Even so, the doctrines of polygamy and unilateral repudiation obviously constituted formidable obstacles, and here the terms of the Ordinance, requiring the consent of the Arbitration Council for a second marriage and suspending the effect of all forms of repudiation pending attempts at reconciliation, are certainly steps in the right direction. But they are short and hesitant steps. Basically the husband's right of repudiation, which undoubtedly occasions the greatest prejudice to woman's status, remains, and the compromise at which the Ordinance aims between the modernist and traditionalist viewpoints seems on balance to favour the latter.

Towards the ultimate notion of equality between the sexes the Tunisian reformers, as we have noted, have progressed considerably further. Yet even here, it may be argued, much remains to be done. For within the structure of traditional Sharī'a law polygamy and repudiation appears as derivative rights of the husband stemming from the root concept of marriage as a contract of sale, wherein the husband purchases the right of sexual union by payment of the dower. However offensive this notion may be to modern moral sense, and however extensive the elaborate superstructure of marital rights and duties, this remains the legal foundation of the Sharīʿa laws of marriage. And if the law is to endorse, logically and satisfactorily, any system of real equality between husband and wife, it is at least debateable whether this basic traditional concept, epitomized by the payment of dower, can be allowed to remain.

Unlike the Muslim countries of the Middle East Pakistan has not attempted any comprehensive codification of Islamic law but has, in the English tradition, simply amended the existing law in a limited number of particulars by direct legislation. Despite the claims of the Commissioners in their report, the Ordinance can scarcely appear as the result of a conscientious application of *ijtihād* on the basis of a reinterpretation of the original sources. As has always been the case since the first legislative interference in the domain of Sharīʿa law in the Indian sub-continent, the problems of the juristic basis of reform, which have so occupied the attention of the Middle Eastern lawyers, have been largely glossed over or ignored altogether. The approach to the problem of polygamy is conditioned not by the Qur'ānic injunctions of financial capability and impartial treatment, but by straightforward criteria of social desirability. And it was precisely this attitude which made possible the introduction of the representation rule, for this cannot genuinely rest upon any text of the Qur'ān or any precedent of the prophet.[1]

In short, therefore, the Ordinance continues the particular tradition of Anglo-Muhammadan law. In so doing it provides yet one more instance of the growing diversity of legal practice in the present world of Islam, a diversity resulting from the varying reaction of the different areas to the stimuli, both indigenous and foreign, provided by modern life. Such divergence, however, is not out of line with Islamic history. The notion that Islam imposes a stereotyped way of life upon its millions of adherents throughout the world is idealistic: its origin lies in the attitude of the medieval jurists and their fictitious expression of each and every detail of the law as the command of Allāh. But because of the great variety of peoples and cultural traditions within the orbit of Islam the Sharīʿa law has always been in practice subject to modification by local influences. Those, then, who think that Pakistan should exploit the common historical heritage of

---

[1] Roussier (*op. cit.*, p. 806) quotes the Karachi journal *Dawn* of March 5, 1961, to the effect that the rule of representation is in agreement with the principles of Islamic law and does not depart from the explicit text of the Qur'ān itself. Roussier speaks also for the present writer when he comments: 'We confess we do not know the text to which the author of the *Dawn* article is referring'.

Islam and, making a clean sweep, formulate a modern code of Islamic family law which will serve as an example for the rest of Islam are perhaps affected by the same detached idealism as their medieval predecessors. The framers of the Ordinance, in remaining faithful to the particular and healthy tradition of the immediate past, have adopted an attitude which is certainly more practical and probably far better suited to the present mood and aspirations of Pakistan.

14

CHINESE LAW IN HONG KONG:
THE CHOICE OF SOURCES

H. MCALEAVY

Lecturer in Chinese Law, School of Oriental and African Studies, University of London

During the hundred and twenty years that have passed since the cession of Hong Kong to the British Crown, the traditional Chinese law has regulated the domestic affairs of many of the Colony's inhabitants, and even today, surviving its decease in its own country, enjoys a vigorous old age under foreign protection. Putting aside any academic considerations, it might have been expected that the practical needs of administration would have long ago brought into being some authoritative statement by the Hong Kong Government at least of the relevant topics of family law. Yet the truth is that no such statement exists, and one can hardly read a page of a Hong Kong legal publication without becoming aware of the obscurity which still enshrouds the Chinese doctrines.

It would be easy, but unfair, to make comparisons with some neighbouring territories. True, the Japanese Government, on acquiring Formosa by the Treaty of Shimonoseki in 1895, carried out a remarkably detailed investigation of Chinese private law, but it could dispose of the services of a considerable number of scholars not merely trained in law but with a depth of Chinese erudition no European can be expected to match. Then again, the French, who did so much to illuminate the closely-related law of Vietnam, had to deal with a country possessing its own legal code and system of government, although both were strictly modelled on Chinese originals. Yet when every allowance is made, it must remain a matter of surprise and regret that the study of Chinese law has been so much neglected in Hong Kong, a place which seems eminently suited for its cultivation.

Of late years, however, there are signs that the subject is arousing more interest than in the past. Two official reports have been published, and English lawyers with experience of the Hong Kong courts have discussed various points of importance.[1] In these circumstances, it is hoped that it will not be considered an impertinence if one whose only acquaintance with Hong Kong has been as a passenger in transit, but who has lived in China and tried to become familiar with the literature of Chinese law, ventures to offer an opinion on what appears to him to be the most fundamental aspect of the question.

This is brought into the open, with great lucidity, by Mr E. S. Haydon on the first page of his article 'The Choice of Chinese Customary Law in Hong Kong'. He writes:

'A considerable proportion of the three-million-odd Chinese, who form the bulk of the population of modern Hong Kong, are now domiciled in that Colony. Their domestic affairs under the rule of Private International Law are generally accepted as governed by Chinese customary law. But the Chinese customary law, which the courts attempt to apply in such cases, is that which obtained in the Kwangtung Province of China, on the border of which Hong Kong lies, on April 5, 1843. At that time Hong Kong was inhabited by about five thousand Chinese who appear to have been employed in agriculture and fishing and intermittently in piracy and other lawless pursuits. . . . Prima facie it is remarkable that many of the Chinese in Hong Kong at the present day, who comprise some of the most cultured people to be found in the Far East, should be at law subject in their domestic affairs, matters which are all important in Chinese eyes, to theoretical concepts of the customs of a riff-raff living in this same region of Kwangtung Province a hundred and twenty years ago. On that ground alone it is submitted that the basis for the choice of Chinese customary law in Hong Kong calls for reconsideration.'[2]

Mr D. E. Greenfield, in his article 'Marriage by Chinese Law and Custom in Hong Kong', goes further. He says:

'Hong Kong Island was in that part of Imperial China known as the Province of Kwangtung. Although the Emperor's decrees had nominal authority throughout all China it seems historically certain

---

[1] *Chinese Law and Custom in Hong Kong*, Government Printer, Hong Kong, 1953 (hereinafter cited as 'Report of 1953'); *Chinese Marriages in Hong Kong*, Government Printer, Hong Kong, 1960 (hereinafter cited as 'Report of 1960'); D. E. Greenfield, 'Marriage by Chinese Law and Custom in Hong Kong', *International and Comparative Law Quarterly*, July 1958, pp. 437–51; E. S. Haydon, 'The Choice of Customary Law in Hong Kong', *International and Comparative Law Quarterly*, January 1962, pp. 231–50.

[2] P. 231.

that his role was very limited in practice. He may have collected and farmed out taxes, appointed some officials, and occasionally enforced a specific order, but away from the immediate presence of the court the only effective law was unwritten and customary, locally upheld and enforced by the people.'[1]

Now it seems to the present writer that both these views are decidedly misleading. The China described by Mr Greenfield, if one substitutes 'central government' for 'Emperor', has it is true a general resemblance to the country of the warlords—say between 1916 and 1927—but surely not to the China even of the late nineteenth century, still less to that of Tao Kuang. Mr Haydon is perfectly justified in drawing our attention to the fact that the original inhabitants of Hong Kong were, by and large, a pretty rough lot, but a Chinese, on the other hand, might be tempted to retort that the British on the China coast in those times could hardly be described as a group of first communicants. All in all, it is probably a case of the pot and the kettle. And if the Chinese at present domiciled in Hong Kong are subject in their domestic affairs, as Mr Haydon says, 'to theoretical concepts of the customs of a riff-raff', then their situation is indeed to be deplored. What these unfortunate people are supposed to be subject to is traditional Chinese law, the principles of which are tolerably well known, and which, outside China, is taught at the University of Tokyo and at the School of Oriental and African Studies in the University of London. In the remainder of this essay it is proposed to discuss some features of that law which pose a problem for the Hong Kong courts today, and to illustrate the subject by reference to a particular Hong Kong legal institution.

STATUTE AND CUSTOM IN MANCHU CHINA

The cession of Hong Kong took place at the end of the second century of Manchu rule in China. The dynasty had many notable achievements to its credit. It had bound Chinese, Mongols, Tibetans and Turkis into a vast and polyglot empire, and to China herself, the only part of the Manchu dominions to concern us here, it had restored orderly government after the confusion of the last years of the house of Ming. Great collections of statutes covered nearly every topic of public law, and voluminous reports testify to the careful supervision of administration. But private law was based on custom, and nothing in the nature of a civil code had come into existence. This customary law,

[1] P. 442.

founded at any rate as regards family affairs on the system of beliefs known to foreigners as Confucianism, was remarkably uniform throughout the country, and was assumed to be sufficiently well-known not to require statutory definition. However, on top of this customary basis there was erected, if one is permitted to borrow the vocabulary of Marxism, a superstructure of legislation. Mr Haydon says that the Manchu Penal Code—and it should be pointed out that the Penal Code was only a part of the vast corpus of statutes—'can by its very nature have little application to domestic affairs, the law of which is essentially civil in character'.[1] In fact, the legislator often took care to confirm the rules of customary law by providing sanctions for breaches of them in domestic and other matters. Even today these penal enactments are of practical importance in the sense that they throw light on some topics that might otherwise be obscure. For instance, it is extremely hard for a foreign student to understand the true nature of family property, or the effect of the contract of betrothal, without the help of the Manchu Penal Code.

But if the legislator's purpose was usually to confirm and defend the customary law, there were occasions when he endeavoured to modify it. The most remarkable example of this concerns a very ancient form of land tenure called *dien*. This institution had several characteristics which rendered it obnoxious to any tidy administration, and in the eighteenth century the Manchu government, then at the very height of its power, promulgated a number of statutes designed to change the nature of *dien* completely. It must be emphasized that such legislation was completely binding on all courts. Yet the Chinese then, as now, were not a litigious people and preferred whenever possible not to invoke the assistance of the state in the settlement of their private disputes. Time passed, and in due course the Manchus fell and were succeeded by a Republic. Thirty years ago the Chinese National Government, in its Civil Code, followed its imperial predecessor and attempted to remould *dien* into a more manageable shape. Yet nothing is more certain than that up to the Communist victory in 1949 *dien* continued to exist throughout China in its original form, quite uninfluenced either by Manchu or Nationalist legislation.[2]

In the Chinese law and custom of 1843, which we must consider to be the starting point of Chinese law in colonial Hong Kong, there were a number of these topics, where the statute law, applied by the

[1] P. 232.

[2] H. McAleavy, 'Dien in China and Vietnam', *Journal of Asian Studies*, May 1958, pp. 403–15.

Chinese courts, laid down one rule, and custom, followed by the great mass of the people, persisted in another. Which of the two, custom or statute, ought to be recognized by the Hong Kong courts? The question is clearly of the first importance, yet strangely enough it does not appear to have been raised, let alone answered. True, Mr Haydon and Mr Greenfield seem to avoid the difficulty by ignoring statute law altogether, but that will surely not do. On the other hand, the Reports of 1953 and 1960 are more respectful to the Manchu legislation. The former especially turns for enlightenment to Staunton's translation of the Manchu Penal Code, and complains only of its meagreness in civil doctrines, which leaves 'ample scope for its amplification by local custom'.[1] However, each report contains a recommendation on a certain topic of family law, the acceptance of either of which (for they are mutually contradictory) would mean in effect that the Hong Kong Government had at last, even if without knowing it, taken sides in the conflict. The topic in question is the institution known as *kim tiu* marriage, and it is important enough in Chinese society to merit a few words of explanation.

RITUAL SUCCESSION AND KIM TIU

The words *kim tiu* are the Cantonese rendering of two characters which are pronounced in standard Chinese as *chien t'iao*. On the surface, they have no connection with marriage at all and signify the conjunction of two lines of ritual succession in one and the same person. It is well known that the corner-stone of the old Chinese family system was the virtue called *hsiao*, usually translated into English as 'filial piety'. This was defined by Confucius as: 'that parents, when alive, should be served according to propriety; that, when dead, they should be buried according to propriety, and that they should be sacrificed to according to propriety.'[2] A law book of the Southern Sung dynasty (twelfth and thirteenth centuries AD) states the matter more plainly. 'The reason a man begets sons', it says, 'is so that they may support him during his lifetime and bury him when he is dead'.[3] But, as an extension of this doctrine, just as one has a duty to render piety to one's ancestors, so one must, for their sake, see to it that one leaves a successor behind to venerate their memory. 'There are three things which are unfilial,' says Mencius, 'and to have no posterity is the

---

[1] P. 14.
[2] James Legge (trans.), *The Chinese Classics*, 2nd edn., 1895, Vol. 1, p. 147.
[3] S. Shiga, *Chūgoku kazokuhō-ron*, 2nd edn., Tokyo, 1951, p. 9, n. 1.

greatest of them'.[1] 'Posterity' means sons, as females had no capacity to continue a succession.

It follows from this that a man was under the strongest moral obligation to marry and beget offspring. If he had the misfortune to remain childless, then the same duty impelled him to adopt a successor. The choice was however governed by strict conditions. The adopted person must be a male from the same clan, and he must be one generation junior to the man he was to succeed.[2] In other words, you could not appoint your brother or your cousin to be your successor. Of the innumerable crimes of the Empress Dowager, none probably shocked public opinion more than her choice in 1875 of her nephew, Kuang Hsü, as Emperor in place of her dead son T'ung Chih. At least one eminent mandarin committed suicide in protest against the atrocity.[3]

There was another condition. The person chosen must not be an only son, whose adoption would deprive his own parents of a successor.[4] Yet this restriction sometimes clashed with other Confucian prejudices. Suppose that of two brothers, A, the elder, had no sons, and B, the younger, had only one. It would be unacceptable for the child to abandon his own father, but on the other hand B had a recognized obligation of deference towards his elder brother, and in the clan structure it was considered to be important to keep alive a senior line. In such a case, the law was relaxed to permit B's son to succeed to both lines. This double succession was called *chient'iao*, the *kim tiu* of modern Hong Kong, and in the Manchu statute law it was permitted solely to preserve the line of an elder brother. But as succession was not merely to the duty of ritual commemoration but also to the deceased person's estate, it is not surprising that custom extended the scope of *kim tiu* to provide successors for younger brothers, and even for cousins.

Even so, great care was taken to ensure that the lines temporarily brought together in one person should be kept distinct, and that they should be separated in the next generation. The most effective way to do this was for the *kim tiu* successor to sustain two personalities. As the successor of his own father B, he married a wife and begot a family. As the adopted successor of A, he married another wife and had a second family, complete in every detail with its own property.[5] Nothing, or so it might appear, could be tidier and more effective.

---

[1] Legge, *op. cit.*, Vol. II, p. 313.   [2] Shiga, pp. 20–9.
[3] J. O. P. Bland and E. Backhouse, *China Under the Empress Dowager*, 1910, pp. 132–47.
[4] Shiga, pp. 29–30.   [5] Shiga, pp. 31–2.

WIFE AND CONCUBINE

Yet there were serious difficulties in the way of such a solution. From the earliest ages Chinese law allowed a man to have only one wife at a time. This wife shared her husband's status in the family and the clan. During the husband's life, the rights attached to that status were exercized by him alone, but after his death many of them passed to his wife. Among these, until any son of the marriage reached maturity, was the right to administer the family estate, and, if there should be no son, to appoint a successor.[1] Concubines, who could be taken without restriction of number, enjoyed no comparable rights, and as a rule were limited, and then only in the absence of a legitimate widow, to expressing their opinion in the family or clan council.[2] It follows that in the case of *kim tiu* it would not suffice, in order to keep the lines distinct, to select a concubine to beget children for line A, while a wife attended to line B. After the *kim tiu* successor's death, the wife would manage the affairs of both lines, very likely to the injury of line A.

This essential difference between wife and concubine must be insisted upon, if Chinese family law is to be understood at all. It was a difference not of degree, but of kind. And here we are confronted with a puzzle in the Hong Kong books. The Report of 1960 states uncompromisingly: 'The taking of a concubine by a man implies another, and nearly always an earlier, marriage to the wife'.[3] And there is a reference to 'mistresses euphemistically called concubines and attached to a Chinese Modern Marriage, a Registry Marriage, or a Reputed Marriage'[4] which leaves in the mind of the reader a strong impression that the validity of a concubine's status depends not only on the existence but also on the nature of her husband's marriage to another woman as a lawful wife.

The Report of 1953 quotes an opinion, written by the Attorney General of Hong Kong in 1936, that: 'The condition which turns a kept woman into a concubine is here acceptance by the wife as a potential bearer of legitimate children to the family. The ceremony usually consists of her introduction in the family house to the wife, to whom she makes obeisance and offers a cup of tea. If this offering is accepted the wife usually assigns to her definite quarters or a court-yard in the principal or some other house belonging to the family and thereafter she is a woman member of the family and, if she bears chil-

---

[1] Shiga, pp. 40–5.
[2] Shiga, pp. 58–66.
[3] P. 1.
[4] P. 17.

dren, her children will be recognized as having equal legitimate status with that of the wife's own children.'[1] Elsewhere, however, the same report gives the view of a Chinese lawyer, Dr Tung, who denies that under the law of the Manchu dynasty a man could not take a concubine unless he had been married. When asked: 'What would be the position if a man took a *tsip* (concubine) before he had ever been married?' Dr Tung answered: 'It is a rare case where a man takes a *tsip* before he has ever been married'.[2] Mr Greenfield in the article already referred to says: 'Although a concubine could be taken before a *tsai* (wife), this appears to have been of very rare occurrence.'[3]

Now the reader, bewildered by these contradictory statements, may fairly complain that no authorities are cited in support of the views expressed. Surely nothing would settle the question one way or the other more convincingly than a reference to a Chinese text? And such texts exist. The law-book from the Southern Sung dynasty already mentioned tells of two men who remained unmarried but begot sons by concubines, and under the early Republic the Peking Supreme Court held that an agreement to marry was not broken if the man, before marriage, took a concubine.[4] From these examples it can be affirmed without any hesitation that concubinage did not depend for its validity on the existence of a marriage.

KIM TIU AND MARRIAGE

The practical necessity, then, of having a wife for each line, if the lines were to be kept distinct, prevailed in the customary law to the extent that it became common for a *kim tiu* successor to marry two women as legitimate spouses. This practice was noticed among the Cantonese immigrants in Formosa in the early years of this century.[5] It was, however, disliked by the Manchu government, which already in the middle of the eighteenth century declared that the keeping of two wives in *kim tiu* was not to be permitted. This looked as if the custom ought to be treated as bigamy, and bigamy was visited by severe penalties for the guilty parties and the separation of the couple concerned. Yet in 1821, the first year of the Emperor Tao Kuang, who ceded Hong Kong to the British, it was held in a case that arose in the province of Shantung: 'Marriage of a wife for each line in *kim tiu* is for the purpose of begetting offspring for the succession, and should not be punished, as in the case of ordinary bigamy, by the

[1] Pp. 137–8.   [2] P. 189.   [3] P. 443.   [4] Shiga, p. 60, n. 7.
[5] Taiwan shihō, Vol. II, Pt. 2, Tokyo 1911, p. 266.

separation of the couple. Yet, as a matter of propriety, a man may not have two wives, and the second woman must be treated as a concubine.'[1]

This ruling, in itself, shows very well the attitude of the Chinese nineteenth-century courts to domestic affairs. So grave an offence as ordinary bigamy, which struck at the heart of Confucian tradition, called for the intervention of the State to suppress it. What amounted to bigamy in *kim tiu* was ignored, but if a dispute came to the courts for settlement only the woman first married would be recognized as a wife. In fact, such disputes were not in general taken before the magistrate, and the custom thrived without hindrance and survives in Hong Kong today. As a matter of interest, it is worth noting that under the early Republic the Peking Supreme Court reaffirmed the 1821 ruling that a second *kim tiu* spouse may be accorded only the status of a concubine.[2]

It is much to be regretted that Dr Vermier Yantak Chiu in his note on *kim tiu* in the Report of 1953, after an accurate statement of what is in fact the customary law, i.e. that a man may in such a case marry two wives, goes on to assert that 'the law of *kim tiu* was made by the Emperor Ch'ien Lung in the eighteenth century'.[3] In fact, as has been shown, although the Manchu Government, as a special privilege, permitted a man in certain circumstances to succeed to two lines, it utterly refused to recognize the marriage of two wives. *Kim tiu*, in other words, affords a striking example of a conflict between custom and statute.[4]

One form the problem may assume in Hong Kong is illustrated by a case mentioned in the Report of 1953, where a magistrate 'had to consider whether a complainant who claimed to have taken, in accordance with the Chinese custom known as *kim tiu*, two *kit fat* wives, could complain under section 3 of the Chinese Marriage Preservation Ordinance, 1921, of adultery committed by the defendant with the second of these wives'.[5] Section 3(1) of the Chinese Marriage Preservation Ordinance reads as follows: 'If it is proved to the satisfaction of a magistrate that any Chinese person has committed adultery with a Chinese married woman, the magistrate may order such a person to pay to the husband of the woman compensation not exceeding 500 dollars.'[6] Section 2(1) of the same ordinance says: ' "Chinese married woman" means a woman married according to the

---

[1] Taiwan shihō, *loc. cit.*   [2] Shiga, p. 33, n. 6.   [3] Pp. 201–2.
[4] Shiga, p. 33, n. 6.   [5] P. 112.
[6] Revised Edition of Laws of Hong Kong 1950, cap. 178, (Vol. IV, p. 365).

laws or customs of China, and includes only the first wife (*kit fat*) or the second wife (*tin fong*) of any Chinese man.'[1]

It is an undoubted fact that Chinese words, in any kind of romanization, are hard for the foreign reader. When, as in the case of *kim tiu*, no western equivalent exists their use is defensible. But all too often the Hong Kong books think nothing of putting *tsai* and *tsip* where the ordinary English 'wife' and 'concubine' would serve perfectly well. If one must at all costs employ Chinese terms, then surely care should be taken to explain them correctly. In this respect, the definition just quoted from the Chinese Marriage Preservation Ordinance is a masterpiece of bad drafting. To the ordinary English reader two meanings are possible: either a Chinese man may have two wives, but no more, at one time, or else, when he loses his first wife by death or divorce, he may remarry once only, after which his matrimonial career, under Chinese law or custom, is at an end. To one who can understand the Chinese crib, the second interpretation is indicated. Yet we are told neither of these is intended. In fact the confusion has arisen through a misrendering of *tin fong*, which on the remarriage of a widower is applied not only to the second wife but to any wife subsequent to the first. The term *kit fat* means that a husband and wife both marry for the first time, and to the complainant in this case it would seem natural to use it of a *kim tiu* marriage, where the husband takes each wife in a distinct capacity. In spite of the wording there is no doubt the legislator intended that a man should have only one legally-recognized wife at a time, but as many wives in succession as the vicissitudes of fortune might dictate. *Kim tiu* marriages were not provided for, and the magistrate held that as the woman in question was the second of the two allegedly *kit fat* 'wives' no complaint could be lodged.[2] 'If the magistrate's decision was correct,' says the Report of 1953, 'the Ordinance must be read as having made another inroad on this particular form of Chinese marriage (i.e. *kim tiu*) in that though, as the magistrate was careful to point out, he was not purporting to decide whether the custom was a valid custom, or in fact anything else except whether a complaint of adultery would lie, the legislature had, by confirming the remedy to adultery in respect of the first *kit fat*, ignored the possibility of there being more than one *kit fat*.'[3]

It may be noted that if the case had been tried before a court in Manchu China it would have assumed an entirely different aspect. True, the second *kim tiu* spouse would have been recognized merely

[1] As in (6).   [2] Report of 1953, p. 113.   [3] P. 113.

as a concubine, but misconduct with another man's concubine was punished as adultery, and the complainant would accordingly have had the satisfaction, for what it was worth, of being revenged on the guilty couple.

This decision did not settle the fundamental problem of *kim tiu* marriage, and the matter was considered by the Committee which issued the Report of 1953. Among the questions on the Law of Marriage put to a group of Chinese informants was the following: 'Should the existing law be amended so that the doctrine of monogamy for Chinese residents in Hong Kong be recommended?' Mr Li King Hong, a member of the Chinese Chamber of Commerce, replied: 'Yes, but the custom of a second *kit fat* for *kim tiu* must be carefully considered.'[1] Nevertheless, in its recommendations the Report advised against the recognition of *kim tiu* marriages for the future.[2] As the whole tenor of these recommendations seems directed primarily against concubinage, it is possible from this to come to the conclusion that the Committee followed the Manchu statute law, in opposition to custom, and decided that a second *kim tiu* spouse was a concubine. However that may have been, the Report of 1960 takes an entirely different attitude and recommends that 'for the present *kim tiu* marriages be recognized as lawful Chinese Customary Marriages'.[3] Here there can be scarcely any doubt that custom is being supported against the Manchu statutes. What, incidentally, is the effect of this on the adoption side of *kim tiu*? Logically, it ought to be liberated from the restriction of the eighteenth-century legislator, who sought to confine it to the provision of successors for elder brothers, and given the full customary scope mentioned earlier. Then there is the custom called in standard Chinese *san t'iao*, where one man may succeed to three lines, with a wife for each.[4] This is not covered by *kim tiu*, which by definition is concerned with only two lines, but what would be the attitude of the Hong Kong courts towards it?

THE BASIC QUESTION

However, even *kim tiu* is apparently not encountered too frequently in the Colony, and the serious question is the fundamental one, namely, whether the recommendation is a sign that the Hong Kong authorities are coming to a decision concerning the conflict between statute and custom in the traditional Chinese law. Admittedly, even

[1] P. 237.   [2] P. 71.   [3] P. 11.
[4] N. Niida, *Shina mibunhō-shi*, Tokyo, 1942, pp. 45, 76, 797.

when this has been answered, other problems remain, notably those concerning the extent to which developments in custom since the cession, whether in China itself, or in Hong Kong, call for recognition. Yet the point of departure must remain the Chinese law of 1843, and no useful advance can be made until the source of that law is determined. After that, the next step, logically, would be a clear and unambiguous statement of its content. If those responsible can be persuaded that this content is known and is expounded in a copious literature of scholarship, the task would not be too daunting. At the moment, such a belief seems withheld, no doubt because the books in question are not written in English.

TABLE OF STATUTES, ETC.

UNITED KINGDOM

(a) *Statutes*

TABLE OF CASES

INDEX

(This Index is intended as a general guide to the contents; it is not an exhaustive analysis)

THE END

For Product Safety Concerns and Information please contact our EU
representative GPSR@taylorandfrancis.com
Taylor & Francis Verlag GmbH, Kaufingerstraße 24, 80331 München, Germany

www.ingramcontent.com/pod-product-compliance
Lightning Source LLC
Chambersburg PA
CBHW060154280326
41932CB00012B/1752